A Sufi Message
of
Spiritual Liberty

Volume XIII
(revised edition)

The Wisdom of Sufism

BY THE SAME AUTHOR

A Sufi Message

OF

Spiritual Liberty

VOLUME XIII
(revised edition)

The Wisdom of Sufism

Sacred Readings from the Gathas

Hazrat Inayat Khan

ELEMENT
Shaftesbury, Dorset • Boston, Massachusetts • Melbourne, Victoria
in association with
The International Headquarters of the Sufi Movement, Geneva

© Element Books Limited 2000
Text © International Headquarters of the Sufi Movement 1982

First published in the UK in 2000 by
Element Books Limited
Shaftesbury, Dorset SP7 8BP

Published in the USA in 2000 by
Element Books, Inc.
160 North Washington Street
Boston, MA 02114

Published in Australia in 2000 by
Element Books and distributed
by Penguin Australia Limited
487 Maroondah Highway, Ringwood,
Victoria 3134

Cover illustration by Qahira Fran Becker
Cover design by Max Fairbrother
Designed and typeset by The Bridgewater Book Company
Printed and bound by Creative Print and Design (Wales), Ebbw Vale

British Library Cataloguing in Publication
data available

Library of Congress Cataloging in Publication
data available

ISBN 1 86204 700 6

CONTENTS

FOREWORD

The word Sufi, according to Greek and Arabic etymologies, means 'wisdom' and 'purity' respectively. However, both concepts clearly suggest one and the same ideal. Wisdom is there only when the mind is purified from preconceived ideas, the burdens of dogma and an unquiet conscience. As to the origin of Sufism, one could say that it is also as ancient as the concepts of wisdom and purity, which have been the inspiration of devotional worship all down the ages. Sufism is not a cult nor is it a school of theology. Sufism is an open door, an attitude of truest sympathy towards all beliefs. As the essence of all religious ideals, Sufism has been appropriated by large cultural and religious streams during different periods in history, but without ever losing its own identity.

When pronouncing the word Sufism, the 'ism' has a tendency to confine the understanding of wisdom, which is in truth beyond limitations and cannot be identified with only one belief, for there are as many descriptions of wisdom as there are seekers on the path. Wisdom might perhaps be recognizable but cannot be tangible nor, even less, subject to definition. Therefore, for the one who is truly wise there is only the reality of wisdom itself, beyond all speculative interpretations.

As soon as one attempts to define abstract concepts, one is taken into the labyrinth of one's own thoughts which descend into speculative descriptions, and one builds up one's own illusions which, added to the many which one acquires, together with numerous other impressions and influences, constitute our mind-world. Then, when putting one's beliefs and understandings into words, these tend to deviate from the original ideas, which were themselves only arbitrary concepts, and it is the result of all this which is so often presented as being the one and only truth.

For a Sufi, the diversity of religious names and forms are like veils covering the phenomena of the Spirit of Guidance manifested at all levels of evolution. This explains why one of the great ideals of the Sufi is the awakening of a broader outlook, with deeper insight into the tragic misunderstandings which divide earnest followers of various cultural and philosophical traditions.

All religions are in their origin of Divine inspiration, but, like the image of water poured into different coloured glasses, as soon as Divine inspiration becomes formulated in human thought it acquires the image of one's thinking. We then call one religion Hinduism, another Buddhism, and still another Zoroastrianism, while others are called Judaism, Christianity, Islam, as well as many other religious denominations, both known and unknown to the world at large.

A Sufi, by definition, is a religious soul whose nature is to be freed from imposed theories, and who is perfectly conscious that life is not necessarily just what one might think it to be. For a Sufi, life is lived not only at the level of physical experience, nor only at the levels of thought and feeling, but also, and most importantly, at a still higher level of consciousness where the self is no more a barrier separating reality from illusion. At this level of consciousness there are no limitations nor opposites, nor any place for dualistic speculation on the subject of the Divinity. When trying to explain God one only fashions an individual concept, limited to the size of one's own mind-world.

Another subject found in Sufi teachings is the alchemy of happiness, which, as we know from fairy tales, is the use of a magic formula to turn base metal into gold. This mystical legend symbolizes beautifully the fundamental principle of the Inner School of the Sufis, where deep consideration is offered to training the ego along a thorny path known as the art of personality, and where false identification and illusory aspirations are no longer a hindrance to the dicovery of the Divine Presence hidden as a pearl in one's heart. This requires constant efforts in forging the character into a living example of wisdom, so as to become a bringer of happiness to brothers and sisters of all beliefs.

Happiness, which is a birthright, although we are not always conscious of that privilege, is only there to the extent that one becomes a source of happiness for others. We find it through trying to appreciate the good in others, and in overlooking that which disturbs us when not in accord with our own thinking; through trying to see the points of view of others, even though these might be contrary to one's own; and through trying to attune oneself to the rhythm of all those one meets, and in whose presence there might be a lesson to be learnt.

Hazrat Inayat Khan came to us with a message of Spiritual Liberty, revealing thereby the real nature of spirituality as inherent to liberty of thought and feeling. Another great teaching of our Master is the Unity of Religious Ideals, which implies being liberated from such feelings as 'my religion' as opposed to 'your religion'. The religion of our time is destined to be the religion of the heart, and since there are many hearts, there are as many religious ideals springing forth from one and the same source, wherein wisdom and purity prevail. When the doors of the temple of the heart are open, humility awakens upon finding oneself face to face with the living God within.

The message of Love, Harmony and Beauty is like a Divine stream of spiritual evolution flowing onwards throughout our daily lives, and this awakening to purity and wisdom is the true essence of all that is understood by the term 'Sufi'.

Hidayat Inayat Khan

INTRODUCTION

In the Gathas the Sufi Movement offers a spiritual treasure to the general reader. In the beginning the Gathas were reserved for the *mureeds*, the students of the Inner School of the Sufi Movement. Different subjects were studied in short teachings which gradually led to the mystical essence of the subject. In this way Hazrat Inayat Khan created Gathas which are jewels of beauty and truth. They are very clear, and yet they ask for deep reflection to reveal their meaning in our lives today.

In this revised edition of *The Gathas*, first published in 1982, the teachings are explained in the same straightforward, personal way in which the Master taught his disciples. They cover seven main subjects, as outlined on the main Contents page in this book; there are three Gathas on each subject and within each Gatha are ten successive teachings. Each Gatha gives a focused insight into aspects of life that are important for our moral, religious and spiritual development. We might say that they distil from the Sufi Message condensed expressions of wisdom for the personal reflection and meditation of seekers on the spiritual path.

In 'Superstitions, Customs and Beliefs' (*Etekad, Rasm u Ravaj*) the Gathas begin with an exploration of the wisdom, intuition and psychic law implicit in many old customs and beliefs. After a general explanation of superstition and belief they go deeper into the meaning of, for example, the Greek mysteries and oracles, and continues to discuss the mystical meaning of important life events like weddings, births and funeral customs, and the influence of numbers, the planets and the days of the week.

Wisdom leads to insight into all aspects of life, just as through insight we can open our hearts to life's lessons which lead us to wisdom. The Gathas on 'Insight' (*Kashf*) begin with subjects like the glance of the seer, movement, expression and qualities of mind; they go on to explore psychological themes concerning the language of the mind, balance in life, intuition, and progress to more mystical subjects like the power of words, the re-echo of the past and tranquillity.

Symbology was an ancient and subtle way of teaching wisdom. As it is poetically expressed in the first Gatha on symbology (*Naqsh Bandi*), 'it is speaking without speaking, writing without writing. The symbol may be said to be an ocean in a drop.' Each Gatha explains a different symbol in a very illuminating way, ending with 'the symbology of religious ideas' and a mystical interpretation of stories from different religious traditions.

To help us come closer to the ideal offered to us in the Gathas, development of the breath (*Pasi Anfas*) can be extremely helpful. Breath plays an important role in the training given in the Inner School of the Sufi Movement and the Gathas on breath explain many aspects of the breath which have a great mystical meaning. For example, we look at its channel and rhythm; the direction and fineness of the breath and the ideal of being conscious of every breath; and some of the effects of this development, such as inspiration, thought reading and magnetism, all of which culminate in the great mystery of the breath.

Wisdom and purity are constantly tested in our relations to other people. Morals (*Suluk*) are of essential importance on the spiritual path. The Gathas on this subject – also called Cultivation of the Heart – use deep psychological and mystical insight to go into the development of personality and training of the ego. The results of this training encourage qualities such as friendship, respect and modesty in the creation of a beautiful personality.

As Hidayat Inayat Khan, son of Hazrat Inayat Khan and present Head of the Sufi Movement, explains in the foreword to this book, Sufism means both wisdom and purity. These are related in that wisdom arises when the mind is purified. The Gathas on 'Everyday Life' (*Taqwa Taharat*) help us to develop many important practical aspects of purity, starting with purity of the body, the breath and the diet, leading to purification of the mind; and then going more deeply into themes such as purity of the heart, radiance of the face, innocence and exaltation.

In essence the Gathas culminate in the final teachings on 'Metaphysics' (*Tasawwuf*). Here different qualities are discussed which can lead the student to a deep understanding and experience of life. Beginning with subjects like faith and belief, hope and patience, they explore will-power, thought, dependence upon God and spirituality; and go on in great philosophical depth to subjects like attitude and the will, human and Divine.

There are subtle links between the Gathas on different subjects with the same number in the same series. Hazrat Inayat Khan was conscious of the importance of all-round progress in all ways and in all aspects of life, so that a deeper insight into each subject would help to gain more understanding of the whole. In classes in the Inner School, Gathas on different subjects with the same number were therefore studied together. In this edition the teachings on one subject are grouped together to give a clearer overview. For those who wish to study the Gathas progressively, through all subjects simultaneously, an alternative list of contents is given at the end of the book.

In this edition we have reproduced as faithfully as possible Hazrat Inayat Khan's words as they are to be found in the first stencilled edition of *The Gathas*, preserved in the archives of the Sufi International Headquarters. These were produced during Hazrat Inayat Khan's lifetime with his consent and under his supervision. In the course of time several stencilled editions were issued, some differing slightly from one another. In a few cases, when a new idea was added later, this has been included in this edition. These words are taken to be authentic.

Hazrat Inayat Khan did not always give titles to the Gathas. As far as the subjects 'Insight,' 'Breath' and 'Everyday Life' are concerned, titles are rarely found. For 'Moral Culture' only two titles exist: 'The development of the personality' and

'The training of the ego'. Most of the titles of the Gathas on 'Superstitions, Customs and Beliefs', 'Symbology' and 'Metaphysics' are authentic. The others have been given later for the first edition of *The Gathas* in 1982.

Originally no Questions and Answers were included in *The Gathas*. Questions were not encouraged as the intention of the 'sacred readings' has always been to develop a responsive attitude in the student, the simple opening of mind and heart to receive the teaching which leaves no room for questioning. However, as these questions have been raised and as they are helpful in elucidating and sometimes enlarging the subject, they are included here at the end of the book.

H J Witteveen
September 1999

Towards the One,

the Perfection of love, harmony and beauty,

the Only Being,

united with all the illuminated souls

who form the embodiment of the Master,

the Spirit of Guidance

PART ONE

◆

SUPERSTITIONS, CUSTOMS AND BELIEFS

Etekad, Rasm u Ravaj

GATHA I

Every country appears to have certain beliefs which are held as beliefs by the believers and are called superstitions by those who do not believe. Some beliefs arise from subtle experiences of life, while others spring from intuition. They are believed by some who are inclined to believe, but are mocked at by some who cannot understand their meaning, and often by those who do not wish to trouble themselves to investigate the truth in them. It is easy to laugh at things and it takes patience to endure and tolerate things that cannot appeal to one's reason. It is difficult to investigate the truth of such beliefs, for it requires something more than reason to probe the depths of life. Those from whom the beliefs come, naturally could not give the explanation of those beliefs to everybody, for the man who is capable of believing a thing, is not necessarily capable of understanding it analytically.

There are natures which would be willing to believe a thing if it is for their good, if it comes to them from someone whom they trust, without troubling to go deeply into the matter. For some it is better that they should *not* seek to analyse their belief, for while the belief is helpful its explanation is confusing. It is a certain spiritual evolution that enables a person to understand a certain belief; a man must not be told what he is incapable of understanding, for instead of helping him it puts him off.

There is a great deal of psychic law which can be traced in such beliefs and in time the beliefs turn into customs. There is a vast field of knowledge in the beliefs of Indians. India is a country where beliefs have existed unchanged for thousands of years, and some beliefs have become customs. At first sight it might seem to an intellectual person, looking no further than the surface of things, that people in India are full of

3

superstitions. Their whole life seems based on them, not only in religion but also in their domestic affairs. In their everyday life every move they make, every word they say is in accordance with some underlying belief.

No doubt a tendency to take an interest in superstition should always be avoided, for the more thought one gives to the subject, the more one seems to be drowned in the thought of superstition. Wherever the superstitious man looks he gets an impression of some fear, some doubt, some suspicion, which generally leads to confusion. But for the wise man a disregard of superstitions is not satisfactory either, for by wisdom man becomes capable of understanding. To understand superstitions is better than to mock them or even to believe in them; for the one who believes is, so to speak, in the water and knows that he is in the water, but he who mocks is in the water but does not know that he is in the water. By understanding, man is capable of swimming in the water; by mastering them he walks on the water. The man who knows all things, and acts according to his knowledge, becomes the master of life.

I:2 BELIEF

The term 'belief' is used for an idea in which one believes but for which one cannot give a reason. Such ideas, when of an ordinary nature, are termed superstitions and, when of a sacred nature, they are called beliefs.

Often man confuses belief with truth. Many people, without understanding their own belief, hold it not as *a* truth but as *the* truth, and thereby ignore all other beliefs which seem to them different from the truth they possess. In reality belief is not the truth nor is the truth a belief. When a person has risen to the understanding of the truth, it is no more a belief for him, it is a conviction.

Beliefs of a sacred nature, which come in the realm of religion, are as steps towards the goal which is called truth, and when man stops at a belief, the belief holds him and he holds the belief. Neither can the belief push him onward nor can he advance. In many cases belief, which should serve as wings on which to soar towards the height, becomes as nails fixing man onto the earth. Every belief in the beginning is a step in the dark, but as man approaches the goal then every step becomes more and more illuminated. Thus there is hope for the believer, but the case of the unbeliever is hopeless.

There are souls who are capable of believing, even capable of understanding their belief, who yet for some reason are not willing to believe and reject a belief before the understanding comes. The wise course in life would be to try to become a pupil – a pupil of one teacher as well as a pupil of all beings. It is then that one will become a pupil of God.

Then the wise course would be to investigate the truth of belief instead of giving up one's belief, also to be patiently tolerant of the belief of another until one sees from his point of view the truth of his belief. When man sees only from his own point of view, he sees with one eye and the other eye is closed. The complete view is in seeing from both points of view, however contrary they may be. It is this which will balance things and will give the right idea of things. In order to view a building one must stand in the street and view it, instead of standing inside it and wanting to see the outside.

In understanding beliefs one must be able to neutralize one's spirit, and to the extent to which it is neutralized man becomes capable of seeing the belief in its right sense. When man says, on hearing something from another, 'That is not what I believe,' he shows his weakness, he shows his incapacity to view the belief of the other from the point of view of that other. Knowledge comes from readiness to learn it, and when we refuse it in life it is by lack of readiness. No matter from what source knowledge may seem to come, it is from one source in reality, and when the mind becomes a free receptacle, knowledge flows freely into the heart.

There is some truth hidden in every religious belief and often it is of greater value than it may seem to be. And believing in a thing without understanding is a first step forward to knowledge, and refusing to believe when a belief is presented means taking a step backward. When a person is content with his belief, that is a comfortable state of being, but it is the understanding of the belief which is ideal.

I:3 CUSTOMS (1)

M any customs that have existed in different countries for a very long time have some psychical significance, and it is barely understood. Customs such as greeting one another and asking after one another's health, even such habits as that of talking about the weather, arise from a psychical basis. This shows that the ancient peoples in the East or West had more magic in their lives than the man of today. The world has lost the magic charm, so to speak, which was the inheritance of the human race, owing to ever-increasing materialism and ignorance of things that are beyond matter.

Recently, however, science *is* discovering some psychological truths concerning human life. The process that science follows in discovering these truths is contrary to that of the mystic. The scientist wishes to climb the mountain from the level ground. The mystic tries to reach the summit of the mountain by way of meditation, and from there he sees the whole beauty of the mountain. Naturally, therefore, the horizon before the eyes of the mystic is incomparably wider than the horizon before the scientist. Certainly, the scientist may see things clearly, distinctly and in detail, whereas the mystic has a general idea of things. Often the vision of the mystic is vague in comparison with the analytical examination of a scientist and yet, while the mystic sees through objects, the scientist can only reach as far as their surface.

Owing to the greater activity in Western life all things change more quickly in the West, while in the East changes come very slowly. Therefore one finds many customs of ancient origin in the East which signify the development of Eastern people in psychical things.

Even ordinary customs such as shaking hands or rising from one's seat to receive someone, bowing, bending, waving or clapping the hands, have a psychical significance. When two people shake hands with one another, magnetism is exchanged between them and a balance of life force is made between them. The one who lacks strength, energy or magnetic power gains, and through the one from whom they overflow they are used for a better purpose.

By rising to show respect to a person and by walking a few steps to receive a person, a man makes himself ready to withstand the forces of the one who is coming. By rising to his feet and walking a step or two he makes his pulsation regular and puts his circulation in order, thus making himself psychically and morally ready to defend himself, if the one who is coming should happen to be a foe, and ready to meet him harmoniously and on the same level, physically, mentally and morally, if he happens to be a friend.

Inclining the head in a bow quickens not only the circulation in the head but also the magnetic current in it, for the head is the chief moral and spiritual factor in man. You will always find that a person with a habit of bowing is thoughtful, and it often happens that the one who keeps his head erect and avoids bowing is foolish.

Man's life depends upon rhythm, rhythm in his breath, in the pulsation, in the beats of his heart and head, and it is irregularity of the rhythm of his heart or of his pulse that shows disorder in his health. It is regularity of rhythm that keeps man in a fit state to go on through life. And when people applaud a speaker, a singer, a player, it is a suggestion for him to continue his rhythm, physical, mental or moral. Even waving one's hand in parting from a friend suggests the same meaning: continue to be in a fit state to live and enjoy life.

There is a custom in the East that, when a person is yawning, a friend by his side claps his hands or snaps his fingers. Yawning naturally makes the rhythm slow; it is going down, so to speak, and the clapping of the hands or the snapping of the fingers on the part of the friend is suggestive of continuing the same rhythm as before.

Different peoples have different customs, and customs that one is not in the habit of seeing seem not only strange and meaningless but often also ridiculous. It is the work of the seer to see into things, and it is this way of viewing which is called insight.

I:4 CUSTOMS (2)

There are different customs in greeting, and in every custom there is some suggestion that explains some psychical meaning behind it. The Hindus greet by joining the palms of the hands, which has the significance of perfection, since the right hand represents the positive power and the left hand the negative power; and when the positive and negative are joined together this sums up in perfection. The idol of Buddha which is worshipped by millions of people in the world signifies perfection – sitting cross-legged, the two palms joined, the eyes closed, all showing that the negative and positive powers are united and made into one.

The greeting of the Chinese is the clasping of the hands, each touching the clasped hands of the other, which means that the perfection of power from both should meet. For the same reason the Arabs shake hands with both hands, for giving one hand is like giving half of one's magnetism, but by giving both hands you show that you keep nothing back.

The Persians touch the heart, which suggests the friendly feeling expressed from the bottom of the heart – that the greeting is not merely superficial, that it comes from the very depth of feeling.

Among a great many people around the world there is a custom of greeting by embracing one another and no doubt there is a great psychical meaning in this. The two arms are the two directions of magnetic power, positive and negative, and in the breast is the centre of these two powers. The custom is that they embrace twice, distinctly on the right and left sides; this is also the exchange of *prana*, the very life, the centre of which is in the breast.

There is a custom both in Persia and in India that, when a younger person greets an older one, he bows his head bringing it closer to his breast, and the elder person, taking his arms, raises him up as if the younger person wanted from the elder person love, light and life; and the elder person gives it to him and raises him with it. It also suggests a sentiment of modesty and humility on the part of the one, and help and encouragement on the part of the other. Customs have sometimes been much exaggerated and yet, if the sentiment is a true one, no external expression can ever be an exaggeration.

Among people of religion and culture in all periods of civilization there has been a custom of kissing the hand. The custom has originated from a natural instinct in life. What smells good the animal first wants to bite, and everything that interests the infant it first puts in its mouth. This shows that the lips are the most sensitive part in man, and that they are capable of the giving and taking of life which may be called magnetism. The greatest fondness, therefore, that one can show to another in greeting can be shown by kissing the hands. This custom may be seen all over the world, in the East and in the West.

A skeleton plan of man's spirit can be drawn as a sun in the midst and five rays shooting out around: one straight upwards, two at the sides rising upwards and two downwards. It is this which makes the five-pointed star. Man's head, two arms and two legs are the outward expression of these rays. The idea of the Hindus in touching the holy feet of the saint is to reach first the two rays that can first be reached; and when one reaches these two, the three other rays naturally fall over one's head when the saint puts his arms over one's head and bends his own head while blessing, looking at the centre of the head of the one who is blessed.

I:5 HANUMAN

There is a custom in the East of offering oil to Hanuman, the idol that is pictured in the image of a monkey. This idol is worshipped by pouring oil upon it. The custom can also be seen at Indian weddings: young women anoint with oil the head, shoulders, arms and hands, knees and feet of the bride and bridegroom. One sees this custom in some churches, for instance in the Catholic church. In Russia there was a custom of anointing the tsar's forehead with oil on the day of his coronation.

Oil has the significance of softening. Leather, iron or steel is either made softer or smoother by putting oil on it. Anointing as it is done in India is a psychical suggestion to the bride and bridegroom that the hands and feet of each shall be ready to serve the other, and that they shall not show themselves stiff one to the other; that if there were any hardness in their nature it should be softened, since harmony is the blessing of a home. It teaches that forgiveness is required for becoming friends and keeping friendship; the mate is not so flexible and docile as one's own imagination conceives.

The idol of Hanuman is suggestive of primitive nature in man, and in the pouring of oil in the service of Hanuman there are two lessons that the worshipper has to learn. One is that however great your evolution may be, regard and consideration for the primitive nature is necessary, for all adjusts itself in the wider scheme of nature. When man stands with his hands folded in humility before the image of a monkey, it is to learn the lesson that life is such that, with all your evolution, you lack something if you have no regard to the primitive nature that is in man. Christ taught us, 'Resist not evil,' and 'If one sue thee for thy coat, give him thy cloak also.' This teaches the same lesson: that life becomes difficult without regard and consideration for the primitive nature. By resentment one partakes it, by rebelling against it one gives fuel to that fire. One should soften it in oneself and in another by wisdom, patience and gentleness.

The anointing of the forehead of the king signifies that he should have an easy expression – not frowning brows and a puckered face, but a 'smiling forehead', as the Persian phrase is. Poor and rich, all must come to the king with their troubles and difficulties and his glance must comfort them and bring them ease.

The great lesson one can learn from this custom is that the great education in life is to soften one's feelings, one's thoughts, words and actions, that they may give ease to ourselves and that we may create an atmosphere of ease that may benefit all who come in contact with us.

I:6 BELLS AND GONGS

The secret of the religious custom of having gongs and bells in temples and churches lies in the great science of the Hindus which is *mantra yoga*. In the first place this custom unites several religions, since bells are rung in Christian churches, in the temples of the Hindus and in Buddhist pagodas. Many think that it is a call to prayer, but from a mystical point of view it is something more than that. The idea of the mystic is to make his heart capable of resonance, that every voice that rises on earth or descends from heaven may have its re-echo in his heart.

The Sufi prepares himself by his exercises of *zikar* and *fikar* to make his heart capable of producing that resonance that may be caused on earth or descend from heaven. When the centres of the body and the faculties of the mind are prepared to produce that resonance, then they respond to every sound. And every time the bell is rung it has its re-echo in the heart of the mystic, and every centre of his being begins to think of God and to feel God.

Vibration is a greater stimulant than wine. Wine gives intoxication to the brain, but vibration produces ecstasy in the heart. Therefore Sufis have called it 'wine'.

The custom of having flowers in the house of prayer and the custom of burning incense in the place of worship also exist in almost all religions and have existed in almost all periods. Colour and beauty also have a power, an influence upon the mind and body, and those who can enjoy the beauty of colour and the delicacy of the flower receive help by way of the eyes. Its effect opens the heart which then responds to the blessing from above. This shows that the beauty of the earth can be best used to obtain the blessing from heaven.

The perfume of flowers or incense has a deeper effect still, because colour and beauty are only reflected upon the heart through the eyes, but perfume and incense, rising through the breath, touch the heart, making it capable of spiritual exaltation.

But nothing has a greater influence on the human soul than sound. Therefore hymns are sung in all churches, prayers are offered and chants are recited, all in order to wake the spirit within to life, which enables the soul to respond to the perfection of God.

1:7 THE CUSTOM OF DRINKING
TO THE HEALTH OF FRIENDS

This custom has a psychological meaning. Wine has an influence that takes away the worries and anxieties of life and makes one unconscious of one's environment, and this only is the condition which may be called the proper one for concentration. Those who cannot concentrate will realize by studying the condition of their mind that they are either worried or anxious about something, or they are conscious of the environments of their life. It is that which keeps them back from concentration.

All those who have become great in the worldly, artistic or spiritual aspects of life have arrived at their destination by the power of concentration. It is by concentration that a person from being poor becomes wealthy; it is by concentration that one invents things that the world has never known; it is by concentration that one arrives at a desired position in life; and it is by the power of concentration that man enters the world unseen.

The custom of drinking to a person's health therefore proves to be based on a psychological idea, the idea that one holds a wish in one's mind at a time when one's mind will be put into a state of concentration, that during the time that one's mind is in that state the thought of one's friend's health will be predominant.

There is a custom of making the glasses touch each other, which is supposed to be a promise of friendship. It can be defined symbolically in this way that a cup is the symbol of the heart, for in the heart there is the capacity of holding the divine love, which is the sacred wine. So the cup touching the cup means heart united with heart. According to the mystical view it is two becoming one.

I:8 THE ORIGIN OF THE CUSTOM OF THE SECLUSION OF WOMEN

The custom of the seclusion of women has its source in mystical thought. There used to be the mystical Orders of people in the East who contemplated in solitude and lived in seclusion. The magnetism and power of influence that they developed by seclusion was in itself a marvel. This gave power to their gaze, power in their word and influence in their atmosphere.

This custom of seclusion was then imitated by the kings and people of high rank. They had two ways of veiling themselves when away from home. One was to put a covering over the back of the head, which was made to hang down in front so that the eyes could be half covered, and the other was to put a veil over the face. It was a sort of mantle that they put on their head. Every prophet of Beni Israel had this. In the ancient pictures of the prophets of Semitic race one will always see the head covered with a mantle.

In the Hindu race also many Orders of Buddhists and Yogis wore a mantle over the head. The veil, which the kings also used, which was called *miqna*, later became customary in the East, and ladies of high rank wore what is called in Turkish the *yashmak*. For thousands of years it has been the custom among Parsees that during their religious services the priest covered his head with a turban together with a mantle. And the Parsee women have kept the custom of covering the head with a white cloth, though it is less observed at the present time. In India, among Hindus as well as among Muslims, there is a custom at weddings of veiling the faces of bride and bridegroom with a veil of jasmine flowers.

Under all these different customs of veiling the head and face one finds a mystical significance. Man's form is considered by Sufis as consisting of two parts, the head and the body; the body for action and the head for thought. Since the head is for thought, its radiance is incomparably greater than that of the body, and the hairs are as rays of that radiance in a physical form. It is a constant outpouring of light that one observes in a person's life. Every action of looking or breathing or speaking robs so much of the radiance out of a person's life. By preserving this radiance the mystic develops within him that influence, power and magnetism which in the average person are wasted. For instance, closing the eyes, which is a custom among mystics, not only helps in concentration and repose of mind, but during the moment when the eyes are closed it preserves the radiance from flowing out.

These customs were helpful to the kings and commanders for developing their power and influence, and they were valued for ladies of rank for preserving their beauty and charm. We learn by this that a life but little exposed to the outer world, whether through seclusion or silence or a perfect state of repose with closed eyes, clasped hands and crossed legs, has a great influence.

I:9 THE CUSTOM OF
THE SECLUSION OF WOMEN (1)

The custom of the seclusion of the mystics remains only in the mystical Orders, but one finds the seclusion of women prevalent in the East. When a custom takes root in a section of society it certainly can be used and abused as people may choose. No doubt jealousy, which in human nature is a proof of love, can be the source of a great many crimes. Man has always guarded the treasures that he values most and, since that which a man can love most is a woman, he has often through ignorance tried to guard her in the same way as all things of value and importance. The custom of seclusion has been in his hand a means that has enabled him to control his household in the manner he likes.

However, it is not true that this custom was the outcome of the teachings of the Prophet. There are only two places in the records where an utterance of the Prophet on the subject is to be found. In one place it is told that, when some coarse dancing was taking place among the peasants of his land, he said that women must be properly clad; in the other, that when the ladies of the Prophet's household were returning home after taking care of the Prophet and his army during a battle, they did not wish to look at the battlefield and to show themselves to their enemies. The only advice that the Prophet gave was that now that peace had been made, if they did not like to show themselves, they might veil their faces.

In India one sees the custom that an aged woman covers her face, a widow covers her face, and a bride veils her face. There is some psychological meaning in this. It is the nature of every soul to wish to hide its sorrow; by veiling her face the widow veils her sorrow from others, and the veil that one sees on the face of an aged woman is there for the reason that in age the emotions become more visible and one has little control so as to hide them from others. When the heart has become softened, at every little touch however gentle it is easily moved, and the covering is as a shield over it. On the face of a bride the veil is for the preservation of her charm, of magnetism. At the same time the finest beauty in human nature is modesty, in whatever form it appears.

I:10 THE CUSTOM OF
THE SECLUSION OF WOMEN (2)

From both the physical and the occult point of view woman is more impressionable than man. The task of woman as a mother is of a greater importance than that of man in any position. Woman with her thought and feeling moulds the character of the child, and as she is susceptible to outward impressions, her impressions always have their influence on her child.

During the period before motherhood very great care must be taken, for any word spoken to her reaches the depth of her being, and it re-echoes in the soul of the child. If a word made her bitter at the time or cross at a moment, it can create bitterness or crossness in the child. Especially during that period woman is more sensitive and susceptible to all impressions, beautiful or ugly; anything striking impresses her soul deeply. A colour, lightning, thunder, storm, all make impressions upon her; conditions of life, misery or joy, all tell upon her more than on every person. Having this in consideration the custom of seclusion has been kept in the East and still exists among certain communities.

No doubt there is another side to consider: that home and state are not two separate things. Home is the miniature of the state and if woman performs a part equally important at home, why must she not perform an equally important part in the outward life? No doubt these ancient customs, even with their psychological importance, often make an iron bar before the progress of the generality.

In the East, for both maid and mistress, there are days set apart for rest in every month in all different religions, among

Hindus, Parsees and Muslims. The life in the world is a constant battle, and a hard battle one has to fight if one has any fineness of feeling, any decency of manner. The position of woman in this battle is worse than that of man. It greatly robs her of her womanly fineness and delicacy of sentiment.

Man is more dependent upon woman than woman on man. From the first moment any child, whether boy or girl, opens his eyes in the world, he seeks the protection of woman. Woman, as his mother, sister, daughter, friend or wife, in every form, is the source of man's happiness, comfort and peace. In whatever form he may express it – in a crude custom like the seclusion in the East or in many different ways – to guard her against the hard knocks which fall on every soul living in this world of selfishness is the first duty of a thoughtful man.

GATHA II

There is a remarkable phrase in the Bible, where Christ says, 'Eat my flesh and drink my blood.' What does he mean by saying this? He means in the first place that what a living being loves most is his food; what he loves most he eats. It has been proved in ferocious and dreadful times in the world by people eating their own children that food is dearer than their own child.

The word of Christ therefore means: 'Find out what it is in me that you love which may become your nourishment, which may become your food. It is not this, my flesh and blood; this will not suffice to satisfy your appetite. There is another part of my being which is in abundance and can nourish my numberless devotees. Therefore before trying to eat my flesh and blood, try to find out on what plane I really exist and what is my true being.'

The lives of all the great saints show that not only their adversaries and opponents, but also their near and dear friends have proved to be among their worst enemies. There is a creature which loves its mate so much that it eats its mate.

Now about the question what it is that Christ speaks of as his flesh and blood. His flesh is the knowledge of God and his blood is the love of God, because it is love that has a tendency, so to speak, to excite the circulation, and it is knowledge which has the tendency to strengthen, making man firm, which is symbolized by flesh. One thing without the other would be abnormal. For instance, flesh without blood or blood without flesh – neither are normal conditions. What gives normal health to the body and to the soul is flesh and blood both. In the religious custom of the sacrament of bread and wine this secret is symbolically expressed.

II:2 Customs of courtesy

There was a custom in the old, aristocratic times which is adhered to even now in the East and even somewhat in the West of walking backwards when leaving someone who was respected. It was not only a custom but had a psychological point of view. When two people are talking together facing each other, a current of sympathy is established which runs chiefly through the breath and through the glance; necessarily one of them is expressive, the other receptive. When the back is turned that current is broken, and the ancient idea was to retain that current which they thought was valuable for every possible moment.

There was another custom of courtesy of the ancients which still exists in certain places, that in order to show a sign of respect to someone they bent their knees. This had the psychological effect that every influence of love, affection or sympathy, benediction or blessing is poured through the glance, the breath and words; and if the receiver were taller than the bestower, the influence would go into the ground instead of touching the person. Especially the influence of the glance which surrounds one with sympathy and good wishes has mostly its direction downwards, and it is naturally so with the breath.

In the salutation made by putting one knee on the ground, the knee resting on the ground expresses readiness to receive the command, and the knee that is up is ready to go forwards to carry it out.

But besides their psychical influences different manners of courtesy have been the outcome of human progress in the direction of refinement. Yet progress is like unto a wave in the sea: it rises and it falls. So it is with manner. This time seems to be the time when the wave is returning. However, doing is one thing and understanding what one does is another thing. Whether one does a certain thing or does not do it, that is another question, but in the understanding of all things lies the purpose of life.

II:3 CUSTOMS OF THE MARRIAGE CEREMONY

India, the land of mysticism and philosophy, has symbolism in all its customs. Even in the marriage ceremony everything that is done as a custom or rite is symbolical. Both bride and bridegroom wear on their hand a pearl-embroidered heart; they wear saffron-coloured garments for the ten days the wedding ceremony lasts; they are anointed during the wedding ceremony on their heads, shoulders, elbows and chins, and on their knees and feet. The bridegroom has a sword in his hand during all those ten days. On the last day of the wedding both bride and bridegroom are veiled with a low-flowing veil made of jasmine flowers and trimmed with roses, and after the conclusion of the marriage ceremony they are unveiled.

Now the meaning of this veil of flowers is that a new phase of life for them begins. They are no more the same as before; they have new responsibilities, new hopes and a new life to begin. The meaning of the sword is that the bridegroom shall uphold the honour and dignity of his family, of his wife, that he will stand in arms to defend the honour and dignity that the connection of the bride and bridegroom has completed. And the heart on the hand denotes that both of them will let their action be directed by their heart. The anointing means that the hands and feet and head of either will be ready to serve the other when occasion arises, that they will not be stiff at any time when their service is called for.

The colour of saffron in the East is considered to be the colour of all sorts of good luck; it is the imperial sign; love letters are also written in saffron yellow. The invitations for the wedding are written in this colour, for this colour represents light. Light in heaven and gold on earth both are yellow. Therefore the yellow colour is preferred to all other colours when it is to become the omen of some good occasion in life.

II:4 THE HORSE

The horse has been considered a lucky animal in all ages, for it represents energy, strength, activity and life. Among the Ancient Greeks the horse was a prominent feature of their art; so was it among the Persians of old times. In the courts of the ancient kings in the East there used to be *chama*, fans made of horsehair, also emblems of the horse's head have been used as decorations in the palaces, and before every entertainment there was something spoken about the horse first. The jesters of India still have that custom; the first item of their programme is an imitation of a horse. A story of a horse is always interesting. A sportsman and a philosopher, who are so different in the objects of their likes, may unite in the admiration of the horse.

The Prophet Mohammed has admired the horse as one of the objects worth attaining in life. The most interesting part of the *Ramayana* is where Lava, the son of Rama, goes in pursuit of Kalanki, the ideal horse. In the sacred book of the Hindus, *Mahabharata*, it is Krishna who is the charioteer of Arjuna. Hassan and Hussein, the great martyrs of Islam, whose day is celebrated each year, are represented with their beautiful horse called Duldul.

The horse is the symbol of the mind. When the mind is under control it is as though one were riding a horse. When it cannot be controlled it is a restive horse; when its rein is not well in hand it is a wild horse roaming about in the wilderness.

The horse is also the symbol of life, representing its energy, activity and beauty. The horse with its strength and activity is harmless, useful, intelligent, and has feeling and yet is different from the donkey. The horse is the companion of war and is the dignity of great warriors. The unity that is sometimes established between the soul of the rider and the spirit of the horse is most wonderful.

The metal horseshoe is considered lucky in all countries for it bears the sign of the horse and gives the impression of the horse's vigour, activity, life and beauty.

II:5 ORACLES AMONG THE ANCIENT GREEKS

In Ancient Greece often a question was asked of an oracle which very often was answered by a woman, who sometimes gave a straightforward answer, and sometimes one with a meaning which was veiled. It was the same thing manifested today in a spiritualistic séance, a mediumistic answer, which has a continuing interest in all ages though in different forms. Among all the occult and mystical interests the interest in the medium has a greater attraction for the average mind.

A woman was often chosen for this work for the reason of her sensitiveness which always exceeds that of man and which is the secret of intuition in human nature. Especially a celibate woman was chosen for this purpose, as in her is to be found more susceptibility to intuition. The question was supposed to be asked of a god, a god who was distinguished by a particular attribute – of poetry, of the sun or some other attribute.

The secret of all this is that the priests by their hypnotic power and suggestion wakened in the woman that particular attribute of the Spirit within who is the possessor of all knowledge, especially that pertaining to the attribute with which he is identified. God is already in the heart of every person; only, to wake Him and to make Him rise He ought to be called upon. He then, so to speak, takes birth from the heart of a sensitive woman whose innermost being can be easily touched.

God has many attributes, He has many ears and many tongues to speak with, and through every form He answers whenever one reaches Him. Spiritualists call Him a spirit, but even through the spirit of an individual, dead or living, when God is called, God answers. Those who play with spiritualistic séances would give it all up in a moment if they only knew that God always answers, when He is called upon.

II:6 THE GREEK MYSTERIES (1)

The little that is known of the Greek mysteries has been very variously interpreted. Some have supposed them to have been a course of agriculture taught secretly, others a mummery carried on for centuries by the priests. What is known with certainty is the high esteem in which they were held and the strict secrecy which attended them. The word means 'silence'; to be initiated was 'to be made silent'.

Access to the lesser mysteries was easy; tens of thousands were initiated. The temples in which the rites were practised were under the protection of the state. In them were enacted the lives of the gods in whose name the mysteries were celebrated, and great use was made of music. The mysteries were held to remove the fear of death and to give assurance of the survival of the departed. Those who had been initiated were believed to be happy after death, while others led a dismal life hereafter, clinging to their graves.

The preparatory training for the greater mysteries was very severe. Fasting was undergone, abstinence of all sorts, extremes of heat and cold had to be endured, and the candidates swam through water for days and had to walk through fire. The training often lasted many years. After initiation, first all was darkness, dread and dismay; then a marvellous light was seen and shining forms came to meet the initiate.

The initiate experienced while on earth the state of the soul dissociated from the body. As a Greek writer says, 'Here all instruction ceases, one beholds the nature of things.' Apuleius, who had received all the initiations of the mysteries, says: 'I went to the boundary between life and death, I passed through the four elements, I stood on the threshold of Proserpina, at the time of deepest midnight I saw the sun shine in brightest splendour. I saw the greater and the lesser gods and revered them near at hand.' The initiate was said to be received, while living on earth, among the immortal gods and made as one of them.

II:7 THE GREEK MYSTERIES (2)

This was really a Sufi institution, though not called by this name, for exactly the same thing is to be found today in the Sufi schools in India and Persia. The lesser mysteries were *ilm-e-rabbani*, the mystery of the gods; in other words, the mystery of the different attributes of God. For when the proper name of God is repeated a certain number of times, some particular effect is produced by it, resulting in a desirable object. Before Islam the different names of God were considered to be different gods known by different names and identified with different attributes and characteristics. By invoking the names of different gods a person accomplished his object in life, as now *wazifa* is practised by the Sufis.

The music which the ancient Greek knowers of the mystery had as a means of their spiritual development – the same is used even now in the Chishtia schools of Sufis where the Qawwali meeting which is called *sama* is held, in which music is played and sung in order to awaken the emotional nature, which is the secret of revelation.

II:8 THE GREEK MYSTERIES (3)

The fasting and abstinence and all these things were taught in order to develop the will-power, which results in self-discipline and which is the secret of all mastery. It is by this power that the kingdom within is attained. Once man has touched his self within, the illusion becomes dissolved. The fear of death is caused by the consciousness of mortality. As long as one is unaware of one's immortal self, one has the fear of death. Once the immortality of the soul is realized and the realization is no longer in one's imagination but has become a conviction, then one rises above the fear of death. This knowledge is gained fully when an adept is able to detach his soul from his body. It is this state which is called by Yogis *samadhi* and by Sufis *nayat*.

Every soul that treads the path of initiation takes his first step through the darkness. As Ghazali says, 'The spiritual pursuit is like shooting an arrow through the darkness.' No doubt as one approaches the goal the light comes. As the *Qur'an* says, 'God is the light of the heavens and the earth.' Then, once the sight has become keen, there is no further instruction needed. One gets insight into the hidden laws of nature, all things seem to speak to the seer of their character, nature and secret. This realization removes the boundary between life and death. One rises above the elements which have formed this mortal abode – the body and mind – for the soul's experience, when one touches one's true being, the soul.

It is the soul-realized man who stands above all matter, and in this way the spirit gets victory over matter. Under all conditions of life which produce obscurity and confusion the soul-realized man sees the light, and to him all men of lesser or greater degrees of evolution are nothing but different forms of the divine immanence.

In this way the man who has probed the depths of the mystery of life becomes God-realized. When he no longer has his limited self before his view, then only he experiences the state of which Christ has spoken, 'Be ye perfect as your Father in heaven is perfect.'

II:9 THE BANSHEE

There is a very widespread belief that in certain families warning of the impending death of a member of the family is given always in the same way. In some families a certain bird is seen by some member of the family before a death, in others the church bell rings without being tolled, in another one or more flagstones of the pavement of the chapel are seen to be wet while the rest are dry and the number of wet flagstones tallies with the number of deaths.

In Ireland such warnings are particularly frequent and often occur in the form of what is called the banshee[1] – a screech heard by members of the family, but inaudible to others. This explains the truth that life is a revelation in all forms – and not restricted to any particular form.

The death of an individual is seemingly the death of one person having its effect to some extent upon that individual's surroundings and on those concerned with him or her. Yet inwardly the influence of the death of one individual reaches the whole circumference of the universe; no object, no being is left untouched by it. The banshee manifests herself to those who are particularly subject to this influence. To them the warning of death takes some form that is perceptible to them and, told by them to their relations and descendants, that form becomes a special alarm clock of death for that particular family. This may continue for a considerable time, until someone is born in that family who ignores it absolutely by his disbelief.

One learns by this that life is revealing by nature; it is man who becomes blinded by nature. There is no creature in this world so absorbed in the outer life in the world as man. So man, with greater capability of knowing, knows least of all creatures. There are birds who give warning of death; dogs, cats and horses perceive the coming death of their friend or neighbour or of their master. If man is open to the knowledge that life continually reveals, his body and mind with his intuitive centres and perceptive faculties can know the secret and the meaning of life most.

II:10 THE PSYCHOLOGY OF THE SHADOW

Among the Hindus there has been an old belief which is now taken to be a superstition even in India. Every Brahmin took great care to keep himself, his shrine of worship, his food, a woman during her maternity period and the new-born child,

---

1 A banshee is a spirit whose wail portends a death in a house.

away from the shadow of a *shudra* or outcast. Now the times are different, so naturally that belief seems meaningless, but in point of fact there was an occult meaning hidden behind it. A shadow is caused by the wall of a person standing against the sun – the sun which is life-giving to plants and human beings, to animals and to all other things, and the direct rays of which give all things new life. Places which are hidden from the sun, flat or mountainous, become the centre of much disease.

The personality which stands in the light of any person, thereby causing a hindrance in the life of that person, is an example of this. The difference between the true teacher and the false, both of whom have always existed in the world, has been distinct. The false one stood in the light of his pupil; the true one showed him the way by standing on the side.

The psychology of the shadow is very complex. The shadow of an unholy person falling upon food will certainly take away the living substance from it. If it falls upon a person in a negative state, a woman sitting aside or a child, it produces exhaustion and lifelessness; it does this also in the souls who are going through a process of recuperation or growth. Very often a tree standing above a plant, keeping from it the light, hinders the growth of the plant. So is the shadow of the unholy; it can for the moment darken the soul of those passive and receptive of spirit. No doubt the power of darkness and illusion itself, as shadow, has no existence in reality; however, it is evident. So is the influence of immature souls.

The spiritual souls have a contrary influence to this. Their presence is a stimulus to intelligence; their influence is comforting and inspiring. The phenomenon of a spiritual personality is that in his presence the memory becomes keen, the waves of inspiration rise, the clouds of depression clear away, hope springs from the depth of the heart and the soul within begins to feel alive, love manifests through thought and feeling, and all that was once dead lives again.

This shows that personality is a mystery. It gives life and causes death; it raises one to heaven and throws another back to the depths of earth. The influence of personality may change one's life, one's environment and all one's affairs. Its influence can turn the wheel of life to the right side or wrong side, diverting thereby the trend of all the affairs of life.

Very often innocent, good and pure-minded souls, because of the lack of positiveness in their natures, become the victims of undesirable personalities, personalities that stand in their lives obscuring the light for which they crave, and this may continue for a long period of time. Once a person is accustomed to being in the shade, then he is afraid to come out in the sunlight, though inwardly he may be drawn to it.

The denser a person is, the grosser is his shadow. In other words, the more material a person is, the heavier is his influence.

The whole idea of life is to live freely, to look through space freely, having nothing to hide or conceal; the light of truth to shine from within and the light of the sun without; light all around, no shadow of any kind hindering the light which is the soul of every being.

GATHA III

There is a custom prevalent in the Western world of propos-
ing toasts, one significant psychological truth behind
which is a wish for a certain thing to happen at a time when one's
own wish is being granted in some form or other. This shows that
the moment when one's wish is granted is that moment when
one is satisfied. We should not therefore wonder why people go
to spiritual souls for their blessing. Those who are spiritually
blessed, their innermost wish has been satisfied, and a wish made
by them acts as a quick blessing in the life of everyone.

But this also teaches one to catch the opportunity of getting
the good wish of every person at the moment when his wish is
being granted. Having known this psychological law the people
in the East look for the opportunity of offering food to the
hungry or a gift to the one who needed it, for the wish that
naturally rises from the heart of such a person while accepting
it will certainly be granted.

Very few in the world know how much power is hidden in
the wish of a person whose heart is, so to speak, in a state of
dancing, full of joy. We read in the legends of sages calling upon
their friends, pupils or followers at a certain time and asking
them to make a wish, for they knew the moment when the wish
could be granted.

There is a story of Hafiz, that near the home of the Shaikh
there were eleven pupils whose name was also Hafiz. But among
them there was only one who used to engage himself in his
night vigils, and the others used to rest all night. One evening
the Shaikh called, 'Hafiz!' There was only one Hafiz awake, all
others asleep. The Shaikh was holding a bowl with the thought
of the wish to be granted. With his eyes closed he gave it to
Hafiz. But then as he knew there were ten more he again called,
'Hafiz!' and as all others were asleep the same Hafiz came

again and received the bowl. Eleven times the teacher called, and the same Hafiz went again and again. In the morning ten were disappointed, and that one Hafiz was blessed with eleven-fold blessings.

It would not be an exaggeration if one said that even God has a time when He grants wishes, and if one knows that time one certainly becomes benefited and blessed. Since Sufism teaches, 'Look for God in the heart of man,' the wise *mureeds* therefore see the pleasure and displeasure of God in everyone they meet, and they carefully regard the pleasure and displeasure of those they come in contact with, knowing that in doing so they regard the pleasure and displeasure of God.

Besides having one's wish granted, the joy of giving another happiness – that itself is greater than a wish granted, if one has risen to that plane of human evolution when one can enjoy pleasure with the pleasure of another, when one can feel satisfaction in the satisfaction of another, when one can be happy in bringing happiness to another. No one will give another happiness and will not have the same come to him a thousandfold. There comes a stage of evolution in the life of man when he feels more satisfied by seeing another person satisfied with food than by his having eaten it himself, when he feels comfortable in seeing another person comfortable, when he feels richly adorned by seeing another person clothed nicely. For this stage is the stepping stone to the realization of God. (*See* Questions and Answers p 289.)

III:2 WEDDING CUSTOMS IN EUROPE

There are many superstitions and customs connected with a wedding observed in Europe, such as throwing an old shoe after the newly married couple as they go away, and throwing rice. The rice signifies flourishing, multiplication, prosperity and providence, whereas an old shoe is times past and a new life has begun.

The rings that bridegroom and bride put on each other's finger are the sign of bond, which is the real meaning of marriage. The hands of the two joined by the priest are the possession of one another, suggesting that each holds the other.

The custom of the Greek Church, where wreaths are put on the heads of the bride and bridegroom, is the exchange of thoughts and feelings; walking three times round the altar is suggestive of God between them, uniting them both one with the other in a divine link, the link which is everlasting as God Himself.

And the old custom of the bride's kissing the hand of the bridegroom, still continued even at this time when the rhythm of the world is quite changed, explains the response from the bride, in which is the secret of nature's harmony. Although what generally happens later is just the opposite – but that brings about the happy medium!

III:3 FUNERAL CUSTOMS

The human body represents the five elements, and nature's law is that every element returns to its own origin. Naturally, therefore, the being which is the air element turns into air, the heat is absorbed by the heat, the fire element has left already.

The body belongs either to earth or to water, but the body which is born on earth, not in the water, and has sought its comfort on earth, not in water, and has also been afraid of the water, an element foreign to it, had better be saved from it and had better be buried.

Again, every living being, whether man or animal, has a fear of fire. A powerful animal like the lion is afraid of the fire; the elephant with all its large body and strength runs away from fire. If that is the nature of all living beings – to be afraid of fire – then imagine for a person who is not yet dead to know that as soon as he is dead his body will be put in the fire.

Although his mind is separate from the body, yet his mind will suffer a shock just the same.

The reason for mummies is to show that if the body, which is dead, can be kept for a long time, then the life, which is real life, is eternal.

Among the ancient Egyptians there was also a custom (the same tendency exists in the East) that at every banquet a mummy was brought in for a moment and then taken away. This was in order to waken man, in the midst of his great joy, enthusiasm and pleasure, to the consciousness that there is such a thing as death, that there is something awaiting him and that he must not stay ignorant of that truth, absorbed in all the pleasures of the world. But at the same time they put the mummies also in the grave. (*See* Questions and Answers p 290.)

III:4 THE SWANSONG

It is said that the swan sings once, just before it dies. The meaning of this is that a full expression given to one's joy puts an end to life, for in the fullest expression lies life's purpose. In the life of an artist a single finished work of art, in the life of a musician his best piece of music, brings to him the warning of his departure. Sa'di says, 'Every soul is born with a purpose and the light of that purpose is kindled in his heart.' It applies not only to the soul of every person but to every living creature, however small and insignificant. Even to every object this rule can be applied.

There is a saying in the East that the elephant dies at the sight of fever, in other words, that death robs one of that which one has made oneself. If this be explained in another way, one makes one's death while making oneself. The heavy flesh that the elephant gathers around itself naturally gives power to the fever that becomes the cause of its death. The same is to be seen in the life of man; every difficulty, even death, man makes with the making of himself. It is to suggest this idea that Christ has said, 'The spirit quickeneth, the flesh profiteth nothing.'

The soul was to be immortal, but mortality it earns for itself. There is nothing that man would have been afraid of, if he did not possess something which he is afraid to be robbed of. When the hermit Machandra said to Gaurikha on their journey through the wilderness, 'Gaurikha, I feel afraid,' Gaurikha answered, 'Throw away the fear.' Machandra answered, 'How can fear be thrown away?' Gaurikha said, 'Throw away that which causes your fear.' Machandra took out from his wallet two bricks of gold and said, 'These bricks of gold, must I throw them away?' 'Yes,' said Gaurikha, 'What is it!' Machandra threw them away and as he went on his face turned pale. Gaurikha looked at him and said, 'Why are you sad?' Machandra said, 'Now we have nothing.' Gaurikha said, 'We have everything. Look before you. What do you behold?' And he beheld mountains of gold. Gaurikha said, 'Take as much as you can if that is your soul's striving.' Machandra's soul awoke, and he said, 'Nothing will I take, for I know the riches of possessing nothing.'

III:5 CUSTOMS AT THE BIRTH OF A CHILD IN INDIA

For three days from the time that the child is born, and sometimes for six days, no friends are allowed to enter the room where the child is – only those relations who are most esteemed in the family. The meaning in this custom is that the mind of the newborn child is like a photographic plate, and the first impression that it receives goes deeper in it, and other impressions have less effect. Therefore the impressions of early childhood make the foundation for the whole life.

The mother does not appear before friends for the first six days; even some relations are kept away. The meaning of this custom is that, in that negative state in which a mother is at that time, she is too sensitive to be exposed to inharmonious and coarse vibrations. In the case of the child it is not only that his mind is affected, but the first impression even influences the construction of his face and form.

At the birth of a son the occasion is celebrated by the beating of drums and gunfire. This custom no doubt comes from the ancient Rajputs whose *dharma* or sacred duty was warfare. This first noise of drums and gunfire was meant as the child's first experience or as a first lesson in warfare.

An entertainment is given in celebration of the birth of a child at which there is singing, playing and dancing. It is meant by this that a joyous atmosphere works as a push given to a swing in the life of a child on earth at its commencement.

III:6 THE SUPERSTITION OF THE DAYS, EXISTING IN THE EAST

In the East the influence of the days of the week is taken into account by all, learned or illiterate. Every time has its peculiar influence and particular purpose. The mechanism of the cosmos has a certain action and a certain reaction on the part of the planets, producing a certain effect in every hour of the day, in every day of the week, in every week of the month, in every month of the year and in every year of the cycle.

The characteristic of Sunday is godliness. Anything spiritual can alone be successful. Anything else besides a spiritual thing, something of a worldly nature, begun on Sunday or continued on that day, must come to naught.

Monday is a negative day, a day for things of a passive character. To receive teaching, to obtain information, to search for anything this is the auspicious day.

Tuesday is a day of enjoyment, for amusement, joy and pleasure. For picnic, feast and wedding, for music and dancing and for sports this is the fitting day.

Wednesday is a day for business. It is a day for taking an initiative and undertaking. All that is done on this day must bear fruit.

Thursday is a central day – to make a determination, to decide things, to settle in a new place. It is a day of inspiration, of revelation, because the influence of this day touches the summit.

Friday is a day of power and a day of aspiration. On this day prayer is granted and wishes are fulfilled, thoughts materialize and dreams become realized. However, this is not the day of sowing, it is the day of reaping. Friday is a day of exaltation.

Saturday is a winding day. If loss is wound it continues for days and days. If the mechanism of gain is wound it continues for weeks. It is a day of upliftment to those who raise their soul to a higher pitch so that the machinery of the spirit may be wound and continue for a long, long time. Every planetary influence that begins on Saturday must always continue its effect upon one's life.

The influence of the day is unavoidable upon every mortal, except upon souls to whom day or night is the same, those who are beyond the laws of this mortal world.

III:7 UNLUCKY NUMBERS

In the East, three, thirteen, nine, and eighteen are numbers which must be avoided in beginning some profitable act. There are some psychological reasons which prove these numbers to be best avoided.

Three denotes all. All means everything, and everything means nothing in particular. Things of the world which are profitable are something particular. Three therefore annuls the distinction, for three resolves into one. One is three, and three is one.

Thirteen destroys balance by unbalancing the rhythm, as it cannot be evenly divided. Besides, twelve hours of the day and twelve hours of the night complete the day and night. So the thirteenth has no place either in the day or in the night. Besides, after twelve o'clock comes one, and it marks thirteen.

Thirteen is a number which has no accommodation. Among Western people there is a superstition that the thirteenth person at table must die within the year. This also explains that the number thirteen has no accommodation; that a person dies means that the earth accommodates him no longer.

Nine falls short of perfection. Besides it is three times three. And so is eighteen, for eight and one are nine. It has the same effect as three.

All numbers besides three, thirteen, nine and eighteen are considered in the East fit to be used.

III:8 The mysteries of omens

The secret of what we call 'an omen' is to be found in the law of impressions. For example, there is a belief that when you are going to do something, if a cat crosses your way you meet with ill luck. It is easy to understand. The swift action of the cat makes a great impression upon a person; it forms a line before you, a line of action, and that line, impressed upon you, gives you the thought of a cross. You are intending to go straight and your line is crossed by a horizontal action against your vertical action, which means in action one's hands nailed and feet tied. It gives the picture of the idea.

The whole mystery of omens, which used to be believed in ancient times and is considered to be superstitions, has behind it this mystery of impression. Naturally when a person is starting to accomplish a certain work, and he happens to see beautiful flowers or fruits, that gives a promise of his desire being fulfilled, of its bearing flowers for him, the sign of success. A person going forward with this impression will certainly meet with success, whereas if a person sees burning wood or a sack of coal, which all show destruction, fire which burns up – a person going to do something impressed by this, certainly loses.

There used to be a custom that when someone in a family was going out to accomplish something, no one must say any word that would hinder his success. They did not even ask the person, 'Where are you going?', because even to ask raises a question. The question stands before one: 'Why?', 'Where?' A person would become discouraged even in answering. The strength of will with which he is going may be exhausted in answering 'Why' and 'Where' and then he may not find sufficient energy and power to accomplish what he hoped to do.

This is the inner psychology of mind, the knowledge of which makes things easy. One must not become impressed by holding different beliefs, but one must know the science, the mystery which is hidden behind all such things which may seem insignificant. But their result sometimes is most important.

III:9 THE INFLUENCE OF TIME

It has been a custom among the people in the East to start every enterprise at the waxing of the moon in order to follow the course of nature and to join forces with the increasing power and light of the moon. The sun represents divine light, the moon represents the human heart. To join forces with the waxing of the moon is like drawing divine light and power into one's own heart to accomplish a certain thing.

It is also considered lucky to rise with the sunrise and, better still, to begin an enterprise with the rising of the sun. This again indicates the wisdom of following nature's tides. The sun represents divine power; therefore it is desirable to perform any spiritual action – a prayer offering or a meditation, a devotional worship – with the sunrise.

However, the night vigils are performed by the seers and the knowers of truth in the midst of the night, when the old day ends and the new day begins, for that is a time of *kemal*, which offers to the soul a perfect stillness. When the sun is at the zenith, that is *kemal* also, but it has not the quiet of midnight, and therefore it is considered by those who know such things as inauspicious for taking up any enterprise.

As time has influence upon weather, upon the sea, upon the trees and plants, so it has a subtle influence upon living creatures. Man appears to be most independent of the influences and yet man is most under the influence of time – not only his body and mind, but with all his affairs of life.

Verily, the one who knows the influence of time knows the secret of life.

III:10 PLANETARY INFLUENCES

Belief in planetary influences has been maintained in all ages by man. However many times a person may have been disappointed in finding truth in the horoscope, yet no thoughtful person can deny the fact of the influence that the planets have upon people's lives. It is possible that not every method is the correct method of making a horoscope, every book on astrology is not the right book, and every astrologer is not a prophet, nevertheless there is as much truth in the influence of planets upon the lives of men as there is truth in the effects of drugs upon one's physical body.

The whole cosmic system is based upon a certain rhythm, a rhythm which relates planets, multitudes and individuals, and manifests as a hidden law governing the action of the whole creation, and yet silent and covered.

There are two aspects that constitute an individual: a spiritual and a material. The spiritual aspect remains untouched in every man, while the material aspect is moved and turned by conditions brought about by planetary influences. The spiritual aspect is as a witness of his life, a soul from within which knows not what it itself is, which identifies itself with this other aspect, and therefore takes as a reality that which it witnesses, that which goes on before it as a course of life.

When once this real aspect of man's being is awakened then it begins to see that it has a voice in the matter too, and then it sees that it must fight for its rights in order to gain liberty. It therefore fights with its own kingdom which is the other aspect of man's being, which it so long witnessed, and so it gains that strength which enables it in the long run to battle with outer conditions caused by planetary influences. It might take one a lifetime to combat. And yet it would be short to gain the mastery which belongs to the soul. (*See* Questions and Answers p 291.)

PART TWO

◆

INSIGHT

Kashf

GATHA I

It is the faculty of the soul to see and the eyes are its instruments. Therefore it is not necessarily the instrument that sees, but it is the soul that uses the instrument to see. I have given the eyes as an example, but in reality it is the whole body that is the instrument of the soul to have life's experience. It is the seeing of the soul which, through the ears, is called hearing and, through the tongue, tasting. It is the knowing of the soul of the external life; but the soul uses different instruments to obtain different experiences.

Between the body and the soul there is another instrument which is recognized by both scientists and mystics as unexplainable; that is the mind. The scientists call it the brain, but the brain is the instrument of the mind and mind goes beyond it. Plainly speaking it may be said that the mind is the instrument of the soul and the body is the intrument of the mind, but both mind and body are the instruments of the soul. Although these instruments give the soul knowledge of things clearly, these instruments at the same time limit the power of the soul.

There are two aspects of sight: one is penetration and the other expansion. The idea of short sight and long sight explains to a certain extent expansion and length of sight. By expansion I mean the width of the range of sight. Through the eyes the soul can see a short or a long distance or have a wide or narrow horizon, but by using the mind as its instrument it sees through another mind in the same way as the eyes see within their range of sight.

When the mind uses the body to experience life, it limits its experience, for the body alone is not sufficient; if the mind were free it would see further. But as from childhood man has the habit of using the body as the instrument of the mind, hardly anyone knows how to make use of the mind without the body. And as the soul has always taken the mind as its instrument, it also limits its sight and experience. If the soul could see independently of mind and body it would see infinitely more.

As it is even difficult for mind to see independently of the body, it is more difficult for the soul to see independently of mind. Therefore the Sufi tries to make his mind independent of the body, and his soul independent of mind and body. In order to accomplish this object different concentrations and practices are given. It is like effacing the external form from the mind, and erasing from the soul the form of the mind. It is this experience which is called *safa*.

1:2 AS THOU ART, SO AM I – *TAT TVAM ASI*

There are three aspects of life, and by seeing the oneness of these three one comes to divine knowledge. To the mystic therefore the idea of the trinity suggests this philosophy. This idea exists in the Hindu religion and is known as *trimurti*. They have a religious instrument with three points – a kind of fork – as a symbol of this, the idea being that it is the three different aspects of the one life which confuse man and prevent him from realizing the one life beneath these three aspects.

The first aspect is the knower, the second is the known and the third the knowing. In other words they may be called the seer, the seen and sight. These three are three turnings on the same road which hide it and divide it into three aspects. Therefore in the spiritual path this puzzle must be solved as the first thing and the last thing. If the barriers which divide these three aspects are removed, then the mystic realizes one life and not three. Occult power is the power of knowing or seeing, the faculty of knowing or seeing.

The seer is the greatest of these aspects, the second is that which is seen, the seeing power is the third. The reason of this is that the seer is the source and origin of what is seen and of the seeing power. Therefore Jesus Christ called him Father. That which is seen has in it the light inherited from the seer. Whether flower or fruit, it has radiance in it which makes it appear. There is a verse of a Persian poet which explains this:

The nightingale has borrowed from Thee his beautiful song
And the rose has borrowed from Thee its colour and fragrance.

But the means that the seer takes is his instrument – as the mind is the instrument of the soul, and the body the instrument of the mind. Therefore the first lesson the mystic has to learn is to know the relation between himself and the thing he sees. As soon as a mystic sees life from this point of view – that he connects himself with the thing he sees – he can understand it much more than the average person.

Sufism is not a religion because it does not give any doctrine or principle, but it is a point of view. The ancient Vedantists adopted this point of view in teaching the sacred words *tat tvam asi* – as Thou art, so am I. With this point of view, when the sight becomes keen, even objects become clear to the seer and speak to him, and what is called psychometry or such phenomena become as a play to the seer. The whole life begins to unfold before him like an open book, but there is nothing so interesting for the seer to see or know as human nature. And it is the seer who can see and know another person.

Ordinarily there exist many barriers between one person and another, such as prejudice, hatred, reserve, remoteness, and all aspects of duality. A person considers another his greatest friend in the world if he realizes that the other understands him. There is nothing that brings two people closer together than understanding. And what is this comprehension? It is trinity with unity. Often one wonders, 'Why do I not understand this person?' But one does not realize that one creates oneself the barriers which separate one person from another. If the barriers are not created, the soul has freedom to see and nothing can stand in its way. Do you think the sages and saints try to see the thoughts of other people? Not at all.

That does not concern them, but the thoughts of another person manifest themselves to the saint. Why? Because there is no barrier. This barrier is of duality.

The idea of the Sufi is to uncover himself, and this he can accomplish by contemplating upon the idea of God which is the absolute oneness. When one realizes this, all such sciences as physiognomy or phrenology begin to become like play, because by these sciences one sees a part, but by the light of the soul one sees the whole.

I:3 THE GLANCE OF THE SEER

The glance of the seer is penetrating, and in this it differs from the glance of the average man. It has three qualities. The first is that it penetrates through body, mind and soul. The second quality of this glance is that it opens, unlocks and unfolds things; it also possesses the power of seeking and finding. The third quality of the glance of the seer is more wonderful. It is this: as it falls upon a thing it makes that thing as it wants to make it. It is not actually creating, but it is awakening in it that particular quality which was perhaps asleep.

This is quite natural, as we see in the ordinary course of life that by fear we create in others fearful tendencies, and when we love we create kindness. It is possible to turn a friend into an enemy by thinking he is that, and also it is possible to change an enemy into a friend by expecting him to be so. Therefore the tendency of the mystic is to turn everything into what he wishes.

To turn what is ugly into beauty or beauty into ugliness, this is what the vision can accomplish. This proves to deep thinkers that things are not what they appear to be, but we make them as they are. The whole life may be made into a thing of complete ugliness, or it may be turned into a sublime vision of perfect beauty.

The Lord of the Yogis, Shiva, is pictured with a cobra on his neck, which means that death which frightens everyone is accepted by him as life. That shows that even death can be made into life, and it is only the difference of the point of view that makes life death.

The first characteristic of the glance of the seer, penetration, depends upon clearness of vision. The second characteristic, the uncovering of objects, depends upon the illumination of the soul. But the third, the greatest, comes from confidence in the self, called *iman*.

I:4 DIVINE EVIDENCE

The first thing in the study of human nature is observation of the external part of man. There are two aspects: one is the head of man, the other his form. And this can be seen from two points of view: the first is the analytical point of view, the second the synthetic. The former is the understanding of the character of each organ and the meaning of its form, and the latter is the harmony of the different organs. A person understands half if he considers one organ only and not its combination with other organs.

The study of physiognomy can help one as an interesting study, but one must have intuition also to help and guide him who wishes to judge. Nothing in life is so interesting as the study of human nature, and in attaining to knowledge of God knowledge of human nature is the beginning. Therefore in occult study one must begin by studying human beings, and the first lesson is to study their form.

The prominence of particular organs and muscles shows the vitality which exists in these organs, and lack of it is lack of energy in these organs. Therefore the straightness of any organ suggests straightness in the nature, and curve where it is natural shows subtlety of nature; a point wherever it is natural shows sharpness of nature; roundness makes for subtlety, and the oval form shows acute intelligence. Proportion of head and body and of each part of the head and body shows balance, and lack of it shows lack of balance.

Every organ represents a certain part of man's nature that may have no connection with that organ.

A particular mode of standing or sitting denotes a certain nature.

Crookedness where there should be straightness shows lack of straightness in the nature.

Organs which should be even and are not show lack of balance.

In every face and form there is always some resemblance to the lower creation, and a person with keen insight can recognize it and intuition helps us to understand it. Sometimes in face or form, sometimes in movements we show a sign of one or other of the lower creatures, and this signifies some resemblance with the nature of that particular creature.

The more one observes from this point of view, the clearer will the view become, and it shows the marvel of the Creator. It makes one tolerant and forgiving to everyone by reason of understanding that none can act against his nature. Also he who looks at this marvel begins to see the divine evidence in every face, as a person can see the painter in his painting. And it is only natural to wish to study this part of occultism in order to recognize the divine part in the creature and worship Him.

I:5 OPENNESS

Every atom of man's body expresses his past, present and future. The reason is that in the first place every impulse creates its vibrations and takes a particular direction of activity. This influences the heart whence the blood is circulated through the whole body. In this way the thought is, so to speak, written on man's face. Man's continual agitation in regard to others, his satisfaction or dissatisfaction, his love or hatred, all show in his appearance. Everyone can know it more or less, but the seer can read more correctly.

It is difficult to tell definitely the marks that are shown in one's appearance of one's thoughts and feelings; nevertheless, partly by intuition and partly by experience, man reads them. There are some in whom self-control is developed, who are capable of hiding their thoughts and emotions, and yet it is impossible to feel deeply and to hide one's feelings from the eyes of others.

No doubt form and movement speak aloud of one's condition, but the expression of man's face speaks louder still. There come distinct changes at every impulse, at every change of emotion, making distinct marks which are an open book to a seer. The word *kashf* means opening, and it is used by the Sufis with the meaning that the human heart is as a rule a closed book, and the one to whom it becomes open can read it like an open book.

No doubt reading man's condition of mind from his appearance is not such a difficult thing. Even dogs and cats can know this and sometimes they know better than man. What gives one insight into another is in the first place one's sympathy. The seer first develops the quality of love. He whose heart is kindled with the love of God is capable of the love of humanity. The heart thus kindled with love becomes a lighted lantern which throws its light on every person the seer meets, and as this light falls upon the person he meets all things about that person, his body, heart and soul, become clear to him.

Love is a torch that illuminates all that comes within its light, but it is the knowledge of God which is the key which opens the hearts of men.

I:6 MOVEMENT (1)

Every movement that one makes suggests to the seer some meaning. A person is not always conscious of his movements, not every movement is made intentionally, and many movements that man makes unconsciously and thinks nothing of mean something to the seer.

The seer notices them from two points, the beginning and the end. No motion to a seer is without direction; in other words every movement is directed by a preceding cause, and no motion to him is without a certain result. The purpose seems to be in the cause, but in reality it is in the effect. It is born in the cause, but it is finished in the effect.

The first thing that a mystic understands by a movement that a person makes is the nature of the person, and the next thing that he understands is about his affairs. And the law holds good about straightness suggesting straightness and crookedness suggesting crookedness, grace of movement suggesting beauty and lack of grace the lack of that element. Rhythm of movement suggests balance, lack of rhythm suggests lack of balance; the upward tendency of movement suggests rise, the downward tendency fall; the horizontal spread, movement inward and outward, is suggestive of within and without. Also the law of the tendency of the five elements to different directions helps the seer to recognize the different elements working in man's nature. The movement can be recognized in sitting, walking, lying, and in laughter or in crying.

The study of these laws of movement and direction is helpful only when the intuitive faculty is developed. If the study is intellectual it is limited and rigid, and one cannot probe the depths of human nature far enough by intellectual study alone.

I:7 MOVEMENT (2)

The condition of the mind is expressed not only in the countenance but also in the movements. Every movement denotes a certain change of thought and feeling. The more one understands the language of movements the more one comprehends this. In every thought and feeling the waves, so to speak, of the mind rise and fall, and as by seeing the waves one can notice whether the sea is rough or calm, so by noticing the movements of a person one can read the condition of his mind.

Upward movement suggests wrath, revenge, conceit or pride; downward movement depression, helplessness, meekness. Movements toward the left and right also have their significance: the right shows struggle and power, the left art and skill.

A contracting tendency suggests fear, indifference, coldness; a stretching tendency shows desire for action, strength and power. A tendency to turn shows confusion. A tendency of pinching and pressing shows uneasiness or agony of mind. Expansion and ease of movement show joy and happiness, and stillness without stiffness is expressive of calm and peace.

I:8 THE STUDY OF THE WHOLE

Man's form can be divided into two parts, the head and the body; one part is for action, the other for thought. Therefore the face can explain the attitude of mind and depict the nature and character more fully than the body and its movements. Every little movement of the eyes, the movements of the lips in smiling or in laughter, the movements of the eyebrows or of the head itself explain the condition of the mind.

The ends of the eyebrows turning upwards denotes egoism and shrewdness. The puckering of the lips suggests pleasure, as the twitching of the lips shows a tendency to humour or indicates pleasure. The rolling of the eyes or a restless movement suggests confusion. The movement of the eyes towards the outer corners denotes a clever brain. The puffing of the cheeks denotes joy, the drawing-in, sorrow.

One can get a full conception of the character by studying the full countenance and not a part only. The study of a part always gives only a partial knowledge; complete knowledge is gained only by a study of the whole.

Keen observation with the desire to understand helps a person to read the condition of man's mind, his nature and character. Yet the view is often coloured by the personality of the one who sees. His favour or disfavour, his liking or dislike stands between the eyes of the one who sees and the one who is seen. Therefore sometimes innocent people have a better understanding of a person than clever people with deceitful minds. There is a saying of Sa'di,

O my subtle cleverness!
Thou often becomest my greatest deceiver.

I:9 THE MYSTERY OF EXPRESSION

Man's expression is more indicative of his nature and character than his form or features. In the *Qur'an* it is said that man's eyes and gestures will confess what he tries to hide in his heart. The strength, the weakness, the power, the fear, the happiness, the joy, the uneasiness, the praise or blame, the love or hatred, all these are shown by the expression. The more capable one becomes of reading the expression, the more clearly one can read character. This shows that there is a mystery that lies behind movement.

There are certain vibrations which take a particular direction under certain conditions, and the visible signs of all vibrations can be seen in man's movement or the expression of his countenance. It does not take one moment for the expression to change from pleasure to pain, from calm to horror, from love to hate. That shows that all the atoms of man's body, the veins, tubes and muscles and the lines formed by their movements are under the control of the heart; and every change that takes place in the heart shows on man's face, so that one who knows the language can read it. People who see each other often can read such changes from the expression, because each grows accustomed to know and recognize the changes of facial expression in the others, but it is the development of intuition which gives the clearness of vision by which one can see more completely.

The eyes are more expressive of thought and feeling than anything else. A person who can read the language of the eyes, their appearance and their movement, has the key to character. The eyes can ask and answer questions, and it is in the grade of speed and direction of the glance that the mystery of expression lies.

1:10 DIFFERENT QUALITIES OF MIND

As there are different qualities of the sight, such as long and short sight, so there are different qualities of mind. There are minds which can see a certain distance and no further, and others that can see a longer distance. And what is called foresight is not a supernatural, superhuman faculty but a long range of sight.

When one person can see the action of another person, the seer can see the reason for the action too, and if the sight is keener still, he can see the reason for the reason. One cannot give one's sight to another; he can tell what he sees, but that is not sufficient, for in order to be sure, every soul wants its own experience.

The faculty of seeing through life can be developed by observation, which is called study, and the focusing of the mind upon the object of study is called concentration. As by making a habit of lifting one thing a person can learn to lift several different weighty things, so by observing one object of study a man becomes capable of observing any object in the same way.

Keenness of observation is a phenomenon in itself. In the first place the sight penetrates, so to speak, the object one sees; and the next thing is that as the light of the sun has the power to open the buds, so the power of keen observation commands the objects observed to unfold themselves and to reveal their secrets.

Every object has a soul in it, which may be called its spirit. In ancient times the seers recognized the spirit of all things, the spirit of mountains, trees, stars and planets, of the rivers, lakes, pools and seas. Penetrating through objects means touching their spirit. No doubt it is easier to touch the spirit of man than to touch the spirit of objects, for the very reason that man is more living than any other form of creation.

The person whose eyes are not steady cannot observe fully; so also the mind that is not steady cannot observe things well. Therefore the mystics prescribe certain postures in order to make the body stable, and steadiness of body reacts upon the mind, making it steady also. The mind and body react on each other and the steadiness of the one gives steadiness to the other. So a self-mastered person who has control over his body and mind has balance and wisdom. Wisdom comes from steadiness and insight follows wisdom.

Gatha II

Every line which is deeply engraved on the surface of the mind may be likened to a vein where the blood runs, keeping it alive. And while the blood is running it is productive of offshoots of the deep-set line. There are moments when there comes a kind of congestion in a certain line where the blood is not running: there are no offshoots. But this congestion can be broken by some outer influence, and when that congested line is touched by an outer influence which is related to that particular line, then again it sets the blood running through and offshoots arising, expressing themselves in thoughts. It is just like a waking or sleeping state of these lines.

As one note of music can be fully audible at one time, so one line of offshoots can be comprehensible at one time, and it is the warmth of interest that keeps the blood running in that particular line. There may be other lines where the blood is alive also; still if they are not kept warm by one's interest they become congested and thus paralysed; and yet the blood is there, the life is there, it awaits a moment to awaken it. The sorrows of the past, the fears of the past, the joys of the past can be brought to life after ages and could give the same sensation, exactly as one had experienced before.

The more one knows the mystery of this phenomenon the more one learns to understand that there is a world in one's self, that in one's mind there is the source of happiness and unhappiness, the source of health and illness, the source of light and darkness, and that it can be awakened either mechanically or voluntarily, if only one knew how one must do it.

Then one would not blame one's misfortune nor would one complain of one's fellow man. One would become more tolerant, more joyous and more loving to one's neighbour, because one knows then the cause of every thought and action, and one sees it all in the form of the effect of a certain cause. A physician would not take revenge on a patient in the asylum even if the patient hit him, for he knows where it comes from.

The psychology of mind is the higher alchemy, and one cannot only study it and not practise it. Its practice and study, both must go together, which opens the door for every soul to happiness.

II:2 IMPRESSION

The mind is likened to a record of the talking-machine. But as it is a living mechanism it does not only reproduce what is impressed on it, but it creates as well as reproduces.

There are five different actions of mind which can be distinguished:

1 creating of thoughts
2 the sense of discrimination
3 memory
4 the factor of feeling
5 the principal faculty, the feeling of I-ness or ego.

Therefore every thought which mind creates has some connection with some idea already recorded, not identical, but akin to it, varying more or less at different times. For instance, one deeply engraved line on the mind may have several small lines shooting out from it like branches from the trunk of a tree. The Sufi therefore learns and practises to discern the more deeply engraved lines by the observation of their offshoots. Therefore he is able to learn more from a person's thought than anybody else, just as by looking at a leaf of a tree one can find out what tree it is.

As a rule every thought a person expresses has at the bottom of it a connection with some deep feeling. The reading of the deep-set line is like reading the cause of the person's thought.

The knowledge of the cause can give greater understanding than knowing only the thought – just like standing on the other side of the wall. Thought is like a wall; behind it the source. Often the difference between cause and effect is like that between sour and sweet. It is often confusing, yet simple, that the same fruit may be sour when unripe and sweet when ripe.

When one begins to understand life from this point of view, the opinion one forms of thought becomes different. There is a great difference between reading a thought externally and reading it from the inside, the source. The one who forms an opinion of the shadow has not seen the beauty. The effect of a thought is but a shadow, the reality is the cause, the source.

What is this deep line whence offshoots come? These deep lines are the deep impressions which man gets in the first time of his life. In the East, taking account of this theory, they observe certain rules in the family concerning the expectant mother and the child to be. Not one undesirable impression may touch their minds. This tells how important it is that this question must be studied.

The word 'man' comes from the Sanskrit *manas*, which means 'mind'. This shows that man is principally his mind rather than his body, and as mind is impressionable in its character, that means that man is impressionable by nature. Most often his illness, health, prosperity, failure, all depend upon the impression on his mind. They say 'lines of fate and destiny on head and palm', but I say that the impressions man has on his mind decide his destiny. Lines on head and palm are but reprints of the mind, and once a person has learned the lines of mind there is no need of the lines on the hand or face.

Can this language be learned like shorthand? No, the method is different. The method is that, while every man goes forward from the thought of another, the Sufi goes backward.

All impressions of joy, sorrow, fear, disappointment become engraved on the mind. This means that they have become man's self. In other words, man is the record of his impressions. The religion of the ancients said that the record of man's actions will be reproduced on the Last Day; angels write down all the good and ill done by each one. What we learn from this allegorical expression is that all is impressed on the mind; although forgotten, it is always there and will one day show up.

II:3 THE BALANCE OF LIFE

Every habit makes a line in man's mind, and the continuation of that habit wakens that line from sleep; in other words it gives the line sensitiveness, which is the feeling of life, and in time man indulges in this habit. If a person takes a liking to a certain phrase of music its every repetition gives him a renewed joy; when someone enjoys a certain poetry it cannot be repeated to him too often; if anyone likes a certain dish in time he has a craving for it. And man does not enjoy only praise and flattery, but even insults if they have engraved a deep line on his mind; he will try to tease others or offend somebody in order to receive an insult. He may not outwardly seem to enjoy it, and yet he will revel in it. If a person becomes accustomed to sit on a certain rock in a garden, he forms a habit of going and seeking the same rock every day; if someone has a liking for the scenery of a certain place, he longs to see it every day. Of course it depends upon the depth of the line; the deeper the line, the more one lives in it.

When talking, a businessman explains things in terms of pounds and pence, an architect in the terms of his compass and tools. Every person has his own language and that language is made of the words which come from the deeply engraved line of his mind.

Therefore the work of the mystic is to be able to read the language of the mind. As the clerk in the telegraph office reads letters from the clicks, so the Sufi gets behind every word spoken to him and discovers what has prompted the word to come out. He therefore reads the lines which are behind man's thought, speech and action; he also understands that every kind of longing and craving in life, good or bad, has its source in deep impression. By knowing this root of the disease he is easily able to find out its cure. No impression is such that it cannot be erased.

The mystics have two processes in dealing with these lines. One process is to renew this line by putting in some other colour and therefore changing one impression into a different one. No doubt this needs great knowledge of mental chemistry. Another way that the mystic takes is to rub out the line from the surface. But often, when the line is deep, it takes the rubbing out of a great portion of the mind to destroy one line.

Naturally the mystic becomes tolerant of every sort of dealing of others with him, as he sees not only the dealing as it appears, thoughtful or thoughtless, cold or warm, but the cause which is at the back of it. By reading the human mind a mystic gets insight into human nature and to him the life of human beings begins to appear as a mechanism working.

The mystic learns from this that life is give and take. It is not only that one receives what one gives, but also one gives what one receives. In this way the mystic begins to see the balance of life, he realizes that life is a balance. And if the gain or loss, the joy or pain of one outweighs that of another, it is for the moment, but in time it all sums up in a balance, and without balance there is no existence possible.

II:4 THE LANGUAGE OF THE MIND

Everything man expresses in his art, painting, verse, music is the reproduction of the mind. Not only that, but his choice, his likes and dislikes, his habits, all show what is the state of his mind. Everything man says or does shows the lines already traced on his mind. There is no exaggeration in the saying that man's face is the mirror of his heart. It seems as if the mind begins to speak through every particle of the body. Since the head is the more predominant factor, the expression of man tells most about the condition of his mind. No doubt it is difficult to give a certain rule of reading this language expressed in the face, form or movements. But two things can help one to understand it: keen observation to study human nature and developed intuition. Then one begins to have a sort of key to this language; but if you ask him, he cannot express it.

From different compositions of composers one can imagine their character, their life, and state of mind. As in the science of sound there is a tone and an overtone, so in the music of a certain composer there is a sense which stands together with the music. He who hears the notes only enjoys the music; he who understands the sense knows the mind of the composer. So the verse is the soul of the poet, for the poetry is not only poetry, it has its music behind. He who reads the verse only enjoys the poetry, but he who comprehends the sense in it enjoys the music of this poetry.

One who asks a question of himself on hearing a certain word, on seeing a certain movement, on observing a certain expression in a face, must receive an answer from his intuition, telling him the cause of this effect which manifests outwardly. In this way the Sufi makes his way for his journey in the inner world.

II:5 THE INFLUENCE OF EXPERIENCE

Beneath the five senses there is one principal sense which works through the others. It is through this sense that one discriminates and distinguishes between the impressions which come from outside. Every impression and experience obtained by this sense is recorded on the mind. This record is made of deep lines and the nature of these lines deeply set in the mind is to want the same thing that has already been recorded – according to the depth of the line. And it is according to the depth of lines that one needs the thing that one has once experienced. For instance, the tastes for salt, honey or pepper are acquired tastes, and the sign of this acquirement is the deep line on the mind.

Each line so produced wishes to live upon its impression, and the absence of that experience is like death to that line. Disagreeable flavours such as that of fish or vinegar or cheese become agreeable after the line is formed. Things even more distasteful than these may become most agreeable once the line is engraved on the mind.

The same rule is applicable to notes of music. A certain combination of notes or a certain arrangement, when once impressed on the mind, may become very agreeable. The more one hears the music which has once impressed one's mind, the more one wants to hear it, and one is never tired of it, unless another line forms more deeply; then the first line may be neglected and becomes a dead line. It is for this reason that the music which belongs to a certain people, whether evolved or unevolved, is their ideal music. Therefore it is not the music written outside, it is the music written inside the mind which has influence. This is the reason why the composers resemble each other in their music, for the lines that are impressed upon their minds have created other lines. But as the first lines are inherited from other composers, in their music there is a resemblance. In this way the music of every people forms its own character.

The same law works in poetry. One enjoys poetry from one's former impressions. If the poetry which one reads is not in harmony with one's first impression, one will not enjoy it so much. The more one reads a certain poetry, the more one enjoys it because of the deep impression on the mind.

From this we learn that not only desirable things but also undesirable things may become favoured. But even things that one would never like to have, such as pain, illness, worry or death, if they are deeply impressed upon one's mind, one unconsciously longs to experience again.

It is very interesting to find that, if a man forms an opinion about a certain thing or a person, and after a certain time there has been everything to disprove this opinion, still he will hold to his impression and will not like to change his opinion because of these lines deeply impressed on his mind.

How true it is what the mystic says, that the true ego of man is his mind! I would further say that man's world is his mind. And it is still more amusing to find that, after having spent his life under the influence of these deep impressions on his mind, man still boasts of what he calls his free will.

II:6 INTUITION

The modern psychologist adopts a system of psychoanalysis in order to investigate the state of mind of his patient, and the barrister in the law court cross-examines in order to investigate the truth of the case. All these methods are more or less useful when they are rightly practised, but the chief thing for getting to the mind of a person is to see the person in his form, in his expression, in his movements, in his words, in his imagination and in the way of his action. But the principal thing which helps in seeing the mind of another person is the light of intuition. Nothing else, neither rules nor studies nor standard of understanding can help without the development of intuition.

But one thing must be remembered: that man shows the lines engraved upon his mind in his form, expression, in his movements, words, in his imagination and action; and it is possible to detect a man from his word before his action or from his movement before his action, or from his expression before his words, or from his form before even he had time to imagine. Therefore the knowledge of this can save a great deal of trouble in life – if man only knows beforehand how to act with different people.

The person who acts in the same manner with every person, however good or kind he may be, must always meet with disappointments. As the direction of the fire is upwards and that of the water is downwards, so the direction of one person is different from that of the other. Therefore if you expect a person who is going to the south to take your message to the north, you will find yourself mistaken in the end. Generally a person dealing with others thinks of the affair more than of the person. Really the person must be the chief object of study, not the affair, for the affair depends upon the person.

In the East there is a superstition of a dog or a cat or a horse being lucky or unlucky for the person who possesses it, but the reality of this idea can be most seen in every human being with whom one comes in contact through one's everyday life. He must surely bring something with him, pleasure, displeasure, happiness, unhappiness, good or bad influence. Every man in himself is a world, and every new contact is a new world opened before us.

II:7 EVIDENCE OF THE THOUGHT

When a person is thinking you can see his thought in his eyes, in his expression, in his movements. Things such as opening or closing the eyes, looking up or down and looking out of the corners of the eyes, turning the head to the right or left, raising it or bowing it, scratching the fingers, rubbing the hands, turning the thumbs, a half-smile, puckering the face or the forehead, sitting stiffly or at ease, sitting upright or leaning back, leaning to one side or the other, all show to the seer the line of thought. Especially when a person is asked a question, before he answers the seer knows what will be his answer from his attitude.

The Hindus believe that the creation is Brahma's dream, which means the Creator's dream; in plain words, what the Creator has thought He has made. So, in proportion to his might, man makes what he thinks. What materializes we call 'happening', but what has not been materialized we do not know, and what we do not know still exists in the thought-world. In the *Qur'an* it is said: 'The organs of your body will give evidence of your action on the Last Day.' In reality, not of the action only but evidence even of the thought is given by every atom of the body immediately. The nature of the manifestation is such that there is nothing hidden – except that which one cannot see. And what one cannot see is not hidden in itself, but from one's eyes.

The aim of the Sufi therefore is to see and yet not be interested. Suppose you were climbing Mount Everest and stopped to admire a certain place which you liked – to admire its, or a place that you disliked – to break it. In both cases you have allowed your feet to be chained to that place for more or less time, and by that have lost time and opportunity, whereas you could have gone on forever and perhaps seen and learned more than by stopping there. Those who trouble about others' thoughts, and interest themselves in others' actions most often lose their time and blunt their inner sight.

Those who go farther, their moral is to overlook all they see on their way, as their mind is fixed on the goal. It is not a sin to know anybody's thought, but it is a fault, no doubt, if one professes to do so. To try to know the thought of another for one's own interest is not just or beneficial; at the same time to sit with closed eyes is not good either. The best thing is to see and rise above, never to halt on the way. And it is this attitude that, if constantly practised, will lead man safely to his soul's desired goal.

II:8 THE ACTIVITY OF MIND

The activity of mind can be recognized in three different aspects: mobile, rhythmic and chaotic; and the activity of mind can be seen by the speech and action of a person.

If in speech and action a person shows a friendly attitude, love and kindness, the activity is mobile and every impulse prompted by this activity will manifest in the form of gentleness, generosity, gratitude and goodwill.

If the activity of mind is rhythmic, it will make a person more reasoning. He will be exacting, weighing, measuring, loving and hating; liking and dislike will be balanced. This is not an easy-going person; this person will be more businesslike. All that manifests from him in speech or action will be more substantial, reasonable, also progressive in a worldly sense.

But the person in whom the activity of the mind is chaotic will be agitated, confused, suspicious, horrified. And all that will manifest in his speech and action will be anger, passion, intolerance, imprudence and will be difficult for himself and for others.

No soul is by nature fixed to any of these three aspects of activity; it is what he allows himself to be or what the condition of his life makes him be. Therefore the principle of Sufi teaching is to regulate the rhythm of man's mind. Then the Sufi becomes the master of the rhythm of his own mind, his mind becomes his instrument. He can play on it any music of any rhythm and nothing will affect it, for he is no longer in the hand of his mind, his mind is in his hand.

II:9 LIKES AND DISLIKES

What one dislikes in line, form, colour, smell, taste or sound or in sense or idea, is not disliked because it deserves to be so but because it is foreign to one's nature. Once a person becomes accustomed to anything, he develops love for it in himself. Therefore often some people have a liking for certain things which many others dislike, or a dislike of certain things which many others like. Often when travelling in the train a person feels more comfortable if no one else comes into his compartment, but once someone has come and sat there, if they have spoken together and become acquainted, then they wish to travel together.

All things have their beauty, and so has every person his goodness, and one's dislike of a person very often comes from lack of knowing that person or from lack of familiarity with him. What makes one dislike things and despise people is a certain barrier which very often the one who dislikes does not know, and also the one who is disliked does not know.

The work of the Sufi is therefore to investigate the truth about all things or persons whom he likes or dislikes. By a keen observation of life he gets to that barrier and understands what it is that makes him disliked or make him dislike others. All fear, doubt, suspicion, misunderstanding, bitterness or spite becomes cleared as soon as one touches that barrier which keeps souls apart.

It is true that one need not force one's nature. It is not necessary to dislike what one likes or to take a liking to something that by nature one dislikes. Only, one must know why one likes if one likes a certain thing, and the reason why one dislikes if one takes a dislike to a certain thing. After observation one will come to understand, 'All I like in the world is what I have always liked, and all I dislike is what I have always disliked in life.' It can be said in other words, 'What I know to be loveable I have always loved, and all that I do not know I cannot love at once.'

This shows that ignorance becomes a cover over all that is beautiful or ugly, and knowledge uncovers it. Liking comes from knowledge and dislike from ignorance – although both are necessary. Also it is possible that through ignorance one may like a certain thing and by knowledge one may rise above that liking. However, the higher knowledge must always give liking for all things; and things which do not deserve liking, above them a soul will rise by the help of knowledge.

II:10 ACTING CONTRARY TO
ONE'S NATURE – *VIPARIT KARNA*

In man's speech and in his action the seer sees designs: a straight line, a circle, a crooked line, a zigzag, an oval, a square, a triangle. For instance, there is a person who tells exactly to one's face all he feels; there is another person who proceeds in a roundabout way; one person has a crooked way of mentioning a thing; one will touch two opposite angles before he will arrive at the desired point; there is another person who will go about in a zigzag way, so that you cannot know whether he is going to the south or to the north until he has arrived at a certain point.

These figures represent the lines on the mind of man. Man does not feel comfortable in acting differently from the lines already engraved upon his mind. Therefore a crooked person enjoys his crookedness as much as a straightforward person enjoys his straightforwardness.

A most interesting study of this subject can be made by studying the art of different ages and of different nations. Every nation has its typical lines and forms, every period shows the peculiarity of expression of the art of that period; so one finds in the imagery of poets and in the theme of musicians. If you study one musician and his lifelong work you will find that his whole work is developed on a certain line as the basis of his work. Also, by studying the biography of great people you will find how one thing has led to the other, different but of similar kind. It is natural, therefore, that a thief becomes in time a greater thief; thus the righteous, after some time, may become a saint.

It is not difficult to slide on the line already made on one's mind, the difficulty is to act contrary to the line which is engraved there, especially in the case when it happens to be an undesirable line. Shiva, the great Lord of Yogis, has given a special teaching on the subject, which he calls *viparit karna*, acting contrary to one's nature, and he gives great importance to this method of working with oneself – that by this method in the end one arrives at mastery.

GATHA III

Mind is highly capable of expressing itself in a fitting form. Very often man expresses his thought in any conversation that may be going on which may have nothing to do with what he is thinking. As his nature is, so man looks for scope for the expression of his thought and he easily gets it. In a serious conversation one can find opportunity for a joke. Even in tragedy one can find comedy, and in comedy one can find tragedy if one's mind happens to dwell on sad thoughts. This shows that the mind always seeks for a scope for expression, and situations outside generously offer it.

One finds the same thing again with the mind – that in every situation, every condition, man easily finds out a reason for it from the mind. The one who does right and the one who does wrong – both find the reason for their action. Two people disputing against each other both have reason at the back of their discussion. This shows that the mind provides reason – as the sun shines and the rain falls – for the sinner as well as for the virtuous. Not realizing this fact, man always reasons with another; but it is not a dispute between reason and no reason, it is a dispute between two reasons contrary to one another. This shows that reason has not sprung on the soil of heaven. Reason, upon which man so confidently fixes his argument, is earth-born.

Therefore every conversation does not always follow a pre-designed plan; most often it is an outcome of instantaneously arising impulses. It is most interesting when one can get to the root of a conversation and find out what it is founded upon. And it is still more interesting to find what a very obedient servant reason is, which is ready to respond to the call of its master, even though its truth is coined by itself.

It is when the seer begins to look behind reason that he begins to get glimpses of truth upon which he can depend.

Insight makes life interesting. One who drifts along with the waves of insight will not enjoy life so much as one who has insight into life and yet stands firm on his own feet.

III:2 THE WORD AND THE IDEA

The word is a body of the idea, and the idea is the soul of the word. As the body represents the soul, so the word represents the idea. As the idea can only be expressed in the word, so the soul can only be seen in the body. And those who deny the existence of the soul must also deny the existence of the idea. They must say that only the word exists without an idea, which in reality is impossible. Behind every word there is an idea, veiled in one or a thousand veils, or clearly represented by the word. However, the word is a key to the idea, not the idea itself. It is not the word which is in itself an idea, but only an expression of it.

The ears hear the word, the mind perceives the idea. If the idea were not there, the word would convey nothing to the listener. If one said to a child, 'Sarcasm is an abuse of the intellect', what will the innocent child understand by it? The word 'sarcasm' will be known by the one who is capable of being sarcastic.

This opens up another idea: that those who accuse others with authority must necessarily know the fault themselves. Man, however evolved, will now and then show childishness in expressing his opinion about another, proving thereby guilty of the same fault in some proportion. No one can tell another, 'You told a lie', who did not tell a lie himself once at least in his life.

No doubt the idea is vaster than the word, as the soul is wider than the body. Every idea has its breadth, length, height and depth. Therefore, as a world is hidden in a planet, so a world of idea is hidden in a word. Think therefore how interesting life must become for the one who can see behind every word that is spoken to him, its length, breadth, height and depth. He is an engineer of the human mind; he then knows not only what is spoken to him, but he knows what is meant by it. By knowing words you do not know the language. What you know is the outside language; the inner language is known by knowing the language of ideas. So the language of ideas cannot be heard by the ears alone, the hearing of the heart must be open for it.

The seer must understand from a word spoken to him what even the one who speaks does not know, for every human being sometimes thinks, speaks and acts mechanically, subject to the condition of his body, mind and situation in life. Therefore as a physician finds out more about a complaint than the patient himself, so the mystic must comprehend the idea behind every word that is spoken to him.

One might think: with the continual growth of such perception the life of a Sufi must become very much troubled, for when the average person sees a yard's distance, a Sufi may be seeing the distance of a mile. Yes, no doubt it could be troublesome – if the mystic does not develop all round. The elephant's strength is required to carry the load of an elephant. It is not enough to become a seer alone, but what is needed is to develop that strength which takes all things easily, the power that endures all things, and the might which enables one to surmount all difficulties in life.

III:3 THE EXPRESSION AND THE IDEA

All actions such as a smile, staring or frowning, nodding or moving the eyes or the head, have ideas behind them. Externally a slight movement, inwardly it is a mountain of thought. No movement is possible without a thought at the back of it. Sometimes it is known to the person and sometimes the person himself does not know why he smiled.

The eyes express more than anything else by their movements the idea behind them. Very often intuitive people say,

'I perceived from that person's look pleasure', or displeasure, or his favourable or unfavourable attitude. And yet many do not know what movement, what expression suggested to them what they perceived. Every expression of the eyes – the eyes which change their expression so many times in one minute – suggests the idea behind. This shows that the mind is an engineer, and the body is a mechanism which it controls. If the engineer becomes conscious of his working, he brings about desirable results, but by unconscious working the engineer also becomes a mechanism.

There used to be courtiers in ancient times in India who at every moment would know the state of mind and the attitude of the king, to such an extent that very often everything was arranged as the king liked without his having uttered one word about it. There were nine courtiers attached to the court of Akbar; every one of them knew the state of mind of the emperor at every moment. The Sufi whose duty in the world is to live in the presence of God, and who recognizes His presence in all His creatures, His personality in man especially, he fulfils his duty of a courtier with every man.

A person who lives as dead as a stone among his surroundings does not know whom he has pleased, whom he has displeased, who expects of him thought, consideration, who asks of him sympathy or service, who needs him in their trouble or difficulty. People think insight comes by psychical development. Yes, it does, but it comes most through the development of the heart quality. A loving person is a living person. No doubt the more living one is, the more difficult it is for one to live. Yet no difficulty is too great a price for living a real life.

The method which a mystic takes to perceive the mentality of another person is that he takes the movement of the person and his expression as a guide to arrive at the thought of the man, and he takes that thought as a guide to his nature. By realizing the nature of man he comes to know about the very depth of a person's being, and instead of having partial knowledge of a person he gets to know all about the person. To know that someone has done right or wrong, to know that someone is wise or foolish is not sufficient. To have a complete knowledge of a person one must know not only if he does right, but also why he does right and if he does wrong, why he does wrong; if he is wise, what makes him wise; if he is foolish, what is the reason of his being foolish. Not only this, but also if there be a possibility of making the best of what the person is and trying to improve the person without his knowing it.

A foolish person cannot get on with his own friend, whereas a wise person can get on even with his enemy. The difference is that the one knows life, understands human nature and acts according to it, whereas the other, even if he wanted to act rightly, always fails and becomes disappointed in the end.

III:4 THE POWER OF WORDS

There are two kinds of men: one who speaks subject to his impulse, the other who speaks just like hitting a target. The first may often strike a wrong note and may work against his own interest, but the second will become the master of his destiny. The one who knows while speaking to whom he is speaking, the capacity of the mind of his hearer, the lines on the mind of his hearer, he will speak the words which will pierce through the mind of the listener. It is just like looking for a track before running the cart in a given direction.

Many, content with their honesty, speak just as they like at the moment. They do not mind what effect it will produce as long as they are sure that what they say is true. The truth that strikes like a hammer on the head of the listener is not desirable, one would be better off without it. This shows that it is not the only thing to consider that what one says is true; there is another consideration which is most necessary, and that is what effect it will make on the other.

The seer sees the lines made on the mind of the one to whom he speaks and makes his words suitable to run over that line. If he likes to make another road in the mind of his listener, he first takes the road which is already there, and when once he has entered the mind of his listener then he will make another road, not before. It is like one person going to buy something in a shop and saying before entering, 'I have not got more than fourpence', instead of going into the shop and finding out what he can buy with his four pennies.

Action is one thing and prudence is another thing. Even the animals are active, even they work for what they need in life. What one expects in man is prudence. Before he utters a single word, man must have forethought about its effect upon another. Some say, spiritually wise is not worldly wise, some think that these two worlds are different. But it is not so. The worldly wise is capable of being spiritually wise, but the spiritually wise is already worldly wise. He may not care for worldly things, therefore he may be lacking in experience in worldly affairs. Yet for him worldly wisdom is not a foreign thing, he has only to open his eyes and see. Those who know nothing of the world and who are called spiritual are known more for their goodness than for their balance. The complete spiritual life is not a dreamy one but wide awake, full of thought and consideration.

The word has a magic in it; it can turn your friends into enemies, and it can make your enemies your friends. The mystery of all success in every direction of life is in the word. The word has power to turn the mind of the listener warm or cold. The word can produce the effect of earth, water, fire, air or ether. The word can produce depression or joy. The one who knows the chemistry of the word does not need drugs or herbs; he has medicine for every disease in the world, not only for bodily disease, but for the disorders of the mind which still remain unexplored by science. By a constant study of life, by special thought given to one's word, by careful watching of the effects of one's speech upon others, one arrives at a state of realization where one can heal hearts.

III:5 THE RE-ECHO OF THE PAST

One can easily trace the past of a man from what he says and from how he expresses it. The past is ringing in the heart of man like a bell. The heart of man is a talking-machine record which goes on by itself, or if it has finished talking, one has only to wind the machine, then it goes on again. Man's present is the re-echo of his past. If he has been through suffering, even if he is better, he will vibrate the same; outer conditions will not change his inner being. If he has been happy, even in a troublous time his heart will vibrate the past. People who have been against one another, if by chance they become friends, will still feel in themselves the beating of the pulse of hostility in the past. Great kings who have been dethroned, imprisoned – still one can feel their past vibrating in their atmosphere.

The past lives and one cannot easily destroy it, however greatly one may wish to close it. It takes hold of the human tongue with which to express itself. As every heart is eager to tell its story, so the past is most eager to sing its legend; it only seeks the way how it shall express itself.

A Sufi therefore does not need spirit communications to learn the past, or astrological science to discover what has happened. To him every person explains his past without a single word spoken. But by the speech of a person about his past the Sufi can see what is hidden behind what is being said and what remains unsaid. He need not trace the past in history or in traditions. He who can read has but to open his eyes, and all is written before him.

III:6 INTEREST IN ALL THINGS

As there is a shadow of every form and as there is a re-echo of every sound and as there is a reflection of every light, so there is a re-impression of everything one sees, hears or perceives. But as it wants the musician's ears to sense the overtone of a sound and an artist's eyes to recognize the form from its shadow, and as it requires a keen sight to distinguish the degree of the reflection of light, so it wants the soul of a seer to see through all things in life.

The seer's eye is in the heart of every soul, but it is the attitude that keeps every man looking down to the earth instead of raising his eyes upwards. The average tendency is to see on the surface. It is not true that the average person cannot see any further, but the average man does not think that there is anything further; so he does not give himself the trouble to see any further. There are many who are intelligent enough to perceive all that is behind things, but the first thing that makes their view limited is the narrow range of their interest. They are not enough interested to take trouble about things they neither know nor believe. They would be glad to have intuition if it came without their taking any trouble. There are many who can think, but they do not wish to take the trouble of thinking.

There are two things necessary to perceive: one is openness, the other is effort made in that direction. When contemplating upon anything, the mind must be free from all else that stands in the way. That is called openness. Also one must arrive by the help of concentration at focusing one's mind on a certain object. The next thing is to be interested enough in all things that one comes in contact with and one cares to know about, that one may penetrate below the surface and find out what is hidden in all things.

III:7 INDEPENDENCE AND INDIFFERENCE – *VAIRAGYA*

The presence of man speaks of his past, present and future. When a visitor comes to your house he brings to you his joy or his sorrow; he brings you the effect of his good or bad deeds; he brings you the influence of his high or low mind; he tunes the vibration of the sphere of your home to his pitch; he charges the sphere with his own vibrations. If you can only perceive, he need not tell you one word about himself, you can know if he is experiencing heaven or hell, for one need not wait for heaven or hell in the hereafter, it is here also; only, after death it will be more felt. Therefore the contact of a heavenly person can bring to you the air of heaven, and the contact of the other can give you the taste of the other place.

This shows that every individual is a tone, a rhythm – and a tone which draws the tone of every other person to its own pitch, a rhythm which compels every other person to follow the same rhythm. That is where one feels the pull in life. That is what scares the sage from the life of the world and makes him feel inclined to run away from this world and take refuge in a forest or in a desert.

Why the average person does not feel it is that, just like children absorbed in play, the people in the world are pulling each other's rope. Therefore they do not feel much, for they are pulled but they also pull the rope of another. But the one who is tuned to a different pitch altogether from the average person and whose rhythm in life is quite different from the others' naturally must feel the pull too much.

The only way how the sages manage to protect themselves from this is by the practice of *vairagya* which means independence and indifference both in one – which cannot be learned or taught. It comes by itself. It is not lack of love, or bitterness. It is only rising above both love and hate.

III:8 A SILENT MUSIC

Every soul radiates an influence which charges the atmosphere all around. The more powerful the influence the wider it spreads, forcing its way even through walls. There is no barrier of water or of space which can keep that influence from spreading. The stronger the influence the longer it lasts. It is not difficult for a sensitive person to perceive on coming into a room or in a house what influence it has, or to perceive on sitting on a chair who was sitting there before him. The character of this influence is like light or heat which silently spreads its warmth according to its power of radiance. It is not that man's influence is felt in his presence only, but even after he has left the place his influence remains. The influence of some persons can remain for hours, of some for days, of some for weeks or months or even years. Atmosphere is a silent music; it has its effect upon the listener, exciting or peaceful, whatever it may be.

The atmosphere remains not only in the place but also in objects such as a chair or sofa or a cushion or a carpet. An influence can remain with the clothes that one has worn in one's life. It is something real, not tangible but perceptible. Music comes through the ears to the heart, but atmosphere comes direct. A walking stick can have the atmosphere of the person who held it. A rosary, necklace, brooch or ring can have atmosphere; a pen or an inkstand can have an atmosphere of the person who has used it. Everybody perceives it consciously or unconsciously, but the more sensitive a person, the more he can realize it.

It is not easy for everybody to break a person's influence, although it is possible to rise above it. A person who is of fine and sensitive nature, pure and good, for him the influence from all around in this world can become so troublesome that he would always find himself in the midst of the battle going on constantly around him. Therefore it will not do for a person to become fine and sensitive and yet not learn how to combat all influences around him. The more one studies this question, the more one comes to realize that life is a battle not only outwardly but also inwardly. There are two things that can be done for self-defence: either to become a very well-equipped fighter to counter all those influences attacking one with the power of one's own influence; or to rise above all such influences, which means to live and not live, to be and not be, to come down to act and to rise up to keep in security.

III:9 THREE WAYS TO DEVELOP INSIGHT

There are three important things to be considered in the development of insight: the steady gaze of the eyes and of the mind which helps one in penetration; another thing is losing everything else from one's sight except the object through which one wishes to penetrate, and that comes by sufficient interest in the object of penetration; but the third thing, which helps the most, is to lose for the moment the thought of one's self. When one's body and mind are not before one, it is then that one has the proper insight into things one wishes to know and understand.

Sufis therefore have different concentrations by which they are helped not only in keeping their gaze steady, but in standing firm upon one thought. When a person cannot take interest in any thing or being, then his mind is not steady, for there is nothing that it takes interest in. It is the interest which makes the mind steady. A certain thought which is inspiring or helpful in some way, or a certain form which is inspiring, when once one has concentrated upon it *then* the mind becomes steady; also then it can easily hold an object before it without wavering.

The character of the mind is like that of the eyes, the eyes which take in all that comes within their horizon. So the mind jumps from one thing to another, upon all the thoughts which may be standing within its horizon. And as it is not always easy to keep the gaze steady, so it is with the mind. To keep the mind firm upon one thought, form or image is not easy. But the third thing is more difficult, and that is to lose oneself in the thought of the object that is before one. In this way the self which stands in the way between the soul and its object of penetration is lost from view for the time being. Thus the person is enabled to penetrate through all things, knowing thereby the nature, character and secret of all things.

There is no other cause of all depression and despair than the inability to see through life. There may be many reasons seeming to be the different causes of unhappiness, but this one is the greatest reason, the reason of all reasons. Even animals in whose nature the tendency of fighting is pronounced become friends when they come to know one another by association. Many troubles in the lives of individuals and of the multitude might be avoided if keen insight were developed, for all confusion is caused by misunderstanding. Not only human beings, but all things of this world which seem of use or of no use, which seem to be easy or difficult to obtain, all are for the use of man. Therefore penetration into things is the secret of the success of science, art, philosophy and religion, all. (*See* Questions and Answers, p 292.)

III:10 TRANQUILLITY

The most important thing in life is the opening of that clear vision with the help of insight. The effect of every emotion covers the insight, just as clouds cover the sun. It is for this reason that most clever and qualified people often do things, especially at the moment of passion or anger, which they would not have done otherwise. The reason is that the mind loses its rhythm under the strain of passion or emotion, and so it upsets the rhythm of the body, it makes man perplexed and unable to see any condition or situation clearly.

It is therefore that the seers, the sages, try to keep their tranquillity at every cost, for life in the world brings up many things each day and hour to disturb that tranquillity which is the secret of insight. Every little noise or disturbance in oneself and outside can upset a person who keeps the rhythm of his whole being in the proper order. It is therefore that the sages have chosen solitude and a life away from the world. But the best way of keeping one's tranquillity is to keep this rhythm under the control of one's own will. By doing this one preserves one's tranquillity in the midst of life's greatest turmoil. In the terms of Vedanta life is likened to the sea where there is a continual rising and falling of the waves. Every man by nature seeks peace, and in peace is his only satisfaction, but often he seeks it wrongly. Therefore, instead of producing peace, he creates more struggle in life. The secret of peace is in the will-power. Instead of resisting the forces which jar and disturb one's life, if one could only stand firm against them then one could attain that tranquillity which is most necessary to have a greater insight into life.

Man is made of atoms gathered together around the intelligence, physical atoms and mental atoms which make his body and mind. The power which has gathered them and which controls them and which uses them for their best purpose is the will-power. When this power is absent the body and mind both go to pieces, broken by every jarring effect coming from whatever direction. This is the reason hidden within most illnesses and weaknesses. Every mistake, failure and every disappointment in life has this reason behind it: lack of control, lack of steadiness and strength against the disturbing influences which come from within and without.

The great lesson which one learns, which helps most in keeping that tranquillity in life which helps insight, is to be able to become like ebb and flow: when the first is needed then to become that, when the next thing is needed, then to make oneself in that way. When it is necessary to express, then to express; when it is necesssary to respond, then to respond – at will. In this manner one will always manage to preserve tranquillity in life. (*See* Questions and Answers, p 293.)

PART THREE

◆

SYMBOLOGY

Naqsh Bandi

GATHA I

The wise have given lessons to the world in different forms suited to the evolution of the people at a particular time, and the first and most original form of education that the wise gave to the world has been symbolical. This method of teaching has been valued in all ages and will always have its importance. It is not beauty which is not veiled; in the veiling and unveiling of beauty is the purpose of life. Beauty is that which is always out of reach. You see it and you do not see it, you touch it and you cannot touch it. It is seen and yet veiled, it is known and yet unknown, and therefore words are often inadequate to express the beauty of truth. Therefore symbolism is adopted by the wise.

The religions of the old Egyptians, of the Ancient Greeks, of the Hindus and of Parsees all have symbols which express the essential truth hidden under a religion; there is symbolism in Christianity and in many ancient religions of the world. Man has often rebelled against symbolism, but it is natural. Man has always revolted against things he cannot understand.

There has been a wave of opposition to symbolism in both parts of the world, East and West. It came in the East in the period of Islam and in the West it re-echoed in the Reformation. No doubt when the sacred symbols are made as patents by the religious who wish to monopolize the whole truth, then it gives rise to that tendency in human nature which is always ready to accept things or reject them. However – and one can say this without exaggeration – symbology has always served to keep the ancient wisdom intact. It is symbology that can prove today the saying of Solomon, 'There is nothing new under the sun.'

There are many thoughts relating to human nature, to the nature of life, relating to God and His many attributes, and relating to the path towards the goal that are expressed in symbolism. To a person who sees only the surface of life the symbols mean nothing; the secret of symbols is revealed to the souls who see through life, whose glance penetrates through objects. Verily, before the seer the things of the world open themselves, and it is this uncovering of things in which is hidden beauty.

There is a great joy in understanding, especially things that express nothing to everybody. It requires intuition, even something deeper than intuition, insight, to read symbols. To the one to whom the symbols speak of their nature and of their secret each symbol is a living manuscript in itself. Symbolism is the best way of learning the mysteries of life, and the best way of leaving behind ideas which will keep for centuries after the teacher has passed. It is speaking without speaking, it is writing without writing. The symbol may be said to be an ocean in a drop. (*See* Questions and Answers, p 294.)

1:2 THE SYMBOL OF THE SUN

Light has the greatest attraction for the human soul. Man loves it in fire and in things that are bright and shining, and that is why he considers gold and jewels as precious. Because of its light, the cosmos has a greater attraction for him than the earth. As man evolved he naturally ceased to look down on earth, but looked up to the cosmos, the heavens. The most attractive object that he saw was the sun in the heavens, the sun which is without any support and is more luminous than anything else in the heavens. Therefore, as man was attracted to beauty and surrendered to beauty, he bowed to the sun as being the greatest beauty in heaven, and man took the sun as nature's symbol of God.

This symbol he pictured in different forms. In Persia, China, Japan, India, Egypt, whenever God was pictured it was in the form of the sun. In all ages man has pictured his prophet, master, saviour with a sun around his head. In ancient Persia there used to be a golden disc behind the head of the king, picturing him as the sun, and they used to call this disc *zardash*. The name Zarathustra has the same origin; the word simply meant the golden disc. In Hindu temples and Buddhist temples around the image of different avatars there is this sign of the sun, and this symbol was used both in the East and in the West on turbans and hats. There are now people in India who put on their turbans a brass band which represents the sun.

A deeper study of the sun suggests the four directions of lines that are formed round the sun. It is this sign that is the origin of the symbol of the cross. The ancient traditions prove that the idea of the cross existed in the East long before the coming of Christ, especially among the Brahmins. It is from this sign that the two sacred arms were made: *chakra* and *trishul*.

Islam, the religion which allows no symbolism, has in the building of the mosques the same symbolism of the sun. Whether the name of the sun be written in Persian or in Arabic, it makes the form of a mosque.

Man, as is his nature, has blamed the sun worshippers and mocked at them, but he has never been able to uproot the strong appeal, the attraction for human souls held by the sun.

1:3 THE SYMBOL OF THE CROSS

The symbol of the cross has many significations. It is said in the Bible that first was the word and then came light and then the world was created. And as the light is expressed in the form of the cross, so every form shows in it the original sign. Every artist knows the value of the vertical line and the horizontal line which are the skeleton of every form. This is proved by the teaching of the *Qur'an* where it is said that God created the world from His own light. The cross is the figure that fits to every form everywhere.

Morally the cross signifies pain or torture. That means that in every activity of life, which may be pictured as a perpendicular line, there come hindrances which the horizontal line represents. This shows the picture of life and that, as it is said, man proposes and God disposes. Somebody asked the great Master Ali what made him believe in God who is beyond human comprehension. Ali said, 'I believe in God because I see that, when I alone wish, things are not accomplished.' According to the metaphysical point of view this shows the picture of limitation in life.

The symbol of the cross in its connection with the life of Christ not only relates to the crucifixion of the Master, but signifies the crucifixion that one has to meet with by possessing the truth. The idea of the Hindu philosopher is that the life in the world is an illusion, and therefore every experience in this life and knowledge in this life are also illusions. The Sanskrit word for this illusion is *maya*; it is also called *mithya*, from which comes the word 'myth'.

When the soul begins to see the truth it is, so to say, born again, and to this soul all that appears truth, to an average person appears false, and what seems truth to this soul is nothing to that average person. All that seems to that average person important and precious in life has no value nor importance for this soul, and what seems to this soul important and valuable has no importance nor value for that average person. Therefore such a one naturally finds himself alone in a crowd which lives in a world quite different from that in which he lives. Imagine living in a world where nobody uses your language! Yet he can live in the world for he knows its language. And yet to him the life in the world is as unprofitable as to a grown-up person the world of children playing with their toys.

A human being who has realized the truth is subject to all pains and torture in the same way as all other persons, except that he is capable of bearing them better than the others. But at the same time when, while in the crowd, everyone hits the other and also receives blows, the knower of truth has to stand alone and receive them only. This is in itself a great torture. The life in the world is difficult for every person, rich or poor, strong or weak, but for the knower of truth it is still more difficult, and that in itself is a cross. Therefore for a spiritual Messenger the cross is a natural emblem to explain his moral condition.

But there is a still higher significance of the cross which is understood by the mystic. This significance is what is called self-denial, and in order to teach this moral gentleness, humility and modesty are taught as a first lesson. Self-denial is an effect of which self-effacement is the cause. This is self-denial that a man says, 'I am not, Thou art.' For instance, an artist looking at his picture says, 'It is Thy work, not mine'; a musician hearing his composition says, 'It is Thy creation, I do not exist.' That soul then is in a way crucified and through that crucifixion resurrection comes.

There is not the slightest doubt that, when man has had enough pain in his life, he rises to this great consciousness. But it is not necessary that only pain should be the means. It is the readiness on the part of man to efface his part of consciousness and to efface his own personality, which lifts the veil that hides the spirit of God from the view of man.

I:4 THE TWO FORCES

The Egyptian symbolism is the most ancient, and for the most part the symbolism of other nations originates from the Egyptian. The Egyptian symbol of wings with a centre of circular shape and at the sides two snakes looking right and left is known to many as *karobi*. The word really means 'spirit' or 'angel'. This symbol represents the spirit and the power of the spirit which is different in the two directions, the right and the left. The heads of the two snakes show the direction of life and energy to either side, and the central circular sign represents the light itself, the spirit. And the wings on both sides represent three aspects of the power of the spirit.

One aspect of the spirit is sound, another is colour, and the third is external action. This symbol suggests that the spirit is not only a light in the centre, but a light directed to the right and to the left, and that it shines out according to the degree of illumination. The light of the spirit is in either direction a peculiar force. The symbol also suggests that in either direction the sound, colour and activity change according to the direction.

In the Hindu Vedas these two different forces are called *ida* and *pingala*. The Sufi names these two forces *jemal* and *jelal*. The great Yogis have experienced the mystery of life by the study of these forces. The central point is called by the Sufis *kemal*, in the Vedas this is called *sushumna*.

It is difficult to picture the finer forces of nature, and as it has been the custom to picture the light in the face of the sage as the aura, so these two forces are pictured as wings and not as rays or otherwise. As the body has hands, so the hands of the spirit can only be pictured as wings. Besides this, man who without illumination is an earthly creature, after illumination becomes a heavenly creature.

The idea of the mystic about these two forces is expressed in calling one the sun-force and the other the moon-force. The mystic pictures them as seated in the two parts of the body, the right and the left. He names also the two nostrils by the same names. By some the right direction of this force is pictured as male, the left as the female direction.

The serpent has been considered a sacred symbol, because it is pictured as representing many secrets of mysticism. The Yogis have learned a great deal from the serpent – as there is a hint in the Bible, 'Be ye wise as the serpent and innocent as the dove.'

This sign shows that man is self-sufficient in his spirit, though incomplete in his body; that in every spirit there is both woman and man. It is the direction of the force of the spirit which makes the male and the female aspect. The central point represents the spirit, and the spirit represents God. As spirit is both male and female, so it is beyond both. It is limitation that turns one into two, but when man rises above limitation he finds that two become one.

So this symbol reminds man of the power of the spirit, that man may know that he is not only a material body but that he is a spirit himself, and that man may know that spirit is not an inactive torch of life, but that spirit is full activity, more than the body is.

It also represents the idea that man is not only an earthly creature but that he also belongs to heaven. This symbol suggests that nothing earthly should frighten or worry man, for he may rise above the earth.

1:5 THE SYMBOL OF THE DOVE

The bird represents the wayfarer of the sky, and at the same time it represents a being who belongs to the earth and is capable of dwelling in the skies. The former explanation of the bird represents the idea of a soul whose dwelling place is in heaven, and the latter that of the dweller on earth who is capable of moving about in the higher spheres, and both give the idea that the spiritual man, dwelling on the earth, is from heaven; they explain also that the spiritual man is the inhabitant of the heavens and is dwelling on earth for a while.

The pigeon was used as a messenger to carry a message from one place to another, and therefore the symbol of the dove is a natural one to represent the Messenger from above. Spiritual bliss is an experience such that, if a bird or an animal were to have it, it would never return to its own kind. But it is a credit due to man that, after touching that point of great happiness and bliss, he comes into the world of sorrows and disappointments and delivers his message. This quality can be seen in the pigeon also; when the pigeon is sent it goes, but it comes back faithfully to the master who sent it.

The spiritual man performs this duty doubly. He reaches higher than the human plane, touches the divine plane, and returns with the message from the divine to the human plane. In this way, instead of remaining on the divine plane, he arrives among his fellow men for their welfare, which is no small sacrifice. But then again he performs a duty to God from whom he brings His message that he delivers to the human beings. He lives as a human being, subject to love, hate, praise and blame, passes his life in the world of attachment and the life that binds with a thousand ties from all sides. Yet he does not forget the place from where he has come, and he constantly and eagerly looks forward to reach the place for which he is bound.

Therefore in both these journeys, from earth to heaven and from heaven to earth, the idea of the dove proves to be more appropriate than any other in the world.

1:6 THE SYMBOL OF THE SUFI ORDER

The symbol of the Order is a heart with wings. It explains that the heart is between soul and body, a medium between spirit and matter. When the soul is covered by its love for matter it is naturally attracted to matter. This is the law of gravitation in abstract form, as it is said in the Bible, 'Where your treasure is, there will your heart be also.' When man treasures the things of the earth his heart is drawn to the earth, but the heart is subject not only to gravitation but also to attraction from on high. And as in the Egyptian symbology wings are considered as the symbol of spiritual progress, the heart with wings expresses that the heart reaches upward towards heaven.

Then the crescent in the heart suggests the responsiveness of the heart. The crescent represents the responsiveness of the crescent to the light of the sun, for naturally it receives the light which develops it until it becomes the full moon. The principal teaching of Sufism is that of learning to become a pupil, for it is the pupil who has a chance of becoming a teacher. Once a person considers that he is a teacher, his responsiveness is gone. The greatest teachers of the world have been the greatest pupils, and it is this principle which is represented by the crescent. The crescent in the heart represents that the heart responsive to the light of God is illuminated.

The explanation of the five-pointed star is that it represents the divine light, for when the light comes it has five points, when it returns it has four; the one form suggesting creation, the other annihilation. The five-pointed star also represents the natural figure of man, though that with four points represents all forms of the world. But the form with five points is a development of the four-pointed form. For instance, if a man is standing with his legs joined and arms extended he makes a four-pointed form, but when man shows activity – dancing, jumping – or he moves one leg, he forms a five-pointed star, which represents a beginning activity, in other words a beginning of life.

It is the divine light which is represented by the five-pointed star, and the star is reflected in the heart which is responsive to the divine light. And the heart which has by its response received the divine light is liberated, as the wings show. To explain in brief the meaning of the symbol: the heart responsive to the light of God is liberated.

I:7 THE SYMBOLISM OF THE DOT AND THE CIRCLE

The dot is the most important of all figures, for every figure is an extension of the dot and the dot is the source of every figure. You cannot let a pen touch a paper without making a dot first of all. It is simply the extension of the dot in two directions which is called a horizontal or perpendicular line. And again it is the dot which determines sides; if it were not for the dot the sides as above or below or right or left could not be determined.

The origin of all things and beings may be pictured as a dot. This dot is called in Sanskrit *bindu*, the origin and source of the Whole Being. Since the dot is the source of the perpendicular and horizontal lines, it is the source of all figures and characters of all languages that exist and have existed, as doubtless it is the source of all forms of nature. The principal thing in man's figure is his eye, and in the eye the iris, and in the iris the pupil, which signifies the dot.

At the same time the dot means zero, meaning nothing. It is nothing and it is everything, and the dot expresses the symbol of nothing being everything and everything being nothing. Amir, the Indian poet, expresses this idea in his well-known verse. He says:

If thou wilt come to thy senses by becoming selfless,
free from life's intoxication,
thou wilt realize that what seems to thee non-existent
is all-existing.
And what seems to thee existent
does not exist.

How true it is that in ordinary life we look at reality upside-down. What exists seems to us non-existent, what does not exist in reality, but only seems to exist, that alone we consider existent.

The dot develops into the circle, which shows the picture of this seemingly non-existent developing into all-existing. The iris of the eye is the development of the dot which is called the pupil. A dot added to 'one' makes one ten and with two dots the one becomes a hundred, and this shows that man is small when he is unconscious of God. When the knowledge of God, who is the source of the Whole Being although non-existent to the ignorant eye, is added to man, he becomes ten or a hundred or a thousand.

As the dot enriches the figure, so God enriches man. As all figures come from the dot, so all things and beings come from God. And as destruction must in time break all things into dots, so all things must return to God.

1:8 THE SYMBOLISM OF LINES

The upright line

The upright line suggests the One; therefore also the number one is represented by an upright line.

The upright line suggests heaven or the world above, its extremity being upward.

The upright line is perfection. Through all forms life has culminated in the end in the human form which is upright.

The upright line also suggests straightforwardness, for it is straight upward.

The upright line also suggests firmness, for it is steady.

The upright line also suggests life, for it stands.

The upright line also suggests rising, for it goes upward.

The upward line also suggests unity, as it shows oneness and the oneness of the whole, all being one.

The upright line is the form of *alif*, the Arabic A, and the name Allah in Arabic writing begins with *alif*.

The upright line is the first line, and all forms and figures are nothing but the change of direction of that line. And as all is made by God and of God, so by the upright line and of the upright line all forms are formed.

The vertical line and the horizontal line

The Messenger is pictured symbolically as a Cupid. He is meant to guide the longing soul toward its divine Beloved, and that part of his work is symbolized as the vertical line. He is also used by providence to bring together two souls in light who are seeking each other through darkness, some knowing and some not knowing what they are seeking after – which is represented by the horizontal line.

The horizontal line and the vertical line together make a complete cross, which is the sign of *kemal*, perfection.

The vertical line is the sign of God and the horizontal line is the world.

The vertical line represents heaven, the horizontal line earth.

The horizontal line represents this world, the vertical line that world, the next world.

The vertical line conveys the meaning Yes, the horizontal line the meaning No.

The vertical line denotes life, the horizontal line, death.

The vertical line represents strength, the horizontal line, powerlessness.

The vertical line spirit, the horizontal line matter.

The vertical line the masculine, the horizontal line the feminine.

The vertical line the sun, the horizontal line the moon.

The vertical line the day, the horizontal line the night.

The vertical line the positive, the horizontal line the negative.

The vertical line power, the horizontal line beauty.

The vertical line God, the horizontal line man.

I:9 THE SYMBOLISM OF THE TRIANGLE

The triangle represents the beginning, the continuation and the end. The triangle is the sign of life which has appeared in three forms, of which the idea of the trinity is symbolical. The idea of these three aspects of life has existed for a very long time among Hindus who named it *trimurti*. As in the Christian Church the Trinity consists of the Father, the Son and the Holy Ghost, so among Hindus the *trimurti* consists of Brahma, Vishnu and Mahesh: Brahma the Creator, Vishnu the Sustainer and Mahesh or Shiva the Destroyer. By the word 'Destroyer' destruction is not meant, but change.

The triangle in all its forms is the basic outline of all form that exists in the world. The triangle has a horizontal line in it and a perpendicular line, and two triangles can very well form a square. The hand, the head, the leg, the palm, the foot, all show in their form the triangle as the principal outline. In the leaf, fruit, tree or mountain the triangle is the outline.

The three aspects in which life has manifested and of which

the triangle is the symbol are the knower, the known and the knowing faculty – the seer, the seen and the faculty of seeing.

The triangle is the riddle which has within it the secret of this life of variety. But for these three different aspects which stand opposite each other man would not be able to enjoy life. At the same time it is these three aspects again which are the cause of all the illusion. And if the riddle of the idea of trinity has been solved and out of trinity unity has become manifest, then the purpose of this idea of trinity is fulfilled.

One can understand this by realizing the truth that it is not three that are one, but one that is three. The beginning and end of all things is one, it is the repetition of one which makes two and it is this division which produces three. In this riddle of the ideal of trinity lies the secret of the whole life.

I:10 The symbology of the mushroom

The Chinese philosopher is symbolically depicted holding a mushroom stem in his hand. The mushroom represents the earth and what comes from it and what is close to it, and keeping it in the hand means spirit handling or controlling matter.

At the same time it suggests a moral: that the sign of the sage is to be as tender, as refined, as meek, as humble as a mushroom. It teaches the same moral that Christ taught, 'If one smite you on one cheek, turn the other cheek.' If one strikes on the rock, one's own hand will be hurt, but one will not have the same experience by striking the mushroom.

It also teaches the philosophy that all the product of this earth, however precious, is in the spiritual sense no more than a mushroom which is subject to destruction every moment.

It also teaches the idea of being in life as free and independent as a mushroom which needs no special care and demands no great attention from others. If any will use it, it is ready to be used; if any will throw it away, it is ready to be thrown away without causing great loss.

It also suggests a mystical point: while all other plants and trees respond to the wind and storm and make a noise, the mushroom stands still without uttering one sound. When the body and mind of the mystic are trained to the stillness of the mushroom through all storms and winds of life, then the mystic achieves perfection.

GATHA II

There is a symbolical picture known in the philosophical world of China that represents a sage with one shoe in his hand and one on his foot. It signifies the hereafter: that the change that death brings is to a wise man only the taking off of one shoe. The body of the philosopher represents his soul or his person; the one shoe still on his foot represents his mind which exists after death. And the withdrawal of the soul from the body is like taking one foot out of the shoe. For the mystic therefore the physical body is something he can easily dispense with, and to arrive at this realization is the object of wisdom. When by philosophical understanding of life he begins to realize his soul, then he begins to stand, so to speak, on his own feet; he is then himself and the body is to him only a cover.

The teaching of the Prophet is to die before death, which means to realize in one's lifetime what death means. This realization takes away all the fear there is. By the symbol of the shoe is shown also the nothingness of the material existence or the smallness of the physical being in comparison with the greatness of the soul or the spirit.

Hafiz says in a Persian verse:

Those who realize Thee are kings of life –

which means that the true kingdom of life is in the realization of the soul. The idea that one must wait until one's turn will come after many incarnations keeps one far away from the desired goal. The man who is impatient to arrive at spiritual realization is to be envied. As Omar Khayyam says:

To-morrow? Why, to-morrow I may be myself,
with yesterday's seven thousand years.

97

He means by this: do not bother about the past, do not trouble about the future, but accomplish all you can just now.

Life has taken time enough to develop gradually from mineral to vegetable, from vegetable to animal, and from animal to man; and after becoming man delay is not necessary. It is true that a whole lifetime is not sufficient for one to become what one wishes to be. Still nothing is impossible, since the soul of man is from the Spirit of God. And if God can do all things, why cannot man do something?

II:2 FRUITFULNESS

There is a Chinese symbol of philosophers carrying on their backs peaches, which means that the object of life is to be fruitful. However good or spiritual a person may be, yet if his life is not fruitgiving he has not fulfilled the purpose of life. A person whose life becomes fruitful does not only bear fruit to others, but every aspect of life bears fruit to him as well; for him life becomes a fruit.

If life were only for what people call goodness, life would be very uninteresting, for goodness is dependent for its beauty on badness. As a form cannot exist without a shadow, so goodness cannot be without badness. If life were for spirituality alone the soul had better not have been born on earth, for the soul in its nature is spiritual. The whole creation is purposed for something greater than goodness or even spirituality and that is fruitfulness. Goodness and spirituality are the means, not the goal. Therefore it is the object of life which the symbol of peaches represents.

Fruitfulness has three aspects. The first aspect is when man benefits from his own life; the next aspect is when man benefits from the life outside himself, and the third aspect is when man is a benefit to himself and to the life outside, and the life outside is a benefit to him. That is the moment of the fruitfulness of life. It takes all the patience one has to arrive at this realization, but it is for this realization that God created the world: that man may enjoy fruitfulness therein.

It is the absence of faith and lack of patience which deprive man of this bliss; if not, every soul is purposed for this. For instance, when a musician begins to enjoy his own music – that is the first fruit; when he enjoys the music of others – that is the second stage of realization; but when man enjoys his own music and makes others enjoy it too, then his life has become fruitful.

There is a great treasure of blessing within oneself and there is a vast treasure of blessing outside oneself, and when one has become able to find out the treasure one has within oneself and to exploit the treasure which is outside oneself, and when there is an exchange between one's own treasure and the treasure outside, then one's life has borne the fruit for which one's soul was born. There comes a time in the life of the fruitful souls when every moment of their life bears a new fruit, just like a plant which bears fruit at all times of the year.

II:3 THE SYMBOL OF THE DRAGON

The best known symbolical figure of China is the dragon. The dragon represents both life and death: life in the sense of eternal life, death in the sense of a change from mortality to eternity.

Very often a Chinese dragon has the appearance of a tiger, of a seal, its body that of a snake, together with wings of the birds and the paws of carnivorous animals, also some semblance of man – which means that life is one but it is manifest in many forms, that life lives on life and so hungers for life.

The dragon suggests mortality standing by one's side, awaiting its hour every moment of our life. And yet man is unaware of it, building castles in the air, depending upon the life in this mortal world.

The dragon also suggests that there is an obstacle on the way to eternity, and that obstacle is death, and that can be avoided by conquering the dragon.

The dragon is also a picture of man's selfish ego which is not only the enemy of others but which makes man his own enemy.

The dragon signifies the lower nature, and the conquering of the lower nature is the killing of the dragon, of which St George also is the symbol.

The dragon is a sign of material power which has its transitory reign over things and beings, and often power can govern and cause difficulty even to spiritual beings, for the reason that even spiritual beings have matter which makes their being and which is dependent for its life and comfort on things of this earth. But all stories of dragons prove the dragon to be a failure in the end and the spirit alone conqueror over it.

In Chinese art this symbol is kept to the fore, for this one symbol suggests and touches many things.

II:4 WATER

In the old scriptures such as the Vedanta and the Old Testament spirit is symbolized by water. One wonders why something which is next to earth should be considered symbolically as spirit. The nature of water is to give life to the earth, and so the nature of the spirit is to give life to the body. Without water the earth is dead, so is the body without soul.

Water and earth mingle, so the spirit mingles with matter and vivifies it, and yet the spirit stands above matter as water in time lets earth sink to the bottom, and itself stands above the earth.

But someone may ask, 'Is the spirit hidden under matter as the soul in the body?' I will answer, 'So does the water stay beneath the earth.' There is no place where water has no existence; there are places where earth is not to be found. So nowhere in space is spirit absent, only the absence of matter is possible.

The symbolical way of expressing high ideas does not come from the brain; it is an outcome of intuition. The first step in intuition is to understand the symbolical meaning of different things, and the next step is to express things symbolically. It is in itself a divine art, and the best proof of it is to be found in the symbol of water, which is so apt for expressing the meaning of spirit.

II:5 WINE

Wine is held to be sacred, not only in the Christian faith but in many other religions also. In the ancient religion of the Zoroastrians, *yima Jamsheid*, the bowl of wine 'of which Jamsheid drank deep,' is a historical fact. Among the Hindus Shiva held wine sacred. And in Islam, though wine is forbidden on earth, yet it is allowed in heaven. *Hauz-e-kauthar*, the sacred fountain of heaven, is a fountain of wine. Although the bowl that was offered to the Prophet in the *meraj* was filled with milk, according to what the authorities of Islam say, yet I doubt it. I should not be surprised if that were not an invention of the authorities to keep the faithful followers away from wine, for it is natural that the wine the Prophet drank in heaven, the followers should begin drinking already on earth.

Wine symbolizes the soul's evolution. Wine comes from the annihilation of grapes, immortality comes from the annihilation of self. The bowl of poison which is known in many mystical cults also suggests the idea of wine – not of a sweet but of a bitter wine. When the self turns into something different from what it was before, it is as if the soul were born again. This is seen in the grape turning into wine. The grape by turning into wine lives; as a grape it would have vanished in time. Only, by turning into wine the grape loses its individuality, and yet it does not lose its life. The self-same grape lives on as wine, and the longer it lives the better the wine becomes.

For a Sufi therefore the true sacrament is the turning of one's grape-like personality, which has a limited span of life, into wine, that nothing of one's self may be lost, but on the contrary may be amplified, even perfected. This is the essence of all philosophy and the secret of mysticism.

II:6 THE CURL OF THE BELOVED

In the Sufi literature which is known to the world as the Persian literature there is much spoken about the curls of the Beloved, and many have wondered what it means. The curl is a symbol of something which is curved and round. The curve denotes the twist in the thought of wisdom. Very often a straight word of truth hits upon the head harder than a hammer. That shows that truth alone is not sufficient, the truth must be made into wisdom. And what is wisdom? Wisdom is the twisted truth. As raw food cannot be digested and therefore it is cooked – although raw food is more natural than cooked food – so the straight truth is more natural, but is not digestible. It needs to be made into wisdom.

And why is it called the Beloved's curl? Because truth is of God, the divine Beloved. And truth is God and that twist, given to His own Being which is truth, amplifies the divine beauty, as the curl is considered to be the sign of beauty.

Then what is not straight is a puzzle. Wisdom is a puzzle to the ordinary mind. Besides, the curl hangs low down; so the heavenly beauty which is wisdom is manifested on earth. In other words, if someone wishes to see the beauty of the heavenly Beloved, he may see it in wisdom. Wisdom is traced not only in the human being, but even in the beasts and birds, in their affection, in their instinct. Very often it is most difficult for man to imitate fully the work which birds do in weaving their nests. Even the insects do wonderful work in preparing a little abode for themselves which is beyond man's art and skill. Beside this, if one studies nature, after keen observation and some contemplation, one will find that there is perfect wisdom behind it. Once man has thought on the subject he can never, however materialistic he may be, deny the existence of God.

Man's individuality is proved by his wisdom and distinguished by comparison. The wisdom of God, being perfect, is unintelligible to man. The glass of water cannot imagine how much water there is in the sea. If man would realize his limitation he would never dare question the existence of God.

The symbol of the curl also signifies something which is there, attractive and yet a puzzle, a riddle. One loves it, admires it, and yet one cannot fathom its length and breadth. It is that which is wisdom. Its surface is human but its depth is divine. It could be hell or heaven, and the knowledge of it can enable man always to keep in touch with his heaven, instead of waiting for it till the hereafter.

II:7 THE GLANCE

The Persian poets in Sufi literature speak very often of the glance, and their symbolical expression for the glance is very often a sword, and it is called a sword for various reasons. In the first place the glance has a projecting effect. An intelligent glance has a crossways movement like that of a sword. But besides this, from a psychological point of view a keen glance sees through an object as though a thing had been cut open by the sword and manifested to view.

The glance is a power; very little is known about it. The power of the glance can hold lions at bay. Therefore also it is symbolized as a sword. The glance of a brave person is very often more powerful than a sword, for the will-power works through the glance.

Besides its precious work which makes the eye superior to every other organ of the body, it is the expression of the beauty of body, mind and soul. Sufis therefore symbolize the eye by a cup of wine.

Through the eyes the secret hidden in man's heart is reflected into the heart of another. However much a person may try to conceal his secret, yet the reader can read it in his eyes and can read there his pleasure, his displeasure, his joy, his sorrow. A seer can see still farther. The seer can see the actual condition of man's soul through his eyes, his grade of evolution, his attitude in life, his outlook on life and his condition, both hidden and manifest.

Besides, to the passive soul of a disciple knowledge, ecstasy, spiritual joy and divine peace, all are given through the glance.

One sees in everyday life that a person who is laughing in his mind with his lips closed can express his laughter through his glance, and the one who receives the glance at once catches the infectious mirth. Often the same happens through looking in the eyes of the sorrowful; in a moment one becomes filled with depression.

And those whose secret is God, whose contemplation is the perfection of beauty, whose joy is endless in the realization of everlasting life, from whose heart the spring of love is ever flowing – it is most appropriate that their glance should be called symbolically the bowl of *saqi*, the bowl of the Winegiver.

II:8 THE MYTH OF BALDER

The Scandinavian myth tells that Balder, the god of youth, beauty, kindness and gentleness, was pursued by enemies who wished to kill him. For his protection a spell had been cast upon all the trees of the forest and every plant that has root in the ground and grows upwards to heaven, that no weapon wrought from any of them should have power to harm him. But in this charm the mistletoe had been forgotten, which has no root in the ground, and from its wood an arrow was made with which Balder was hit and wounded to death.

Its interpretation is an answer to the question which often arises in an intelligent mind: why were godlike people continually treated cruelly, through all periods of the world's history? And how could any person in the world think of causing harm to those who attracted the sympathy of almost every soul they met on the earth? Their adherents spread their teachings and the beauty of their life and character among all, wise and foolish, kind and cruel. They all became to a greater or lesser degree impressed by what they learned of the godly souls, even those whose soul had not yet risen to human evolution, who only live like trees and plants, living and yet dreaming, unaware of life except their own activity. But the one who could not be impressed by this spell, whom it could not have reached even had it been cast upon him, is the godless one who is like the mistletoe, living without any root.

The mourning is continued in memory of the death of that god. In reality it is celebrating the birth of what was born from him: it was divine knowledge.

II:9 THE TREE OF WISHES

There is an old Hindu belief, found in the ancient myths of India, that there is a tree which they call *kamna kalpavriksha*, a tree that bears all the fruits that one can imagine. And if a person is under that tree he has but to wish for what he would like and in the same moment all fruits, all flowers, everything he can imagine he will find, brought forth by the tree as its fruits. He has but to wish and it will fall into his hands. If it is within one's reach, one only has to raise one's hand to pluck the flower or fruit of that tree; if it is beyond one's reach, one has only to wish and the branch will reach one's hand that one may pick it without any effort.

There is a story about that tree: that a wanderer, while journeying in deserts, by chance happened to sleep under that tree. And when after a good sleep he opened his eyes and looked up at that tree, he thought, 'I suppose it must be a pear tree.' No sooner had he thought that than two good ripe pears dropped near him. While lying there he picked them up. 'Oh,' he said, 'what a wonderful tree! If it were a grape tree, what a splendid thing it would be!' As soon as he said it the tree seemed full of grapes, and before he raised his hands the branches bent low and without any effort he was able to pick the grapes. But when he thought, 'What a wonderful tree,' he wondered if the tree would yield some roses. And no sooner had he given a thought to it than the whole tree seemed to blossom into roses. This man became so surprised, so amazed and perplexed by this magical tree that he wondered if it was true or if it was only a dream. As soon as he thought of a dream and he looked up at the tree, the tree vanished in a moment.

There cannot be a better example to demonstrate the idea behind the symbolical tree than this story, for this tree is this whole universe, the miniature of which is one's own self. And there is nothing that you ask that this universe will not answer, for it is the nature of the universe to answer your soul's call. Only, if you ask for the pears, there are pears; if you ask for a cactus there is a cactus; if you ask for the rose there will be the rose and its thorns together. And it is the lack of knowledge of this great secret hidden in the heart of the universe which is the only tragedy of life. When a person seeks for something in the universe and he cannot find it, it is not true that it is not there. The fact is that he does not see it. Besides, he sees something within his reach, he sees something which he desires, and yet he thinks whether it is possible for him to get it or whether it is beyond the reach of his effort and power.

At the same time the end of the story solves the whole question of life, and that is: it is all there and nothing is there. If we think it is everything, it is everything, but if we realize that it is nothing, it is nothing. It is something of which you may say that it is and it is not.

However, beyond all things of this universe, above all things that this life can offer, there is only one thing and that is God. And what is God? God is truth.

II:10 THE HINDU SYMBOLICAL FORM OF WORSHIP

P*uja* is the name of the Brahmin form of worship which is from the beginning to the end a symbolical expression of what the seeker has to perform in the path of spiritual attainment.

After bathing in the running stream of water which the Hindu calls the Ganges – whatever be the name of the river, he at that time believes that it is the Ganges, the sacred river – he proceeds with flowers to the shrine of the deity. He puts on to the deity the flowers and repeats the *mantram*, and stands greeting the deity with folded hands, and prostrates himself before the deity. Then he rings the bell and repeats the sacred word. Then he takes rice in his hands and puts it at the feet of the deity. Then the red powder, *kumkum*, he touches with the tip of his finger and makes a mark with it on the shrine of the deity and then on his own forehead. Then he touches the ointment with the tip of his finger, and after touching the deity he touches his forehead with the same ointment. He then prostrates himself and makes three circles around the shrine. Then he rings the bell, and thus the service is finished.

Afterwards he goes and stands before the sun and does his breathing exercises while adhering to the sun. And that completes the next part of his worship.

However primitive this form of worship, at the back of it there does seem to be a great meaning. The meaning of the bath in the Ganges is to become purified before one makes any effort of journeying on the spiritual path. The purification of the body and of the mind are both necessary before one takes the first step towards the God-ideal. One must not approach the deity before such purification, the outer purification as well as the inner purification, for then alone, when once a person is pure, he will find it easy to attain the desired presence.

The meaning of the flowers which he takes is that God is pleased with the offerings which are delicate, beautiful and fragrant. Delicate means tenderness of heart, beautiful in colour is fineness of character, fragrance is the virtue of the soul. This is the offering with which God is pleased.

He stands with the thought that his self is devoted in perfect discipline to the supreme will of God. His hands folded express no action on the part of himself but complete surrender. The meaning of prostration is self-denial in the right sense of the word, which means 'I am not, Thou art.'

Whispering the words and ringing the bell is that the same word is rung in the bell of one's heart.

His touching the red powder, the name of which symbolizes eternal life, means touching the eternal life, and when he touches the deity with the powder it means that from this source he is to gain eternal life. When he touches his forehead with it, it means he has gained it for himself.

The ointment means wisdom, and the touching of the God with it and then to his forehead means that true wisdom can be obtained from God alone, and touching his own head with it means that he has gained it.

Then making three circles around the shrine is the sign that life is a journey, and that journey is made to attain his goal which is God. 'Every step I take in my life', the Brahmin thinks, 'will be in His direction, in the search of God.'

In the second part of the service when he stands before the sun, by that he means that God is to be sought in the light. And by the breathing exercises he welds that link of inner communication between God and himself. (*See* Questions and Answers, p 294.)

Gatha III

The legend of Leili and Majnun is a story which is known throughout the East and the Sufi poets have used the characters of Leili and Majnun to express in this symbolical legend the philosophy of love.

Leili and Majnun, when young, were schoolmates devoted to one another. Whenever the teacher looked at Majnun's slate there was the picture of Leili drawn upon it, and when the teacher asked Leili to read from the book she repeated the name of Majnun. So, disappointed with the school, the parents had to take them back home. When difficulties arose owing to the caste differences – that they could not be married to one another according to the ideas of caste – in order to make them forget each other by changing the direction of their minds someone asked Majnun, 'What is there especial in Leili that you love her so much? There are many other maidens in the world.' Majnun answered, 'In order to see Leili you must borrow Majnun's eyes.'

With great reluctance Leili's people consented to the marriage on condition that Majnun did not show himself odd in his love but behave sensibly. On the day for which the visit had been arranged for Leili's people to meet Majnun, Majnun entered the drawing-room with his parents, who had told him to behave sensibly. It happened that Leili's dog which Majnun had known for years came into the room. Majnun could not for one moment hold to his dignity. He bowed at the feet of the dog and kissed its paws. And the visit became a failure.

Disappointed at Majnun's action his parents took him to the Ka'aba and told him to pray as they would pray. He said, 'Yes.' The multitude followed to see what prayer was going to take place. On hearing the name of Majnun, Majnun's parents first prayed, 'God, take away the love of Leili from the heart of

Majnun.' All the others listened. Then they asked Majnun to come and pray as they did. He said, 'Then shall I have Leili if I pray?' They urged him to come and pray. He said, 'God, give me Leili,' and all present said, 'Amen.'

When the parents lost all hope, then they let Majnun roam about as he wished. Majnun at last arrived near Leili's town and stayed outside the town in an old ruin where nobody lived. He was tired so he took shelter there under that worn-out roof. Leili, hearing that Majnun was near the town, sent some of her portion of food by a maid who was in her confidence and who was to carry it to Majnun. When the maid came and looked in that place for the beloved of Leili, there were two persons there: one a person thin and drowsy, the other person rather good looking. The maid thought certainly this person must be the beloved of Leili. With the basket of food in her hand she asked the man, 'Are you Majnun?' 'What is it you have brought?', he asked. She said, 'Some food for Majnun.' He said, 'I am Majnun, give it to me.' He was glad to partake of it and said, 'I shall be gladder to have it every day.' So Leili starved for days sending her food, and that food was given to this man who for the time became Majnun.

One day Leili asked, 'How is my Majnun?' The maid said, 'He is better looking every day.' Leili said, 'It cannot be.' The maid said, 'Certainly, be sure of it, he is better looking every day.' Leili said, 'Today you need not take the food. Take a knife and a saucer and tell my Majnun that I need a drop of his blood.' When the maid came, the man came with anxiety, with eagerness to have the dish, but instead there was a knife. He said, 'What is this?' She said, 'Leili asks a drop of your blood.' He first looked perplexed, then he said, 'I am not Majnun. That may be Majnun, he who is sitting in that corner.' By that time Majnun had grown very thin. Yet when she asked for a drop of blood, Majnun tried by striking the knife on different parts of his body if he could get out a drop of blood to be sent to Leili. 'Ah,' he said, 'there cannot be anything more delightful for Majnun than to give his blood when it is asked for Leili.'

III:2 LEILI AND MAJNUN – CONCLUSION

The end of the story of Majnun is that he sat a long time under the shade of a tree, and he grew in time like the tree. Being near the tree his body and the tree became one, and when a woodcutter came and instead of cutting the wood his axe struck Majnun, Majnun said, 'Leili,' for that was the only thought in his mind. Leili on hearing this, when she had freedom for a moment, was drawn by some way to Majnun at his last moment on the earth, and called him, 'Majnun!' He answered, 'Leili.' She said, 'I am Leili.' But he said, 'I am Leili.' And so Majnun fell and died, and Leili followed him instantly.

The path of the Sufi is the path of devotion, and therefore 'Leili and Majnun' is the symbol that a Sufi takes for God and man. The soul who journeys in the path of God does not need much learning. What he writes on his slate is the name of God, what he reads in his book is His name. That is the only learning which is essential in the path of God, and no one can distract the mind of the godly towards anything, however attractive, though he may find not one reason to give for his devotion to God. He can only say, 'In order to become the lover of God you must borrow my eyes.'

While people think of the differences of their religions and creeds, the godly bows before the humblest person, as Majnun to Leili's dog.

When the prayers of different people will be for themselves, the prayer of the godly is only to attain to the presence of God, and therefore, whatever be his religion, his prayer will be followed by every sincere soul.

Besides, both the path of God and of love, if sincerely trodden, need sacrifice from beginning to end, and the one who is not ready for sacrifice is like that pretended lover of Leili who was ready for the food, but was not willing to suffer.

Verily, who pursueth the world will inherit the world, but the soul that pursueth God will attain in the end to the presence of God.

But to what does the love of God lead? It leads to that peace and stillness which can be seen in the life of the tree which bears fruit and flowers for others and expects no return, not even thanks in return. It serves and cares for nothing else, not even for appreciation. That is the attribute of the godly. And the godly, in the end of his attainment of God, forgets himself, as Majnun said even to Leili, 'I am Leili.' And what happens then? Instead of man pursuing God, God follows man.

III:3 THE SYMBOLOGY OF RELIGIOUS IDEAS: CHRIST WALKING ON THE WATER

The phenomenon of Christ walking on the water, from a mystical point of view, is suggestive of a greater philosophy rather than a phenomenon. The whole universe in all its forms is one single vision of continual activity. From beginning to end every aspect of life represents motion, and it is the perpetual motion of the whole universe which is called life.

Therefore the universe is, so to speak, an ocean of vibrations, and every movement represents a wave. Therefore the wise have called it in Sanskrit *bhavasagara*, the ocean of life. And the great devotees have constantly prayed to be liberated, that they may not sink in this ocean, but that they may be able to swim in it, which is called *taran*.

It is the master spirit that can arise above these waves of the enormous ocean of life in which generally the souls are drowned. To be in it, and to be able to stand above it and to walk on it, is the phenomenon of Christ's walking upon the water.

III:4 THE SYMBOLOGY OF RELIGIOUS IDEAS:
THE OPENING OF THE BREAST
OF THE PROPHET – *SJAQQ-E-SADR*

There exists a legend in the world of Islam – and some believe that it really did occur, some say once and some say it happened more than once – that the angels from heaven descended to earth and cut open the breast of the Prophet; they took away something that was to be removed from there and then the breast was as before.

From the Sufi point of view, this is a symbolical legend. It explains what is necessary in the life of man to allow the plant of divine love to grow in his heart. It is to remove that element which gives the bitter feeling. Just as there is a poison in the sting of the scorpion and as there is a poison in the teeth of the snake, so there is poison in the heart of man which is made to be the shrine of God. But God cannot arise in the shrine which is as dead by its own poison. It must be purified first and made real for God to arise.

The soul who had to sympathize with the whole world was thus prepared that the drop of that poison which always produces contempt, resentment and ill feeling against another was destroyed first. So many talk about purification of heart, and so few really know what it is. Some say to be pure means to be free from all evil thought, but there is no evil thought. Call it evil or call it devil, if there is any such thought it is the thought of bitterness against another. No one with sense and understanding would like to retain a single drop of poison in his body. And how ignorant it is on the part of man when he keeps and cherishes a bitter thought against another in his heart. If a drop of poison can cause the death of the body, it is equal to a thousand deaths when the heart retains the smallest thought of bitterness.

In this legend the cutting open of the breast is the cutting open of the ego which is as a shell over the heart. Taking away that element means that every kind of thought or feeling against anyone in the world has been taken away, and the breast, which means the heart, was filled with love alone, which is the real life of God.

III:5 THE SYMBOLOGY OF RELIGIOUS IDEAS: THE DREAM OF THE PROPHET – MERAJ

A story exists in Islam about the dream of the Prophet, a dream which was an initiation in the higher spheres. Many take it literally, and discuss it, and afterwards go out by the same door by which they came in. It is by the point of view of a mystic that one can find out the mystery.

It is said that the Prophet was taken from Jerusalem to the Temple of Peace, which means from the outer temple of peace to the inner temple of peace. A *buraq* was brought for the Prophet to ride upon. Jibra'il accompanied the Prophet on the journey and guided him on the path. A *buraq* is said to be an animal of heaven which has wings, the body of the horse and the face of a human being. It signifies the body together with the mind; the wings represent the mind, and the body of the *buraq* represents the human body, the head represents perfection. Also this is the picture of the breath. Breath is the *buraq* which reaches from the outer world to the inner world in a moment's time. Jibra'il in this story represents reason.

It is said that the Prophet saw on his way Adam who smiled looking to one side and shed tears looking to the other side. This shows that the human soul, when it develops in itself real human sentiment, rejoices at the progress of humanity and sorrows over the degeneration of humanity.

The *buraq* could not go beyond a certain point, which means that breath takes one a certain distance in the mystical realization, but there comes a stage when the breath cannot accompany one. When they arrived near the destination Jibra'il also retired, which means that reason cannot go any further than its limit.

Then the Prophet arrived near that curtain which stands

between the human and the divine, and called aloud the name of God saying, 'None exists save Thou.' And the answer came, 'True, true.' That was the final initiation from which dated the blooming of Mohammed's prophetic message.

III:6 THE SYMBOLOGY OF RELIGIOUS IDEAS: THE FLUTE OF KRISHNA

Krishna is pictured in Hindu symbology with a crown of peacock's feathers, playing the flute. Krishna is the ideal of divine love, the God of love. And the divine love expresses itself by entering in man and filling his whole being. Therefore the flute is the human heart, and a heart which has been made hollow, which becomes a flute for the God of love to play. When the heart is not empty, in other words when there is no scope in the heart, there is no place for love.

Rumi, the great poet of Persia, explains the idea more clearly. He says that the pains and sorrows the soul experiences through life are holes made in a reed flute, and it is by making these holes that the player makes out of a reed a flute. Which means: the heart of man is first a reed, and the suffering and pain it goes through make it a flute, which can then be used by God as the instrument to produce the music that He constantly wishes to produce. But every reed is not a flute, and so every heart is not His instrument. As the reeds need to be made into flutes, so the human heart can be turned into an instrument and can be offered to the God of love.

It is the human heart which becomes the harp of the angels. It is the human heart which is the lute of Orpheus. It is on the model of the heart of man that the first instrument of music was made, and no earthly instrument can produce that music which the heart produces raising the mortal soul to immortality.

The crown of peacock's feathers leads to a further revelation: that it is the music of the heart which can be expressed through the head. It is the knowledge of the head and the love of the heart that express the divine message fully. In all ages peacock's feathers have been considered as a sign of beauty, as a sign of knowledge: beauty, because they are beautiful, knowledge because they are in the form of an eye. It is by keen observation that man acquires knowledge. Knowledge without love is lifeless, so with the flute the crown of peacock's feathers makes the symbol complete. (*See* Questions and Answers, p 296.)

III:7 THE SYMBOLOGY OF RELIGIOUS IDEAS: TONGUES OF FIRE

The symbolic meaning of the legend, of the myth, is that there is a period when the soul of the earnest seeker is seeking – which means that it has not yet found the object it is seeking after. In the lifetime of Jesus Christ the beauty of the Master's wonderful personality and the great intoxication of his presence and the constant outpouring of the message that he had to give, was so much for his disciples that it was beyond what may be called a joy or a happiness or something which is explainable; and all the blessing that they received and experienced during his presence was covered by the Master's personality. And the time of realization of that which they had constantly gained came in their lives after that great change when the external person of the Master ascended and the capacity of realization became open.

But after the Resurrection, when they had had sufficient time to recover from the feeling that had overtaken their hearts, the seeming separation from their beloved Lord prepared them, so to speak, in time and opened the doors of the heart, giving capacity for the illumination which was constantly pouring out from the Spirit of Guidance, the Alpha and Omega who always was and is and will be.

The symbolic interpretation of the tongues of flame rising from their foreheads is the light of the message, the rays of the Christ spirit in the form of thoughts which were expressed in words. There is a stage in the life of a seer when the tongue of flame becomes not only an interpretation of the reality but a reality, his own experience. The head is the centre of knowledge and when the centre opens, the light which was covered becomes manifest – not only in idea but even in form.

And the phenomenon that was shown the next day, when the apostles spoke all different languages, can be rightly interpreted in this sense that every soul hears its own language, for every soul has its own word, as every soul has its peculiar illusion. And it is therefore that one person cannot understand another person in this world, and it becomes more than a miracle when one friend, perhaps one person in the world, can understand one fully. Which means: in this world the language of each one is not understood by another, and if someone understands a little, one feels at-one-ment with that one.

It was the illumination of the Christ spirit which brought exaltation in their lives so that they began to see in every soul the master, and they became at one with every soul, inspired by sympathy and love of Christ. And they understood the souls as they saw them, and so they spoke with souls whose language was never understood. Plainly speaking, they heard the cry of every soul and they answered each soul's cry.

The message means the answer to the cry of every soul. Every great prophet or teacher had in his life many followers attracted to his personality, to his kindness and love. But those who became as the instrument of his message, whose hearts became as a flute for the Master to play his music, have always been some chosen few, as the twelve apostles of Christ.

III:8 THE SYMBOLOGY OF RELIGIOUS IDEAS:
THE STORY OF LOT'S WIFE

The ancient method of revealing the mystery of life was to give it in the form of a legend. The legend of Lot tells that it was to Abraham that Lot was related, and it was by the love and help of Abraham that the two angels were sent to Lot to warn him of the coming destruction of two cities and to advise him to flee to the mountains. And Lot was not willing to leave the cities but in the end he agreed to. His sons-in-law failed him by not accompanying him, but his wife and two daughters accompanied him on the journey to the mountains. They were told that his wife must not look back, and when she did she was turned into a pillar of salt. Lot and his two daughters were spared this fate and they reached the cave in the mountain which was Lot's destination.

The two cities that were to be destroyed represent the north pole and the south pole, the two poles of the world; for all the treasure of the earth, all possessions and power and fame that belong to the earth are subject to destruction. And that was taught to Lot, the human soul who was the relation of Abraham, the human soul which is from Brahma, the Creator. The relationship of Lot with Abraham represents the relation of the human soul to the Creator. The two angels were the angels of light and of reason. When the light comes to man, its first teaching is to warn the soul of the disaster that awaits all that is subject to death and destruction. It is this lesson that is called in Sanskrit the lesson of *vairagya*, when man's eyes open to see that all he loves and likes and wishes to hold and possess is subject to destruction and death.

There are five bodies considered by the mystics of old to be the vehicles of the soul which are called:

anandamayakosh	body of joy
vijnanamayakosh	body of wisdom
manomayakosh	body of mind
pranamayakosh	body of ether
annamayakosh	body of earth.

This last is the receptacle of food. It lives on earthly food and if it is starved of that it dies, for it is made of earth, it lives on earth. Another is the receptacle of ether. That part of man's being lives by breath and by taking in the air; if it is starved of air it cannot live. These two bodies form the material part, the physical part of man's being, and it is these two receptacles which are termed in the legend 'the sons-in-law'.

Then there is *manomayakosh* which is mind, the mental body, and this body has its action and reaction on both sides. It acts and reacts on the earthly bodies and it acts and reacts upon the soul. Therefore, when Lot left the two cities which represent the physical plane to journey toward the goal of immortality, his wife was still with him, for it is not necessary that the mental body should stay behind when the journey towards illumination is begun. It is capable of going with the soul towards eternity, and yet its attachment to earth and the physical plane is great, because it is made, it is built of physical impressions, of all impressions that come from the physical world. And of necessity it wants to turn to see if the physical being or the spiritual being is leading it aright. The principal nature of mind is doubt whether one is doing right or wrong, and doubt and faith are enemies. While faith leads to the destination, doubt pulls back. When the mind was so pulled back, attracted by all the impressions of earthly life, it could neither take hold of the earth nor journey with the spirit and remained neither earth nor water, but salt.

The only two bodies which are close to the soul followed the soul. Naturally they would follow for they are closely related to the soul, *vijnanamayakosh*, the body of wisdom and *anandamayakosh*, the body of joy. The soul bound towards the eternal goal, as it is called the top of the mountains, then proceeded towards the mountains. And before they reached the top of the mountains there was the cave which is called heaven – in metaphysics, 'capacity', in Sanskrit, *akasha* – which has the power of holding the soul from going to the top and using the soul for some purpose. And the soul which was bound for the eternal goal remained so intoxicated by the ecstasy that it received from the plane of joy and the plane of wisdom. And as it ever happens that ecstasy produces purpose, so this joy resulted in a great purpose, in the birth of the messenger, which in Sanskrit is called *bodhisattva*. The messenger was born of the soul's experience, the knowledge and the happiness, to bring good tidings to the world.

A question may arise: why *manomayakosh* should be the mother, and *anandamayakosh* and *vijnanamayakosh* should be the daughters. And the answer is that they are born of mind, born of mind and soul. If there were only the soul there would be neither joy nor wisdom. Mind and soul together produce joy and wisdom. Therefore the latter are the daughters, because mind is the mother. The two lower planes are represented by the sons-in-law because they were not born directly of mind and soul; it was a separate substance mind and soul have taken into their life.

By this story the process is taught how the soul can journey from mortality to immortality, and what experiences the soul has to have on its way. But when the messenger is so created, then the father, the soul, rests in peace. It is therefore that the messenger was called the son and the original soul the Father.

III:9 THE SYMBOLOGY OF RELIGIOUS IDEAS

The idea that is meant in the New Testament by the words of Christ, 'Eat my flesh and drink my blood', is suggestive of the inner being of the Master. It is the eternal life which he meant by his blood, and it is the omnipresent existence which he meant by his flesh. The idea of the Master was to make his disciples know that his physical form that they were attracted to was not his being, his true being was the all-pervading, everlasting life of God. And it is in this meaning that the Father, Son and Holy Ghost are One.

Christ said to the fishermen, 'I will make you fishers of men.' That meant, 'As you spread the net and the fishes come into it, so by spirituality your personality will spread in the atmosphere and the hearts of men hungering for love will be attracted to you as fishes.'

The love of Christ for the lamb expresses symbolically that to the Master that soul made a greater appeal which was simple and harmless as a lamb.

The crown of thorns represents tolerance of the thorn-like personalities of which there are so many in the world, constantly pricking their thorns, consciously or unconsciously. And it is this which makes the sensitive annoyed with life in the world. But the teacher, whose heart represents both the divine mother and the divine father, cannot but be tolerant and can willingly take all the thorns that would come to him, for that is his crown, the sign of his sovereignty in the kingdom of soul.

Christ said to Peter, 'Thou wilt deny me three times before the cock crows.' It explains human nature. The faith of man is generally dependent upon the faith of the multitude. If the multitude calls the pebble a diamond, then man calls the pebble a diamond; everyone will begin to consider it so and say so. And if the multitude thought that the diamond was a pebble, then everyone would follow the belief of the multitude.

The soul of the Messenger that comes from above – which the dove represents – which is not made by the world, not known by the world, remains unrecognized till the cock crows and the sun rises. His words shine and spread the light to the world and the souls, privileged with some little recognition but with a great deal of doubt, may believe for a moment, impressed by the power and grace of the Master's personality, and yet may deny a thousand times and doubt and suspect, being impressed by the influence of the multitude. How true it is, the saying in Hindustani that generally a soul follows the multitude.

There are rare souls who believe in their conviction and remain steady even if it were that the whole world was against their own inner conviction. Verily, to the faithful belongs every blessing.

III:10 THE SYMBOLOGY OF RELIGIOUS IDEAS:
THE TEN VIRGINS

There is a story in the New Testament about ten virgins, the five who were wise and the five who were foolish. It was said that the bridegroom was to come and they were to light their lamps. And five were in time and brought the oil and lighted their lamps, and the other five waited until the bridegroom came. And when the bridegroom came, then they went to the five who had lighted their lamps and asked of them oil and were refused.

This story is a symbol of receiving the Message of God. By virgin is meant the soul which is awaiting illumination, innocent, and responsive to the light, and by five is meant the multitude. And there are two classes of people: one class are those who have prepared themselves and made ready to receive the Message of God which is pictured as the bridegroom, and the five foolish virgins are the other class of mankind who wait and wait until the message has come and gone. In all ages there have been these two kinds of souls: one kind who are called in the scriptures believers, the others who are known as unbelievers.

In every age the prophecy has been by the Messenger of the time as to the next advent. Sometimes it is said, 'I will come,' and sometimes, 'He will come.' 'I will come' has been told to those who would recognize the same Spirit of Guidance in every coming of the Messenger. 'He will come' has been told to those to whom name and form make a difference, and who cannot recognize the same spirit in another name and another form. For example, the coming of Jesus Christ was the coming of that Spirit which was expressed in this myth as the bridegroom, and how few at the time recognized him and how few received illumination. Only those whose lamps were ready to be lighted. Oil in this parable is love and the light is wisdom. And when their lamps were lighted then so many came afterwards, but that blessing and privilege which had come with the personality of the Master had then gone. They had to take the benefit of the light that came from the lamps of those whose lamps were lighted, but the chance of lighting their own lamps was lost.

The same is with all things in life. Every moment in our lives is an opportunity which brings a benefit and blessing, and the one who knows how to be benefited by it and how to be blessed by it receives the benefit and the blessing. Everyone seems living and awake, but few souls really are living and awake. There are opportunities of benefit and blessing on every plane of one's life, on the physical plane, on the mental plane, on the spiritual plane, and every opportunity is invaluable. But often one realizes the truth when it is too late. There is no greater and better opportunity than the moment that can give a spiritual illumination, a moment when one can receive the blessing of God. It is a priceless moment. Who knows it and understands it and tries to be benefited by it, is blessed.

PART FOUR

◆

BREATH

Pasi Anfas

Gatha I

It is difficult to define breath in a few words. Breath is the very life in beings, and what holds all the particles of the body together is the power of the breath, and when this power becomes less then the will loses its control over the body. As the power of the sun holds all the planets, so the power of the breath holds every organ. Besides this the breath purifies the body by taking in new and fresh life and by giving out all gases that should be put out. It nourishes the body by absorbing from space the spirit and substance that are necessary, and more necessary than all man eats and drinks.

The whole mechanism of the body works by the power of the breath, and every disorder in the working of this mechanism is caused by some irregularity in the breath. Therefore physicians feel disorder in the health of a patient by feeling his pulse or the beats of his heart. The difference is that the physician will say that it is the physical illness of the body which has caused the change in the pulsation and in the beats of the heart, but the mystic knows that it is caused by the breath.

Breath in its different aspects acts differently; in every direction the breath does a special work. The breath has a special work with every organ of the body, and it has its particular influence upon every element which constitutes the physical body. Every movement that one makes is directed by the power of breath; at the same time the breath alone has the power to stop any motion. For instance, walking, running, sitting and standing are actions that take place by the power of breath, and trembling, shivering or waving the hands or feet without control show lack of power in the breath.

Breath has various works to do in the mechanism of the body. Hunger and thirst, the power of eating and drinking are given by the breath; the closing and opening of the eyes and

127

the activity of all the organs is directed by the power of the breath; the expelling of all gases and excrements also is directed by the breath. Therefore every activity of the body, outward and inward, is directed by the breath. Therefore it is disorder of the breath which causes illnesses, and its order regulates the health. Many physicians now point out reasons for diseases where mystics think of the breath and point out reasons in breathing.

Diseases, especially such as nervousness, palpitation of the heart and paralysis, all come from a lack of power of the breath. All lung diseases are caused by unclearness of the breath. Troubles of the brain and troubles with the intestines are also caused by lack of regularity of the breath.

This shows that breath is the key to health, which is all happiness in life.

I:2 THE CULTURE OF THE BREATH

The air inhaled and exhaled that one feels through the nostrils or lungs is what we ordinarily call breath. In reality however, that is as the stem of a tree whose branches are many. A mystic sees the whole body as a plant of the breath. According to the physician the lungs are the channel of the breath, but to the mystic the lungs are the branches of the tree, and other branches reach all parts of the body. The mystics call all the branches by different names. This tree has a root in the body and has centres where the branches meet the stem.

There are five such centres in the body of man. The breath has its particular work in every centre. By the study of mysticism one finds that man's life depends upon the working of the centres. Generally the centres are blocked up on the inner side of the body, therefore they give but a dim light, if the breath be pictured as a gas and the centres as lanterns. When the centres are not in a fit condition they are wasted. Not only this, but man is deprived of the full experience of life.

Powers that are considered supernatural become natural when man leads a natural life. The first lesson of a natural life is right breathing. Many people breathe a half breath, many a quarter and many still less. It is a certain direction that the breath takes that brings about sleep, and it is the direction of the breath that brings vigour or fatigue. A man may, by the help of the breath, become stronger by doing physical exercises, and another by physical labour may become exhausted and worn out. The labourers in India who have to lift heavy weights have a certain way of breathing and work a great deal and yet feel little fatigue.

According to the point of view of the mystic a natural, full breath gives perfect health, and to a mystic's view in a hundred people not one breathes rightly. Every Brahmin teaches his child the way of breathing when he is nine years old. As it is a common thing that everybody breathes incorrectly, it rarely occurs to the mind that one's breath is incorrect.

There are many reasons why people in general do not breathe rightly, but one among them is the lack of education in this. As health is more important than anything else on earth, and as health depends entirely upon breath, which is the very life, it is necessary that the culture of the breath should be considered as of the highest importance.

I:3 BREATH, THE VERY LIFE – *PRANA*

Breath in the Sufic terms is called *nafs*; in Sanskrit it is called *prana* which means the very life. It spreads life and magnetism in all parts of the body, for breath in itself is life and is magnetism.

Deformity of form and feature is often caused by disorder of the breath. Lack of proportion of the body in form and strength is also caused by lack of order in the breath.

By exercises for physical culture and exercises of voice production breath can be developed in different parts of the body. It can especially be noticed in the fingers of the violinist that by constant practice on the violin he puts a sort of magnetism, of life, into the strings his fingers touch. This example is a plain proof that it is not the fingers that play nor the violin that sounds, but that they are instruments of life.

The importance of breath is now becoming known to the scientific world, and there is much of this mystical subject which is unexplored. But mysticism has been founded on the science of breath. There is no mystic, whether Buddhist, Vedantist or Sufi, who makes use of another process than that of breath. Breath is the first lesson and it is also the last.

A mystic becomes capable of sending breath to any part of his body; thus he is able to send life, radiance and magnetism to any particle of his body. The question, 'Does he send the breath by his power of will?' can be simply answered by 'Yes.' And yet that is not enough. If there are no strings on the violin, you cannot play on it by will-power. So long as the adept has not balanced his breath and controlled it and mastered it, it cannot bring about the proper result. Therefore it is of no use to try to make use of breath for psychical or occult attainments until one has caused the breath to be in such a condition that it can work properly in the body. Many therefore are not successful in spiritual attainments because, before making use of the breath in the body, they want to produce psychical phenomena.

The body is the instrument for every experience, worldly or spiritual. By a deep study of breath a seeker after truth will find that, as every particle of his body is formed and nourished by breath, so from that and according to that his character is formed.

I:4 Five aspects of breath

The mechanism of the body is dependent in its work upon five different aspects of breath, and these aspects are the five different directions of breath. In the *Qur'an* and also in the Hebrew scriptures these five breaths are known as the five angels; these aspects are thus pictured in their finer work in human life. Often their direction is spoken of by the prophets in symbolical terms, as it is said: 'One stands on the left side of man, one on the right, one before, one behind, one within him.' When one aspect of these five is not working properly it brings disorder in the whole mechanism of the body. In eating and drinking, yawning and stretching and in all actions of everyday life these five aspects of breath have to take the lead.

Among these five aspects the first is the breath which is like the stem in the tree, and which one feels through the nostrils. By the purification, development and control of this breath all five aspects are developed. There are atoms in man's body which form a certain organ, which are more or less active in different rhythms according as the breath reaches them. The atoms which do not receive the proper breath remain undeveloped and therefore are inactive. As the centres of the body are situated in the centre of the whole mechanism, it is natural that in the average person the breath does not reach their innermost part as it ought to.

The question, 'If it is natural that it should reach them, why does it not?' may be answered by saying that it is because man leads an artificial life. If man led a natural life it would not be necessary for him to develop by certain meditative processes the qualities that are latent in him. A horse, a dog or a cat knows intuitively of death, disease or distress in the house in which it lives. The animals are considered by modern psychology to be without mind, and man who is far superior to the lower creation and is the ideal of all beings has not that intuitive power. The reason is that the animals lead a more natural life than man, although even that is spoiled by contact with man. The cobra can attract its food from a mile's distance, but man must toil with his hands for his daily bread. In short, there are faculties in man which by the artificiality of his life are closed, and man lives an incomplete life.

To live a fuller life the wise in all religions have taken the breath in hand and awakened atoms and centres which are instruments for those faculties. As soon as breath touches those centres it makes them vibrate and then they do their work. Therefore breathing exercises given to a *mureed* are like the winding of a clock. Once in twenty-four hours the clock is wound, and after that it goes on without effort.

I:5 THE CHANNEL OF THE BREATH

Breath is a channel through which all the expression of the innermost life can be given. Breath is an electric current that runs between the everlasting life and the mortal frame. Those who have attained any intuition or miraculous power or any power have achieved it by the help of the breath. But the first essential thing is a pure channel for the breath, and that channel is the human body. If the channel is blocked there is no possibility for the breath to pass freely. Air in itself is not bad, but when it touches the earth it partakes the influence of the earth and therefore can become polluted. So it is with the breath; breath in itself is pure, but if the channel through which it works is not right it becomes impure.

The breath makes a circuit through the body, and the channel through which it makes the circuit is the spine. The mystics give this channel great importance. They call it the serpent; they picture it as a serpent holding its tail in its mouth. In almost all symbols the serpent represents the channel of the breath. In the terms of the Yogis it is called *kundalini*. When this channel is made clear by the method of breathing, then this is not only a help to the physical health but it also opens up the faculties of intuition and the doors that are within, where lies the real happiness of man.

In order to clear this channel of all that blocks the way, one must follow the rules of mystical ablutions and of rhythmic breathing. People who cannot understand the subject and who hear and read things by halves say that some *chakras*, centres, are opened by breathing exercises and that many kinds of distress may be the consequence. But looking at it from another point of view, one might as well say that the eyes of a child should never be opened, because he will thereby be exposed to temptations of all sorts.

All virtue is in self-control; there is no virtue in being dead. Life is worthwhile only when a person leads it fully. People look for phenomena, but there is no better phenomenon than breath itself, because breath is life and light, and in the breath is the source of life and light. In the mastery of breath the secret of both worlds is hidden.

1:6 THE RHYTHM OF BREATH

Rhythm is the principal thing to be considered in breath, as it is on the rhythm of the breath that the working of the whole mechanism depends. And the chief reason of irregularity of the beats of the heart or head is lack of rhythm in the breath. As man generally neglects to think of his breath, he overlooks the fact that his health entirely depends on rhythmic breath.

Rhythm is the central theme of the whole creation. Therefore the infant moves his hands and legs by turns, forming a rhythm. This shows that nobody teaches anyone rhythm, it is natural to all beings. It is the rhythmic movement which enables the fish to swim and the serpent to climb trees. If rhythm were not an instinct the animal would never have known how to walk nor the bird how to fly. The life of man is so pulled from all sides, so divided, that he often forgets things that are most essential to his life which the lower creatures seem to keep more correctly in their lives.

Neatness in man's work and balance in man's actions show rhythm in him. When man shows lack of balance in his life and when his life is disturbed and all things seem to go wrong, it is most often that the rhythm of his breath has become wrong. Irregularity of activity and repose in the habits of life causes disorder of rhythm in the breath.

Very often the Eastern mystical exercises are wrongly understood by many. When a teacher gives a breathing exercise to his pupil, often he does not mean the breathing itself but rhythm. Thought given to the breath becomes a weight upon it and naturally holds it longer in its movement, altering it from what it would otherwise naturally be. It is the following of the rhythm of breath and the keeping of the rhythm regular which brings about the best results.

I:7 DENSE AND FINE – *KASIF* AND *LATIF*

Breath is termed by Sufis *kasif* and *latif*. *Kasif* means dense and *latif* means fine. Dense breath is that which is noisy and laboured, which strains the nerves and the lungs. The exercises of dense breath are useful for developing the muscles and for gaining control over the nerves; they are helpful also to the lungs and useful to the physical health. But in spiritual development, unless the breath be made fine, it cannot penetrate through the important centres in the body, and it cannot reach far enough into the innermost parts of one's life.

Breath to a Sufi is a bridge between himself and God. It is a rope for him hanging down to earth, attached to the heavens. The Sufi climbs up by the help of this rope. In the Qur'anic language it is called *buraq*, a steed which was sent to the Prophet for his journey to the heavens. Hindus call it *prana*, which means life, but they picture it symbolically as the bird which is named in Sanskrit *garuda*, on which rode Narayana the Godhead.

There is no mystical cult in which the breath is not given the greatest importance in spiritual progress. Once man has touched the depths of his own being by the help of the breath, then it becomes easy for him to become at one with all that exists on earth and in heaven.

I:8 BREATH – THE VEHICLE OF THE SELF

Breath is the mystery; in it is hidden the secret of life. Breath proves the existence of the life unseen. Breath is audible, at the same time inaudible. Breath is visible and at the same time invisible. It is a certain degree of the activity of the breath and the capacity through which it is acting which make the breath audible. This shows that there exists something of which we are conscious, the source of which no one knows, which is active every moment of the day, on the model of which the mechanism of nature and art is made.

No one can explain whence it came into this mortal body, and no one can say whither it goes when it leaves this body of clay. One can only say that something living came and kept this mortal body alive and left it, proving that the same body, which once was thought to be alive, was not really alive, but itself was the life. This proves to the intellect, even to that void of faith, that there is some source whence life comes, and that it returns again to the same source.

Man's true self is the part of his being which knows itself to exist, which is conscious of itself. When that self takes breath as its vehicle instead of the body, then it soars upwards toward the utmost heights, toward that goal which is the source and origin of all beings.

I:9 THE MYSTICISM OF BREATH

Breath is audible and visible, and when a spiritual person by spiritual exercises strengthens and purifies the breath, it becomes more intelligible as a light and a sound.

Life and light in truth are one; the breath is the life, and it is the same breath which is light. Breath in fact is the light of all senses. The senses of sight, smell, taste, hearing and touch perceive all things by the light of the breath. When the breath is absent from the body, the body with all its perfect mechanism becomes useless. It is natural therefore that every sense must become powerful and keen if the breath be developed and purified.

The reason why the ill and weak and people physically delicate generally see visions is that by the lack of flesh, fat and blood the veins and tubes of the body and the organs of all the senses are free and not blocked as they are in a muscular person. Therefore naturally the senses become keen and man perceives more than what is within the ordinary range of perception. Also such a person, when asleep, perceives the impressions from the inner world, because during sleep the inner sense, which may be called the root of the senses, turns its back, so to speak, on the external world and so begins to see the world within.

The mystic, by the help of exercises, develops and purifies the breath. Therefore to him after a certain time all things become clear in the outer and inner world. There are some who see light before them, there are some who notice colours before their view, also there are some who see forms before their sight. When they talk about it to others who cannot observe the phenomena, they are considered imaginative; people often laugh at them. The Sufi therefore does not speak of any such experience to others; he thinks it is not their world and they will not be able to understand, unless they also rise to that sphere.

There is no motive for speaking about one's experiences to others except pride. And if someone does this out of vanity, his next step will be exaggeration. If something makes anyone feel himself above others, it is natural for him to feel inclined to make it still more impressive. Besides, it is in human nature to wish to interest one's friends in one's pleasure, and if someone is pleased with something he sees, he will surely try to make it more interesting by a little added exaggeration.

Therefore there are these two dangers on the spiritual path of which the adept must be aware before making the journey. It is for this reason that mysticism has been made a secret cult: that it may not be for everybody to play with.

I:10 COLOUR AND SOUND

B reath in reality is light, but when it shoots forth its rays, according to the direction of the rays and the capacity which takes this light, the colours manifest. Form and colour both depend upon the direction the light takes and upon the degree of light. Nothing on earth is meaningless, every occurrence has its meaning and every moment has its purpose. Even the colours that manifest in the light of the breath have their meaning, which coincides with the moment and the conditions then.

There are attempts being made to take photographs of thoughts and feelings, and some have even attempted to photograph the spirits. It is difficult to say how far this attempt can be successful. No doubt it gives a great scope to falsehood. If there is any means of seeing a spirit, a form from the inner world, it is only breath: that in the light of breath a form from the inner world can manifest as a picture from the magic lantern. The picture actually is in the lantern, and it is the reflection of that picture which we see. Those who can see the form of the dead, see the reflection before them manifested in the light of their own breath, the real form being still in the inner world; for it is the breath which connects the inner world with the outer world, just as the light thrown from the magic lantern falls upon the curtain.

There are many who believe that there is a colour or a note which belongs to a particular person, and this question gives no doubt a great scope for confusion and puzzle. Many people are anxious to know what note really belongs to them or what colour is their special colour. In point of fact this question can be looked at from two different points of view, one symbolical and the other metaphysical.

From the symbolical point of view every person is, so to speak, tuned to a certain pitch in his particular evolution, and he stands with another person just as C on the piano may stand with the G, or E with A. This shows the reason why a person can get on with a certain person harmoniously and with another inharmoniously. It is not the fault of the F or the G on the piano that they sound inharmonious together, it is the combination which causes the inharmony. It is not always the note which is inharmonious, it is a wrong combination which makes it so. Spiritual perfection makes man the keynote which is in harmony with all notes. And even that perfection shown to the world by Christ caused his crucifixion.

Metaphysically this question may be explained that there is a certain degree of life in a person which can be distinguished by his breath, and that degree shows itself to the seer in colour and sound. Those who have not reached the degree of that power which perceives the tone and colour of breath can perceive it by the voice and expression of man.

GATHA II

The breath is like a swing which has a constant motion, and whatever is put in the swing swings also with the movement of the breath. *Fikar* therefore is not a breathing practice. In *fikar* it is not necessary that one should breathe in a certain way different from one's usual breathing. *Fikar* is to become conscious of the natural movement of the breath and, picturing breath as a swing, to put in that swing a certain thought, as a babe in the cradle, to rock it. Only the difference in rocking is an intentional activity on the part of the person who rocks the cradle. In *fikar* no effort must be made to change the rhythm of the breath; the breath must be left to its own usual rhythm. One need not try even to regulate the rhythm of the breath, for the whole mechanism of one's body is already working rhythmically. So the breath is rhythmical by nature and it is the very breath itself which causes man to distinguish rhythm.

What is important in *fikar* is not the rhythm but the concentration. *Fikar* is swinging the concentrated thought with the movement of the breath, for breath is life and it gives life to the thought which is repeated with the breath.

On the rhythm of the breath the circulation of the blood and the pulsation of the heart and head depend, which means that the whole mechanism of the body – also of the mind – is directed by the rhythm of the breath. When a thought is attached to the breath by concentration, then the effect of that thought reaches every atom of one's mind and body.

Plainly speaking, the thought held in *fikar* runs with the circulation of the blood through every vein and tube of the body, and the influence of that thought is spread through every faculty of the mind.

Therefore the reaction of the *fikar* is the resonance of the same thought expressing itself through one's thought, speech and action. So in time the thought one holds in *fikar* becomes the reality of one's self. So he who contemplates on God, in time arrives at a state where his self turns into the being of God.

II:2 REGULARITY OF BREATH

A s the mechanism of the body depends upon the breath for its subsistence as well as for its health, so the breath is important in sustaining the mind and keeping its work regular. Mostly confusion, depression or any other disorder of the mind arises from the disorder of breathing. All diseases such as hallucinations and delusions are caused by wrong breathing. For instance, if a person comes running or is hurried for a moment, he loses the regularity of his breath for that moment and at that moment he is incapable of thinking rightly.

If science and the State knew this, they could surely cause some change in the present law. Many who are put in prison for some crime which is caused by them during the moments of irregular breathing, the State would send to be cured and taught how to breathe, instead of sending them to prison, for neither does the prison cure them nor does it benefit by their presence there.

By this I mean not only a disorder of mind that comes at a certain time, but also one which comes and goes so often during the day whenever breathing is not rightly done. When people become impulsive or show irritability in nature or become impatient at times, or when they get fits of anger, passion or laughter, when they get spells of tears, this all is caused by irregularity of breath.

The physician has no remedy for it, modern psychology has not found its link, but the mystics of old have for years believed it – not only believed but have practised it – and have found in the end that balance of mind entirely depends upon the regularity of breathing.

II:3 THE LIFE POWER

On breath depends the capability and efficiency with which one does one's work thoroughly. Shortness of breath gives man impatience, lack of endurance, and irregularity of the rhythm of the breath gives man confusion and makes him inclined to be easily upset. Breath being the life-power, it is the same life-power which gives man strength to endure all things. One always will find that those who easily get cross, quickly upset, instantly annoyed, have something wrong with the breath. People, not knowing their difficulty, get annoyed with them; they are put aside and are considered disagreeable people. What they need is the training of breathing. When their body and mind is so repaired, one will find no more disagreeableness in their nature.

Then the artist who gets tired of his work and feels a lack of enthusiasm to complete his work and feels a lack of interest and feels absence of inspiration – it all is often caused by some disorder in the breath.

Regular and rhythmic breathing gives health to body and mind both. Inspiration comes from above, but as a light. It is the work of the mind to receive it. If the mind is not ready to receive it, the inspiration will come but will not be realized. It is just like the difference between the gong of metal and the gong of wood. The former will resound, the latter will not resound. It is not the fault of the one who strikes the gong, it is the gong itself which does not resound. So it is with the mind which is receptive to the inspiration and the mind which cannot conceive it. But to every mind inspiration comes; the only difference is that one receives it, the other rejects it.

Right breathing makes the mind vibrate, and vibration is the sign of life. All that vibrates more is more living, what vibrates less is less living. So it is with trees and animals; they show their life in their vibration. India's greatest scientist, Jagadish Chandra Bose, has spoken at a university in England on the subject of trees breathing. Among horses, the horse one selects as the best is the one whose nostrils are fully open and whose breath is fuller, which the horse shows in its expression in the eyes. A good horse shows vibrations by the quivering of its skin when its back is patted; it is not like a stone-like horse which takes one step after ten whips given on its back.

In man in the same way that life can be seen which is termed in Hindustani *pani*, which means water. They say that a horse or a man has 'a watery nature', which means a liquid nature, living, pliable. And this life breath gives to body and mind.

II:4 FULL BREATH

The importance of the breath in the body is like the influence of the weather in the world. As the body and mind act and react on one another, so the influence of the breath takes the chief place in directing mind and body both. Every emotion is caused by the breath flowing in a certain direction, also by the degree of the force of the breath.

There are three different rhythms of breath which have influence upon the mind. Slow breath gives tranquillity to the mind and all the creative faculties of mind have scope of work given by this rhythm. Moderate breath helps the mind to continue its activities. If one wanted to make out a plan of work or wished to accomplish a certain work, the slow activity of breath, spoken of above, would not be helpful, though for poetry or music the activity of breath which is slow is more helpful. But quickness in the rhythm of breath produces confusion, although it gives a force to physical activities. One can run better or swim well when the breath is in a fairly quick rhythm. When the rhythm of the breath is too quick, it brings confusion to the mind and exhaustion to the body.

One who does not breathe fully, in other words freely and deeply, can neither be well physically nor make use of his mental faculties. Very often one finds most learned and intelligent people unable to work as they wish and incapable of finishing a work which they have taken up. Sometimes a person thinks it is bodily weakness or mental weakness or lack of enthusiasm or loss of memory, not knowing that it is very often a matter of regularizing the breath. Most often people think that it is the external senses being tired or exhausted that prevents their thinking, but in reality it is the absence of right breathing, for right breathing can make the mental faculties clearer and the outer organs of the senses more capable of perceiving. This shows that the mind can live a fuller life by what I call full breath. For a Sufi therefore breath is a key to concentration.

The Sufi, so to speak, 'covers his thought under the breath'. This expression of Rumi's I would interpret as that the Sufi lays his beloved ideal in the swing of the breath. I remember my *murshid's* saying that every breath which is inhaled with the consciousness of the divine Beloved is the only gain, and every breath inhaled without this consciousness is the only loss there is.

II:5 THOUGHT AND BREATH

Thought is conveyed without speech through breath. The true wireless telegraphy is the rightly established current of breath. It is difficult for every man to try it without the practice of concentration and in absence of the development of breath, though unconsciously always thoughts are exchanged by the means of breath. The scientist is ready to believe that contagious diseases are taken by one from another by the means of breath, but it is the part of psychology to realize that thoughts are taken – such as humour, depression, energy or sloth – by the means of breath. In the presence of an angry person one feels excited and inclined to anger, the contact of a humorous person spreads around the atmosphere of humour, in the presence of a cold person one becomes cold, the contact of a warm-hearted person warms one, and this is all done by the medium of breath. If an angry person were to close his breath while angry, much less of his feeling would affect another; if a person who is subject to humour would close his breath in the presence of an expert comedian, he could protect himself from being influenced by him.

Yogis who rise above the thoughts and feelings of those around them attain power by the control of the breath. So the method of the inner cult of Sufis also depends upon the science of breath. Pleasure, displeasure, the message of affection, the warning of hostility, all is received by the way of breath.

The one who is conscious of the rhythm of breath and whose breath is pure from grossness begins to perceive a sense which becomes in time a language to him. Thought-reading is not necessarily an intuition, although many confuse thought-reading with intuition. There is not much difference between the work of these two faculties; the difference is like the difference between the telephone and the telegraph. Thought-reading comes from without, intuition comes from within, although for both rhythmic breath and a clear mind are necessary.

The rhythmic breath helps the mind to be clear. Breath breaks the congestion which in the head produces confusion and in the heart depression, which covers the thoughts of others from one's perception, even from one's own intuition.

A thought is better conveyed to another through breath than by speech, for a feeling put in words becomes half-dead. Feeling in its own sphere is fully living, and when conveyed from there through breath it reaches the mind to which it is sent.

When a person has not developed his mind by concentration and when he tries to send his thought by the breath, he is not always successful. He is like a person trying to hit a target without ever having practised in his life. It is practice which makes man perfect.

11:6 BE CONSCIOUS OF EVERY BREATH

I t is by the power of breath that the animals search for their food; through breath they perceive what they must eat, what they must not eat; through breath the carnivorous animals search for their prey. It is through breath that certain animals receive warning of dangers, and again it is through the breath that some animals, when ill, find their remedy. If the lower creation can do so much by the power of breath, how much more can man do, if he only knows the right way of the development of breath! It is through the breath that the birds receive warnings of the changes of the weather, and accordingly they migrate in flocks from one place to another. Through the breath the herds of deer perceive approaching storms or changes of weather or the approach of a lion or a tiger.

Man who is more capable of perceiving by breath still deeper things, warnings and calls from the earth and from heaven, which places are meant for him to dwell in or to settle in, of discriminating between friend and foe and discerning their pleasure and displeasure, owing to his interest in the superficial things of life, cannot fully benefit by the power of breath.

Yogis and Sufis therefore and all students of the inner cult believe that breath is the means of receiving all intuitive knowledge from every direction of life. Absorbed in a thousand things of daily life man gives very little thought to breath. Therefore he keeps his heart closed to all the revelation that can be received by the help of breath. Man as a rule is never conscious of his breath, of its rhythm, of its development, except at the time when he is so tired that he is breathless or when he is so excited that he feels choked up or when something keeps the breath from flowing.

For a Sufi it is desirable to be conscious of every breath. In the schools of the Sufis in the East the members of a certain association take up as their duty to remind the whole assembly of the same. So one after another, in turn, takes it up as a duty. They call aloud, '*Hosh ba dam*', meaning, 'Keep conscious of the breath', and '*Nazr ba kadam*'. This sentence is added when the Sufis are walking – which means, 'Look down and see whose feet are these that are walking.'

II:7 DIRECTION OF BREATH

It is said that the cobras, enormous reptiles living in dense forests or in the mountains, attract animals or birds by the power of the breath. When the cobra is hungry, which is once in three months or six months, by inhaling the breath it draws its prey near. In its exhaling there is magnetism, power and influence; in its inhaling there is attraction. The mystics of ancient times have learned much from cobras. Mahadeva, the Lord of Yogis, had the cobra as his necklace. The peace and stillness of this creature, the contentment with which it waits for its sustenance are wonderful and most instructive for an adept on the spiritual path. One who masters breath becomes invigorated and strengthened in his mind, becomes quiet and peaceful and achieves self-control.

In the cobra there is the far-reaching breath. So is the breath of the mystic. The mystic's breath is not what is called deep breathing; his is the breath reaching inmost which touches every plane of his being.

Every movement robs one of a great portion of breath, every excitement takes away a great deal of life-force. Therefore those who master breathing, first learn control not only over every passion and emotion, but over every movement. By trying first to make the body still one can practise the breath better. Therefore among Yogis different postures are taught. Every posture allows the breath to take a certain direction, for every direction the breath takes has a different result. It is posture and thought both together that help to direct the breath in a certain direction. As breath is a life-power, whatever centre it is directed to it brings to a new life.

II:8 BREATH IN THE DEVELOPMENT OF MIND

Different conditions and the changes that take place in the world have their effect upon the mind, and the different conditions of the mind have their effect upon the body. As bodily illness makes man irritable, confused and exhausted in mind, so different conditions of the mind cause health or illness in the body. The link between the body and the mind is the breath, a link through which the influences of the body and the mind are exchanged and work upon one another. By the use of breath in physical culture the health and vigour of the breath is projected, so to speak, upon the mind. By the use of concentration, through the breath the light of the mind is thrown upon the body, which takes away from the body all heaviness and stiffness making it light and exhilarated.

Breath in this way acts like a ball in tennis thrown from one side to the other, and the force of its movement comes from the side from which it is directed. Therefore when it is directed from the body to the mind, the mind becomes subject to the influence of the body, but when from the side of the mind it is directed towards the body, in this case the body becomes subject to the mind.

Very often dervishes and fakirs in the East, many of whom live upon alms and go several days without food and spend many nights in sleepless vigil, do things which are difficult for a wrestler, a boxer or any other muscular person. Some dervishes practise jumping into fire, standing for hours in the water, sitting or lying on iron spikes, thrashing their bare arms and legs, cutting themselves with knives and swords and all such things beyond the power of a physically strong man. Often a physically strong man suffers in proportion to his strength when he is exposed to pain or torture.

This explains that, though the power of breath is the main source of physical development, yet breath is the principal thing in the development of mind, in which the influence of the breath is more valuable.

II:9 CONTRACTION AND EXPANSION

The breath has a great influence and entire control over two principles which work by the power of breath: *qabz* or contraction, and *bast* or expansion.[1] The former absorbs, attracts and gathers energy from outside, the latter tendency repels energy from within. In this way body and mind are sustained, nourished, enriched and made light, easy, clear and pure by the power of breath.

Inhaling is contraction and exhaling is expansion. It is upon these two principles and their regular working that the health and happiness of man depend.

A man who has not gained power over his breath is like a king who has no power over his domain. Once man has gained the power of contraction and expansion, then what he needs in life is to know what to attract and what to repel, and this the master of breath intuitively understands. Even the birds and animals know what they must eat and drink and what they must not. By a close study of the lower creation students of nature have learned that animals and birds abstain from food and drink when it becomes neccessary for their health.

I am often asked the question why there should be pain in childbirth. And the answer is that our life has been removed far from nature. Man today lives an artificial life to such an extent that he can hardly understand what real life may be. Man considers the accustomed the natural; he does not think how far the natural is removed from the present life we live. The domesticated animals are also beginning to show the birth-pain through their association with human beings.

Fikar practised for some years helps to regulate the rhythm of breathing, and it helps in all aspects of life to attract and repel all one wishes. By the help of *fikar* not only the digestive faculty

---

1 Hazrat Inayat Khan used the terms 'contraction' and 'expansion' here not for the physical movement of the breath, where contraction is exhaling, but for the influence of the breath which in inhaling 'extracts and gathers from outside' and in exhaling 'repels energy from within'.

and the circulation of the blood and the pulsations of the body are made regular, but the concentration that is developed through the development of breath enables man to repel all disagreeable impressions which cause despair and depression. By the power of *fikar* one helps the power of memory, also the power of retention of thought. At the same time one is enabled by the power of breath to forget any thought one wishes to put out of one's mind and to erase from one's heart any impression deeply engraved.

II:10 COMMUNICATION THROUGH THE BREATH

Breath is the medium between the outer life and the inner life. By the help of breath the elements necessary for the body can be attracted, and by the help of breath thoughts and inspiration can be gained. By the help of breath all that is undesirable in the body and mind can be expelled. The secret of telepathy, of reading the thoughts, has the science of breath as its mystery. When one wishes to draw inspiration from within, breath is the key. Breath is a life-current; its value is known to so few! Breath in itself is a phenomenon, but the phenomenon becomes manifest when once the breath is fully mastered.

The law of transmutation is also the secret of breath. What we give or gain from another without seeing or hearing, which we only realize as a result of the contact of someone, that is the effect of breath, for by the medium of breath there is always something given and taken; so few are aware of it! In the presence of one person one feels an inclination to laugh, in the presence of another one has a desire to cry; contact with one makes a person feel cheerful, with another sorrowful. Sometimes without there being one word spoken between two people thoughts and feelings are transferred, without people knowing it, through the current of the breath.

Breath is a link through which one individual is connected with another individual, and space does not make a difference if once connection of breath is established. The communication will be sure and clear if only the wire is tied to the sympathetic hearts. There is much that is common to the science of electricity and the science of breath. The day is not very far off when science and mysticism both will meet on the same ground in the realization of the electricity which is hidden in the breath. (*See* Questions and Answers, p 297.)

Gatha III

Mind is creative and thought is living, but out of what does mind create a thought? Out of the atoms of the mental sphere, but the current which attracts the desired atoms to complete a thought is the breath. Not that breath which is outwardly manifest – that part of breath, the action of which is not felt by every man.

The more length and breadth the breath has, the more scope it gives for the creation of thought. It is therefore that the thoughts of the sages and mystics who have gained mastery over breath are more substantial and complete in themselves and besides, they prove to be more expressive and impressive.

The breadth of the breath is in its volume. This comes by the facility one has of breathing through wide nostrils and open lungs. The secret of the power of voice is also to be found in this. The voice of the commander of an army which carries through the army and impresses the soldiers, thus encouraging them to fight, has breath as its secret behind it. Ali by his invocation of the sacred word, which he sometimes used to cry aloud on the battlefield, used to cause the enemies to tremble.

The length of the breath shows the length of life; lengthy breath is the sign of long life. This comes not only by wide nostrils and open lungs, but also by the accommodation that the body has for the breath; not only the nose and the chest but also the head and the abdomen.

There are some whose breath has volume or breadth, but not much length, and there are others who have length and no breadth. But it is the balance of the lenght and breadth of the breath which gives balance to the mind.

III:2 INSPIRATION

Inspiration comes from the light thrown upon a certain idea. This comes from the radiance of the breath falling upon the mind. There are two shadows: one that is projected upon the sky and another which falls upon the ground; the former known to the mystic and the latter to everyone. When the breath which is developed is thrown outward, its radiance produces light and it is the different shades and grades of this light which manifest in various colours, suggesting to the mystic the different elements which the peculiar colours denote.

The same breath has a different action when it is thrown within. It falls upon the mind like a searchlight and shows to the intelligence the object of its search as things seen in daylight. Thus man knows without any effort on the part of the brain all he wishes to know, and expresses in the way each individual is qualified to express. Inspiration therefore is one thing, qualification another thing. The inspiration is perfect when expressed by the qualified souls. Nevertheless inspiration is independent of qualification.

The light that the breath throws upon the mind is in every case different in its radiance. When far-reaching it illuminates the deepest corners of the heart where the light has never reached, and if breath reaches further the light is thrown upon the mind of God, the store of all the knowledge there is.

III:3 THOUGHT-READING

It is the vibrations carried by the breath which become thought-waves which carry the thought from one mind to the other. It is therefore that thought-reading much depends upon the position in which two people sit with regard to each other, for a certain position makes it easier for the breath to reach than another, although it is not always necessary that a person must be facing one in order to receive thought-waves through breath. If the thought power is strong and the breath is sound enough to carry the thought-waves a person, whether facing or having his back turned, must receive thought.

The mystics do not only project their own breath and see the condition of their being manifest before themselves, but also they can make themselves responsive to receive the thought-waves of another carried by his breath. This receptivity does not only enable an adept to read others' thoughts, but also to a mystic the condition of another person becomes revealed by the projection of another person's breath upon his heart.

Plainly speaking, souls are likened to mirrors, and two mirrors facing one another become projected on one another, one manifesting the reflection of the other. The mirror which has no reflection is capable of manifesting the reflection of the other mirror.

In this way breath enables a Sufi not only to know and see his own condition of life, but also to know and understand the condition of those he comes in contact with.

III:4 LIVELY BREATH – *NAFSI GARM*

The breath of one person may, so to speak, overpower the breath of another. It is as a little stream can be washed away by a large stream of water. In this is the secret of knowing the condition of another person. A Sufi whose breath is lively, which is called in the Sufic terms *nafsi garm*, has the influence of scattering the thoughts, feelings, the vibrations of the atmosphere of another. In this way he is able to convey his thought or feeling, and create his vibrations as the atmosphere for another who needs it for his own betterment. In this way a Sufi brings life and health to another person; he can have an influence on the character of another person.

There is a great difference between a developed breath and an undeveloped one. There is as vast a difference, or even a vaster, between the breath of two persons as in two voices. A specially produced singing voice is quite different from the uncultivated speaking voice. It is a psychological fact that the voice and word of a person whose voice is cultivated makes a greater impression than the voice and word of an ordinary person. How much more then must the influence of breath work silently. It is in this that is the mystery of the mystic's magnetism which is healing, harmonizing, exalting, at the same time invigorating.

III:5 THE UNKNOWN DIMENSION

The breath is a light in itself and it becomes projected like the beam from a searchlight thrown upon an object. When the breath is coarse, undeveloped, it is full of material atoms which dim its light. But a developed breath is sometimes not different from the light of the sun, but even brighter than that.

Breath being a light from another dimension which is unknown to science today, it cannot be visible to the ordinary physical eyes. The glands of the physical eyes must be cleansed and purified first by *pasi anfas* before the eyes can see the light of breath.

What people call the aura is the light of breath, but it is not everyone who sees it. A radiant countenance is a proof of an aura which lightens it, and the lack of it is the lack of light in the breath. A seer sees the sign of a death more clearly and longer beforehand than a physician can. The reason is that the seer sees in the aura of a person, whereas the physician sees only the condition of the body.

There is a belief in India that there are some cobras that have light in their head, the light by which they find their way through the dark. They make a hole in the earth miles long and illuminate the hole by their own light which is centred in their head. As two wires, positive and negative, cause the electric light to manifest, so the two currents of breath, *jelal* and *jemal*, when connected in a head in the way they ought to be, cause the light to manifest.

Many experience the phenomenon of the light of breath and yet doubt if it can be true, for they think it is perhaps a figment of their imagination. Others who are incapable of seeing that light confirm their doubt. The Sufi, by the developing of breath, experiences this light, which becomes for him a proof of the existence of that dimension which is unknown to the ordinary world.

III:6 BREATHING AND MEDITATION

Why is breath called *prana* by the Hindus? It is because it brings on the surface the essence from within. It is a current which is running from the outer spheres to the inner spirit. What it brings from the outer spheres to the inner spirit is not nearly so great as that which it brings from the inner spheres of life.

This being the condition, breath is vitalizing. Naturally therefore the breath of a man in sound health must give health to another in his presence. The breath of a master-mind must vitalize the thought of another, and the breath of a spiritual person must illuminate those in his presence. By breath a spiritually developed person can impart his physical energy, his thought power and his spiritual influence to the others with whom he may come in contact.

It is natural no doubt that, if the one who wishes to impart has not sufficient power to impart, he becomes broken if there is a greater demand on his power and if there is little left with him. Sufis therefore consider breathing connected with meditation much more important than anything else in the world, their food, sleep or comfort.

III:7 BREATH IS LIKENED TO WATER

Breath is likened to water; the flowing of the breath is like the flowing of a stream. Inhalation and exhalation show ebb and flow.

Parts of the earth which water does not touch remain barren; so the centres in the body with all their intuitive, innate capacities remain unproductive if the breath does not reach them. Besides, various diseases in spite of all their apparent causes often have one principal cause, and that is the lack of free flow of breath. Many operations could be avoided and several diseases could be cured by the knowledge of the phenomena of breath.

The Hindu sacred rivers Ganga and Jumna are outward symbols of *jelal* and *jemal*, the two directions of the flow of the breath, and the place where they meet is called *sangam*, the meeting or unity, which is considered most sacred by the Hindus. That *sangam* is the meeting of these two opposite flows; it is like the meeting of the two directions, in the centre which is called *kemal* by the Sufis.

The water rises, passes, falls and runs zigzag, and stands if held. So does breath. Every above-mentioned action of breath has a meaning and has a peculiar effect, as even water varies in its power and magnetism while going through the above said directions.

Water is a tonic, and breath is life itself. No tonic can be greater and better than breath. A spiritually evolved person's presence therefore brings about a cure in cases where all remedies fail.

Water is the necessity of life, and breath the only condition for living. Without it life is impossible.

Water falls as a rain from above, so breath is from above also, though from another dimension.

Water rises as vapours, so breath rises with gases, also with joys or depressions.

Pure water is health giving, pure breath gives life.

Water partakes of all things mixing with it, so does breath.

III:8 BREATH AND MAGNETISM

The mechanism of the human body shows the nervous system as its principal battery, in which magnetism is prepared by the action of breath. It is when the nervous system cannot function that this battery gets out of order and does not work properly. Many, in order to make this battery of the nervous system work properly, take drugs and other medicines which stimulate the nervous system. But instead of giving power to it they take away power from it, and in the end the nervous system becomes accustomed to all such medicines one takes.

The nourishment of the nervous system is what breath attracts from space. As far as science goes, it says one gets into one's system oxygen. The mystic goes further in saying: not only oxygen, but that life and intelligence, that power and radiance which make the nervous system in perfect order, the result of which is not only good health but ever increasing magnetism which comes forth from the person in his thought, speech, movement and action, charging his atmosphere with magnetism which surrounds him as a fortification and protection against all influences, physical and mental; thus making man live a fuller life.

III:9 THE SUBTLE WAVES OF BREATH

Inhaling shows the power of absorption, which is manifest in all living beings and in all objects. Small germs, worms, trees and plants all absorb, and in that way they breathe. Also in all living beings and in all things there is a tendency to put out an element which does not belong to them, in other words, an element which their system will not assimilate.

It is not only the inhaling and exhaling by the nostrils which accomplishes these two functions absorption and rejection, but there are minute waves of the breath working in different directions of the body, which perform the above said two acts in their own way and in their own rhythm of speed; for instance, the tendency of stretching and contracting, the tendency of blinking the eyes, of expelling water and refuse from the body. When any of these subtle waves of the breath, working in any direction of the body, gets out of order, then an illness originates in that particular part of the body spreading its influence gradually to other parts.

Balance in man's life and being is maintained by the evenness of inhaling and exhaling. The compass of man's being is as large as the reaching point of his breath. One lives a fuller life, another does not live a fuller life, because the former breathes fully, the latter does not breathe fully. Very often the reason why a child is a dwarf is that his breathing capacity does not allow him to breathe fully. And often the reason why a youth does not develop fully is that he does not breathe properly. A person ages sooner also because his breathing is not right. Very often people who have no particular illness feel tired and lifeless, because their breathing is not as it ought to be.

The spirit produces this physical body out of itself; so the body, in spite of all the physical nourishment, entirely depends upon the spirit to live. One can live for some time without food and water, but one cannot live without breathing. The reason is that, as the physical body is made of the spirit, it needs to breathe spirit in, in order to exist. Breath therefore does not only nourish the physical body but it gives subsistence to all the planes of man's existence.

III:10 THE MYSTERY OF BREATH

Breath penetrates, breath permeates, breath strikes, breath absorbs, breath invigorates and breath heals. It is therefore that souls with great powers make their thought and feeling penetrate into the mind and the hearts of others. As breath creates an atmosphere it permeates the bodies of others –

also the sphere, charging the whole atmosphere with its particular magnetism.

The hearts of men are likened to gongs in the temple. Every spoken word strikes them, but by the power of breath one strikes them without a word. It is by the breath that one contracts illnesses, but also one absorbs defects and the depression of others, as well as joy and happiness. The breath of personalities, healthy in mind and body, is vitalizing. The breath of the spiritual beings, whose love and sympathy go out to others, is naturally healing.

It is no exaggeration that the whole phenomenon of life has breath as its mystery, and once the knowledge of breath is attained and breath is mastered by practice, one beholds a most wonderful phenomenon within and without. There are many who remain sceptical till they have fathomed the mystery of breath. Once they know it, they call it, as Hindus have called it for ages, Breath-Life.

PART FIVE

◆

MORALS
Suluk

GATHA I

I:1 THE DEVELOPMENT OF PERSONALITY:
THE SENSE OF BEAUTY AND SINCERITY

Personality is the secret of the whole life, and in the development of personality it is not necessary that the psychic or occult sides should develop first. The beginning of development is natural. There are two things needful in the development of personality: the sense of beauty and the preservation of sincerity.

The sense of beauty can be defined as the adoption of all that appears beautiful in thought, speech or action. For generally man appreciates all that is beautiful in another person, but he overlooks the lack of that beauty in his own thought, speech and action. For instance, a person would appreciate the respectful, humble, gentle attitude of another towards himself, but he often overlooks his own lack of this attitude towards another.

There are two reasons for this. One reason is that man always looks outward, not inward, and he sees another person before he sees himself. The other reason is that man is selfish by nature; he wants all that is good for himself and he hardly gives a thought to giving these things to another. Man is ignorant of the fact that life is naturally a re-echo: what one gives one must take back sooner or later, and it is ignorance of this fact that makes man inconsiderate. Therefore to a sensitive person life all around seems nothing but thorns. But he does not expect thorns, he expects roses. That shows that his soul is longing for what is good and beautiful. And man pities himself, but instead of pitying others he blames them. If he only knew that others are just as much to be pitied as he! But not everyone thinks of the pain and suffering of another. As soon as man in his life begins trying to forget his troubles and think of others, he has taken his first step in saintliness.

Rose and thorn are the outcome of the same plant and come from the same root. Saint and sinner both come from one source, God, the Father of the whole humanity. It is only that the beauty, fragrance and colour in the root have expressed themselves in the rose and have not expressed themselves in the thorn. The difference between the plant and the human being is free will. A human being cannot make the excuse, 'I was born a thorn. How can I become a rose?' As a human being he has his free will, he is responsible if he is a thorn, and it is to his credit if he is a rose. Man must know that as the colour, fragrance and beauty are hidden in the root, so all goodness and beauty spring from the same source. The quality which shone in the life of the Master shines still and will ever shine. What attracts friends is not necessarily power, property and beauty; what really can attract man is personality.

Now the other question of personality – sincerity – that is necessary to be considered in the development of personality. There are many people who in order to behave nicely polish their manner and speech. But polish is not necessarily effective or the effective thing in a person. Beauty is that which penetrates through and through, and the greater the beauty the greater the penetration. What is called manner, which is only manner, is not a deep thing, it is almost a play. Every thought, speech or action has in it a psychic power which makes an impression on another, and the psychic power comes from the true divine essence in man.

No doubt in the name of sincerity people often express their lack of the sense of beauty, saying 'I am a frank person, I tell the truth and I don't mind how you take it.' This shows that sincerity void of the sense of beauty is lack of balance, and beauty void of sincerity is lack of balance. As music depends upon rhythm and tone, so personality depends on the sense of beauty and sincerity.

I:2 THE DEVELOPMENT OF PERSONALITY:
THE JARRING EFFECT OF THE EGO OF ANOTHER

By a keen outlook on life we find that what disturbs us most in life is the ego of another person. It is the ego that has a jarring effect upon life. Those who know the right manner of developing personality know that the first lesson in life is to efface that ego as much as possible. Christ says, 'Blessed are the poor in spirit.' That poorness in spirit is the softening of the ego. When the ego is softened in a person, then in the thought, speech and action of that person there is a charm. Sometimes a person, after going through a disillusionment, suffering, torture, shows in his personality some charm and that charm has come from the softening of that ego. But any virtue that develops naturally, forced by life or circumstances, is not a virtue in the same sense as that which has been developed by one's own effort.

Every beautiful action, thought or speech is derived from effacing of the self or ego. For instance, every manner of courtesy comes from holding the reins of the ego. Beauty of speech always depends on the same effacement of the self, and so it is with thought. As soon as the ego expresses itself without control it hurts the ego of another person. The tendency in the lower creatures to fight is caused only by the ego, and man has this tendency no less than they but rather more. It is this tendency which brings about disturbances in the life of individuals and in the multitude. The family feuds in ancient times and now wars all come from the same source, the ego.

The idea of self-denial in Christianity, if rightly considered, expresses the idea of effacement rather than that of renunciation. Those whose contact brings us comfort, ease, peace, always have a softened ego. It is vanity or pride that hardens the ego, and it is love and light that soften the ego. The greater the person, the finer the ego. No example can be better than that of Christ washing the feet of his disciples.

What builds man's ego is every kind of gratification of the ego, and what breaks the ego is patience and renunciation.

The question whether it would be advisable to so destroy the ego that others might take advantage of a refined person is answered by saying that it is not necessary that one should work against the ego, but one must control it.

It would not be exaggerated if I said that man's worst enemy is his ego, his own ego. When it is not in his control man's thought, speech and action are bent towards the gratification of his ego. And the more he satisfies his ego, the more his ego desires, and it is never satisfied. Nobody else has such power in life of enslaving a man as his own ego.

Man is in fact from the divine essence and, being so, he has the right to be king of his own life, which is his own kingdom. By the gratification of the ego man falls from kingship into slavery, and in the end his own life becomes a burden to himself. In order to gain his own kingdom he must destroy the illusion that in satisfying his ego he shows his power. He satisfies his enemy in satisfying his ego. A Persian poet says:

Each time that I make peace with my enemy
he has the opportunity of preparing again for the struggle.

The great battle that the Sufis and sages and Yogis fight is the battle with the ego. But the sage battles with his own ego, the ordinary man with other people's egos. And the difference in the result of these two battles is that the victory and the failure of the ordinary man are momentary, but the victory of the sage is eternal. The former, when he has finished one battle, must begin another, but the latter, once he has succeeded, is victorious. All that the former gains after all is not his own, because his kingdom is not his own; all he gains does not belong to him. But the sage is king in his own kingdom.

I:3 THE DEVELOPMENT OF PERSONALITY:
WHAT IS THE EGO?

'Know thyself and thou wilt know God,' said the great Sufi philosopher Ali. To know the self is the most difficult thing in the world, because what man can perceive first is a part only of the self, a limited part. When man asks himself, 'What is it in me that is "I"?', he finds his body and his mind, and in both he finds himself limited and apart from others. And it is this conception of his being that makes man realize himself as an individual. If man dived deep enough within himself, he would reach a point of his ego where it lives an unlimited life. It is that realization which brings man to the real understanding of life; and as long as he has not realized his unlimited self he lives a life of limitation, a life of illusion. When man in this illusion says 'I', in reality it is a false claim. Therefore everyone has a false claim of 'I' except some who have arrived at a real understanding of the truth.

This false claim is called in Sufic terms *nafs*, and the annihilation of this false self is the aim of the sage. But no doubt to annihilate this false ego is more difficult than anything else in the world, and it is this path of the annihilation which is the path of the saints and the sages. One may ask, 'Why should one take the trouble to annihilate the ego? Since life is full of pain and suffering, why add this suffering?' The answer is that even if an operation will cause one suffering, it is better to endure it in order to be cured.

The inborn nature of the ego is intolerance; that is its nature because there are other egos that jar it. It is for this reason that when two cocks meet they want to fight. The reason is that the ego of one jars the other. Even a silent life such as that of a rock can jar upon another ego, for instance that of a bull who wants to hurl himself upon it and break it with his horns. It is the nature of the ego to exist alone and it cannot allow another to exist. No doubt the reason is still deeper. It belongs to the deep side of metaphysics but the moral aspect can be understood.

The finer an ego becomes the less it jars upon others. In the different degrees of evolution of man one sees this gradual development of the ego. There are people who seem to have no thorns, and yet they have a thorn which makes itself felt in the presence of another; it is their ego. Others are like the rose with its softness, beauty and fragrance. No doubt not everyone is a rose, but everyone desires the rose and not the thorn. The best training is to try to turn this thorny ego into a rose. It is very hard, and the finer and the more evolved the ego, the harder life becomes for man. The higher and the more refined you are, the greater trials you will have to go through in life. The more sensitive you become, the more you will have to suffer. The thorn cannot hurt another thorn, but the slightest thing can hurt a rose. It is not surprising if an ego that has become a flower does not wish to live among thorns. But that is its destiny, and in spite of all sufferings it is preferable to be a rose rather than a thorn.

To return to the question why one ego jars another, the answer is that one must understand the nature of the other egos. When one dog barks at another and the other wags his tail, it is to let the first understand him and not fight with him. It is this moral that Christ taught from beginning to end. If you wish to experience fully the beauty of life you must make your ego as fine as possible. This allows the grosser egos to come into contact.

It is from this that good and evil have come. It is always from the grosser ego that what we call evil comes, and it is from the finer ego that that comes which we call good.

I:4 THE TRAINING OF THE EGO:
THE EGO IS TRAINED AS A HORSE

The ego is trained by a Sufi as a horse is trained by man. A bridle is put upon it and man holds the reins in his hand. This training is called by the Hindus *hatha yoga*, which means to gain the control of one's self by means of abstinence. Often when man does wrong it is not that he likes to do wrong, but that he is not able to prevent himself from acting in that way. In the first place wrongdoing is almost always the consequence of the appetites and passions – or for the gratification of vanity. Fasting and special postures are often practised by the mystics for the same reason. The more man gives way to the appetites and passions, the more he is enslaved by them, until he reaches a state where he speaks and acts against his own conscience. Such faults as treachery, flattery, falseness and all others of the kind come from lack of will-power and from giving way to the passions.

For training the ego it is not absolutely necessary to abstain from all physical desires. The idea is to master the desire instead of allowing it to master one. The complaint of every soul and the remorse of every soul is always of the same thing: the enslavement of man through yielding to his desires. One allows the desire to master one when one identifies oneself with the desire and one pities oneself – which makes things worse. The desire for the momentary joy becomes an excuse for having given way. For instance, a person who gets up late makes the cold an excuse. He had to, he says, because it was cold. Reason always supplies an excuse for everything; but one cannot escape the consequences, and the remorse that follows proves that a fault has been committed.

Once a person has accustomed himself to his faults, the sense of his faults becomes less keen; then he no longer troubles about them, then he becomes a slave to his faults. He is like a worm and his faults become his life. That is why in the language of the Hindus the word for hell means 'a place full of worms'. In other words, he feeds on his faults and his faults find their nourishment in him. To a keen sight such cases are not rare. There are some cases that everyone can see, others are hidden.

Those who know its value consider the training of the ego the most important thing in life. The first lesson in this training is to ask: 'Why must I have a certain thing? Why must I not have it? If it is not good for me why should I have it? And if it is good for me why should I not have it?' When a person has acquired the habit of speaking with his ego in this way about every physical appetite, he will always be able to do what he ought to do.

I:5 THE TRAINING OF THE EGO:
WHAT THE EGO NEEDS AND WHAT IT DOES NOT NEED

In order to train the ego it is necessary that one should distinguish what is the right of the ego and what is not its right. The ego has a tendency to want what it needs and also what it does not need. The first is its natural appetite and the second is greed. This is like the nature of the dog that after eating the flesh from a bone still guards the bone against another dog. Besides this the ego has a tendency to want more and more of what it likes, regardless of right and justice, also regardless of the after-effect. For instance, a person may eat and drink more and more until this makes him ill. Every kind of gratification of desires or appetite gives a tendency to want more and more. Then there is desire for change of experience, and when a person gives in to it, it never ends.

Excess of desire in appetites or passions always produces an intoxication in man. It increases to such an extent that the limited means that man has become insufficient to gratify his desires. Therefore naturally to satisfy his desires he wants more than what is his own and he wants what belongs to other people. When this begins, naturally injustice begins. Then he cannot get what he wants, then there is pain and disappointment. When one person gratifies his desires more than other people, the others who see this want to take away the gratification he has. One naturally expects a thinker to understand this and to relieve his ego of all that is unnecessary.

The training of the ego is this: to eat to live and not to live to eat, and so with all things one desires. The nature of desire is such that nothing will satisfy it forever, and sometimes the pleasure of a moment costs more than it is worth. And when one's eyes are closed to this, one takes the momentary pleasure regardless of what will come after. The training of the ego is not necessarily a sad life of renunciation, nor is it necessarily the life of a hermit. The training is to be wise in life and to understand what we desire and why we desire it and what effect will follow, what we can afford and what we cannot afford. It is also to understand desire from the point of view of justice: to know whether it is right and just.

If the ego is given way to in the very least in the excess of its desires, it becomes master of one's self. Therefore in training the ego the slightest thing even must be avoided which may in time master us. The ideal life is the life of balance, not necessarily the life of renunciation. Renunciation must not be practised for the sake of renunciation, but it must be practised if it is necessary for balance.

Verily, balance is the ideal life.

I:6 THE TRAINING OF THE EGO: TRAINING BY NOT GRATIFYING VANITY

The first form of the ego is that which the body helps to form, and the next is that which is formed by the mind. This aspect of the ego lives for vanity, which causes a person to do good and also to do evil. Its desire is always the satisfaction of its pride and when this increases, in the end it results in tyranny and cruelty.

A person expects others to see him as he thinks he is, and often his self-esteem is excessive and it is impossible for others to admire him as much as he wants. He wishes to be admired for his clothes, his jewels, his possessions, his greatness and position, and naturally when this desire increases it makes the person blind and he loses sight of right and justice. It is natural that the desire for things that gratify vanity should have no end; it increases continually.

The tendency to look at others, to view them with hatred

and prejudice, to consider them inferior to oneself and all such tendencies come from this ego. There are even cases when people spend money in order to be able to insult another. To make someone bow before him, to make him give way, to put him in a position of inferiority, to make him appear contemptible, sometimes a person will spend money.

The desire for the satisfaction of vanity reaches such a point that a person would give his life for the satisfaction of his vanity. Often someone shows generosity not for the sake of kindness, but to satisfy his vanity. The more vanity a person has the less sympathy he has for others, for all his attention is given to his own satisfaction and he is as blind toward others. This ego, so to speak, restricts life because it limits a person. Coldness, pride, jealousy, all come from this ego.

There is nothing so displeasing to the surroundings as conceit in whatever form, and what is the use of an opinion that is pleasing to us and unpleasing to all our surroundings? In reality a person's true satisfaction comes from the opinion that others have of him, not from his own opinion of himself. There is nothing more repellent than a thorny ego. The outward manner cannot hide an ego that is not soft, even if the manner is very humble. It shows itself suddenly, unconsciously, in a word or an action that jars upon another.

The training of this ego requires more care than the training of the other ego, for it is more difficult and a subtler matter to be aware of the desires of the mind and to weigh them than to be aware of and to weigh the desires of the body. No doubt vanity is natural to the ego, and the ego is natural to every human being. But there are desires of the mind that are necessary and there are desires of the mind that are not necessary. And the more one controls the ego, the more one allows the virtues and merits that are in one's heart to manifest.

This ego gives a false idea of greatness, but the effacement of this ego results in the true greatness.

I:7 THE TRAINING OF THE EGO: CONSTANT BATTLE WITH THE EGO

For the person who walks in the path of God the only struggle is a constant battle with the ego. It is the ego which forms the cover on the light of the soul, and the light hidden under the ego is the 'light hidden under a bushel'. Man's sense of justice, his logic, his reason, his intelligence, his affection, all is covered by the ego. If he judges anyone it is from the point of view of his own interest; if he reasons his selfish mind produces the results; in his affections he puts self first; his intelligence is darkened by self. And this is the condition of the average man.

In proportion as man takes away the covering from the soul, so much juster, truer, more sincere, more loving does he become. Selfishness develops the sense of self-interest, and very often a person may gain earthly prosperity because of it. But as all things in this world are subject to change, death and decay, he remains in the end empty-handed, while the unselfish man, who has perhaps been debarred from earthly good by his lack of the sense of self-interest, at least remains possessed of his sense of reason and is rich in the qualities of love, justice and intelligence.

The whole tragedy of life is in losing sight of one's natural self, and the greatest gain in life is coming into touch with one's real self. The real self is covered by many covers of ego. Those which preponderate above all others are hunger and passion, beneath these are pride and vanity. One must learn to discriminate between what is natural and what is unnatural, what is necessary and what is not necessary, what brings happiness and what brings sorrow.

No doubt it is difficult for many to discriminate between right and wrong, but by standing face to face with one's ego and recognizing it as someone who is ready to make war against us, and by keeping one's strength of will as an unsheathed sword, one protects oneself from one's greatest enemy which is one's own ego. And a time comes in life when one can say, 'My worst enemy has been within myself.'

1:8 THE TRAINING OF THE EGO:
THREE STAGES THROUGH WHICH THE EGO DEVELOPS

There are three different stages through which the ego develops and reaches the ideal state.

The first stage is called *ammarah* by Sufis, and in this the ego is satisfied by the satisfaction of the passions and the appetites.

From this animal stage the ego may rise to a higher stage which is man's ego, and that stage is the gratification of vanity. This ego is termed by Sufis *lawwamah*, and this stage in the beginning causes a person to act in every way that is likely to cause harm and to be hurtful and unjust to others. This continues until he learns to understand the true nature of vanity, since all good as well as all evil is born of vanity.

When vanity ceases to cause man to do evil, he has reached the human stage, *mutmaina*. When vanity causes man to do good the ego becomes humane, using this word in the Oriental sense in which it means more than human, as it is derived from the two words *hu*, divine and *manas*, mind.

The first lesson that the ego must learn in order to develop into the humane state is that of pride in the form of self-respect. As man has the inclination to have good clothes and good ornaments in order to appear in the eyes of others as what he considers beautiful, so he must feel the same inclination towards the building of personality by the ornamentation of every action and manner in the way that he considers good and beautiful.

1:9 THE TRAINING OF THE EGO:
THE ANIMAL SIDE OF MAN'S EGO

There is a side of man's nature which may be called the animal side; and yet it is worse than an animal side, for there are tame animals which have a tendency to love and to respond to love and that are harmless. But there is a part of man's nature which may be likened to a thorn or the horn of a rhinoceros, and this ego takes pleasure in hurting others and gets joy from giving pain. From the scientific point of view this is called mania or disease, but psychologically all that is below the human ideal is a defect in man, and he could overcome that defect if he knew how.

Often a man is seen taking pleasure in whipping a horse or a dog, and the same defect that is shown there may be seen in a pronounced form when a man gets pleasure from hurting or paining another person. This defect is shown in its mental aspect when a person shows contempt or antipathy to another, when he insults another, even when he shows disrespect where respect or reverence is due.

Man gives pain by irony, sarcasm or harshness of expression. There are looks that wound and many slight changes of manner by which it is possible to hurt another and get joy from it. When this tendency is developed a man is naturally disliked by those around him. Some show their dislike outwardly and others do not, and the man resents it only where it is expressed. Man often puts on others the blame for his own fault.

This kind of ego may develop into a monster, and the soul can see this process from within and admits it to itself, though the individual may be too proud to admit it openly. The soul, from within, is often frightened at this monster and dreads the sight of it. And when this monster-ego is so developed that it has created a world of pain and torture, the soul finds itself in hell. This is the only hell that exists, either here or in the hereafter, in external conditions.

Even after creating the ego man can be happy if he can break it until it becomes his friend and servant.

I:10 THE TRAINING OF THE EGO:
SELF-CONSCIOUSNESS

There is a tendency in man to think a great deal about what others think of him, and in some natures this tendency develops quickly. This develops in him self-consciousness which is the root of several defects in man. It enfeebles man physically and mentally and makes him dependent upon the opinion of others. So to speak, he lives on the good opinion of others and he is as dead when they have a bad opinion about him.

This tendency makes a person sensitive, often hypersensitive. It often reaches such a point that at every word he speaks he looks around for approval and every movement he makes in the same way is calculated to produce an effect. This makes his body and his mind both heavy and burdensome to his soul. It develops in nature that weakness which in ordinary words is called touchiness, taking offence at every little thing. And the nature of many people is such that they enjoy bringing out any weakness that may be in a person. It becomes a pastime or pleasure to such people, and the life of the one who is sensitive is made so difficult that he has no rest at home or abroad. Everyone seems to him to be wicked, everyone's presence seems to have a jarring effect upon him, and he seeks to be exclusive and to find a seclusion which life does not permit of his finding. If he happens to be in a position where he has to speak or sing or perform in any way, he fails to do his best, and when he meets people he cannot stand a criticism or reply to a jest. The presence of others has the effect of a weight upon the soul. The desire of the sensitive person is always to be in hiding, keeping away from people, looking at others with nervousness, dislike or fear. Such a person, however great his virtues or merits, is always incapable of free expression of his gift.

Stiffness in walking, also crookedness, is caused by self-consciousness, and sitting in a rigid position without any flexibility is caused by the same thing. Self-consciousness gives hardness to the expression of the lips and it stiffens the tongue and makes the voice toneless, preventing a man from saying what he wishes to say. Self-consciousness is like a chain upon every feature and limb of the body, and in the self-conscious person there is nothing of the smoothness that should flow like a fluid through every expression of life. Its only remedy is forgetting self and putting the whole mind into work in each occupation undertaken.

GATHA II

II:1 THE TRAINING OF THE EGO: VANITY

Man has the desire to do good and to refrain from doing evil because it feeds his vanity. Among one thousand good and virtuous people there is scarcely one who does good and refrains from evil because it is his natural inclination to do so. The majority of those engaged in art, science, religion or politics are conscious all the time of the opinion of others and they can only work upon the lines they are following if there is appreciation from somewhere, and the least antagonism or opposition discourages them and often kills their desire. It is one great soul among thousands that can keep firm and strong in his purpose through life, unshaken and unweakened by opposition from any direction. It is that person who wins in the end and accomplishes things that are worthwhile.

In the lives of all great souls who have accomplished wonderful deeds in life you will surely find this mystery hidden. Those souls have not learned it, it happens to be their nature. And the thinker will see in this a philosophy which teaches that it is the ego that chains man's feet keeping him from progress in all paths of life. The ego does not only make man self-conscious, but it makes of him a coward and renders him helpless. He is timid because he sees his own limitations, and he is helpless because everything stronger overpowers him, as he confines his being within a certain limit.

Besides all the disadvantages that self-consciousness brings with it, there is one thing it does more than anything else: it prevents man from realizing that thought of self keeps him away from God. In the heart of man there is only room for one, either for himself or for God.

II:2 THE TRAINING OF THE EGO:
'BLESSED ARE THE POOR IN SPIRIT'

Jesus Christ says, 'Blessed are the poor in spirit.' Why is not the word ego used instead of spirit? Man's glance, expression, posture – all speak of his ego and tell to what extent it is hard and to what extent soft. People seek to disguise the true nature of the ego by diplomatic language and by good manners, but this does not really hide the ego, which is expressing itself in everything they say and do. Every particle of man's body and every atom of man's mind is controlled by this ego. If there is anything that is meant by the word spirit, as used above, it is this. The least word spoken against it rouses man's anger; praise tickles his vanity and goes to the heart of the ego.

And now the question arises: 'If this ego is the chief thing in man's development why should we fight it? Is it not the essence of man?' The answer is that there is the spirit of man and the Spirit of God. These two are different and yet the same. Think of the sea and of the bubble, how vast the one, how small the other! How dare man claim that he is God! Only the emptiness in which the ego is noise is found in a heart that can claim such greatness as that. The true emptiness is filled by the divine light, and such a heart it is which in humility is turned to nothingness so that that light shines out.

Man's ego is a globe and the Spirit of God is the light. 'Poor' is said in the sense of thin, and when the ego is poor or thin, the Spirit of God shines out. Rich in spirit would mean thick or dense in the ego-nature, which would stand as a wall against the divine light hidden in the heart.

II:3 THE TRAINING OF THE EGO:
THE THREE PARTS OF THE EGO

The ego is divided into three parts: the physical ego, the mental ego and the spiritual ego. The mental ego is the cover of the spiritual ego, and the physical ego is a cover

over the mental ego. The ego indeed is one, but these three are the different aspects of the ego.

The physical ego is nurtured by the gratification of the bodily appetites. One sees that after having a meal or some refreshing drink a sort of feeling of stimulation arises, and no doubt it covers with an additional cover the 'I' within. And therefore there is a difference between sleep and meditation. Although both produce rest, yet one is caused by a stimulus to the body, and the other rest is without it. There have been cases where meditative people have only slept for two or three hours out of the twenty-four without becoming ill. A person who can sleep well shows the sign of health, and yet is subject to any illness.

The gratification of every appetite is a momentary stimulus and rest to the body, but this momentary satisfaction creates a further appetite, and every experience in the satisfaction of the appetites gives a desire for more satisfaction. Thus the ego, the cover over one's mental and spiritual being, becomes thicker and thicker until it closes all light from within.

There are some who eat in order to live, but there are many who live in order to eat. The body is an instrument that the soul may experience the external world, but if the whole life is devoted to the instrument, then the person for whom the instrument exists is deprived of his experience in life.

The blindness that the physical ego causes can be clearly seen among the lower creatures: how the lion is inclined to fight with another lion, how the dog is inclined to watch the bone, the flesh out of which it has already eaten, and does not want another dog to touch it. This same physical ego gives man pride in his strength, in his beauty, in his power, in his possessions.

If there is a spark of light in time it must expand to a shining star, and when there is the slightest darkness, that darkness must expand and put the whole life in a mist. In the intoxication of the physical ego man becomes so interested only in the satisfaction of his appetites that he can readily harm or injure or hurt not only his enemy but his dearest friend. As a drunken man does not know what he says or does, so a person blinded with his physical ego is intoxicated and can easily say or do things regardless of the pleasure, comfort, happiness, harmony or peace of others.

II:4 THE TRAINING OF THE EGO: NECESSITY AND AVIDITY

In the satisfaction of bodily appetites there are two things: necessity and avidity. A satisfaction which is necessary for existence is one thing, and ever increasing joy in the satisfaction of bodily appetites is another thing. When man acts regardless of this, in either way, in satisfying the appetites or in abstaining from satisfaction – in both cases he makes a mistake. In order to train the ego it is not necessary that cruelty be done to nature; discrimination is necessary to understand how far one should satisfy the appetites and how far one should refrain from being addicted to such satisfaction.

Intense desire for bodily satisfaction has a bad influence on one's mentality, which acts psychically unfavourable upon oneself and on one's surroundings. It produces jealousy, envy, greed in the nature, and if the thought-currents are stronger it produces psychically poisonous effects. There is a belief in the East which is known by the name *nazr*, a belief that any food or drink can have a poisonous effect upon the one who eats or drinks it, if it has been exposed to an evil eye. This superstition is known in most parts of the East in some form or other, and the psychical idea behind it is that the intense feeling of envy produces a thought-current which must surely spread its poison, which causes harm to the one against whom the feeling works.

When we consider the whole unrest of the present time in the world, we find that it is caused by the physical ego. The wars and revolutions seem to have the desire for comfort and pleasure and for more earthly gain behind them. And since the happiness of the world depends upon the moral of the standard of the majority, it is upon the education of human nature in the psychic law of happiness that depends the peace of the world.

II:5 THE TRAINING OF THE EGO: HUMILITY

Humility is the principal thing that must be learned in the path of training the ego. It is the constant effort of effacing the ego that prepares man for the greater journey. This principle of humility can be practised by forgetting one's personality in every thought and action and in every dealing with another. No doubt it is difficult and may not seem very practicable in everyday life, though in the end it will prove to be the successful way not only in one's spiritual life but in one's everyday affairs.

The general tendency is to bring one's personality forward, which builds a wall between two souls whose destiny and happiness lies in unity. In business, in profession, in all aspects of life it is necessary that one should unite with the other in this unity in which the purpose of life is fulfilled.

There are two forms of effacing the self which in other words may be called giving in. One way is by weakness, the other is by willingness; the former being a defect, the latter a virtue. One comes by lack of will, the other from charity of heart. Therefore in training the ego one must take care that one is not developing a weakness, presuming it to be a virtue. The best way of dealing with the question is to let life take its natural course, and at the same time to allow the conscience to keep before it the highest ideal: on one side life taking its natural course, on the other side the conscience holding its highest ideal. Balancing it will make the journey easy.

The words of Jesus Christ which teach man to walk with another two miles if the other wanted him to walk one, prove the great importance of harmony in life. And his words, 'resist not evil', show still more the importance of harmony in life; namely that if you can avoid evil, in other words keep it away, that is better than to want to fight it.

And the idea of Christ's teaching of giving in is also expressive of harmonizing with the wishes of another person. No doubt in this discrimination is necessary. That harmony is advisable which develops into harmony and culminates in a greater harmony, not that which may seem in the beginning to be harmony and would result in greater inharmony. In training the ego balance must be taken as the most important principle.

II:6 THE TRAINING OF THE EGO: TRAINING BY ABSTINENCE

There is no better way of training the ego than denying it what it wants for the satisfaction of its vanity. Spirituality in other words may be called a capacity; plainly explained it may be called a depth. In some people naturally there is this capacity, this depth, and in some it may be made. In order to collect the rainwater people dig the ground and make a capacity for the water to collect. So in order to receive the spiritual life and light one must open within oneself capacity. The egoistic has no capacity, for it is his ego which makes the heart, so to speak, solid, giving no accommodation to the essence of God. The more one denies the demands of the ego which satisfy its vanity, the more capacity one makes to be filled by the life of God. It is painful sometimes, it often seems hard to deny all the ego demands, but it always results in a higher satisfaction.

When the will is able to rule one's life, and not one's bodily appetites and mental fancies, then there is the reign of the Golden Age, as the Hindus say; there is no injustice and there is no reward. When man finds disturbance in his life, a lack of harmony in the external, he must take refuge under the reign within which is the kingdom of God. To a Sufi this body is the temple of God and the heart His shrine, and as long as man keeps God away from His temple, from His shrine, his limited ego reigns, and that reign is called the Iron Age by the Hindus.

A person who has not opened his heart to God to abide in may yet be a good person, but as his life will be involved in the activities of the world, his ego will turn from bad to worse, culminating into the worst state of mind, and it is that condition of mind which is personified in the religious term 'Satan'.

In order to learn to realize, 'I am not, but God is', one must first deny oneself for one's fellow men. Respecting another, enduring a person or an action which is uncongenial to oneself, tolerating all, overlooking the faults, covering the weaknesses that one finds in one's fellow men, being ready to forgive, all these things are the first lessons in self-denial.

II:7 THE TRAINING OF THE EGO:
THE TWO SIDES OF THE HUMAN EGO

The human ego has two sides to its nature. One side is to strive for its nature's demands, and that side of the ego may be classed as the animal ego. But there is another side which manifests when the ego shows its agitations for no other reason than intolerance. This feeling is a kind of blindness or intoxication, and it arises from an excess of energy coming out from the soul quite unrestrained. It covers, so to speak, the light of the soul as the smoke may cover the light that comes from a flame. In order to allow the divine Spirit to guide one's life one must clear the soul of its smoke part, leaving there only the flame to illuminate one's life.

It is the nature of the ego during its period of ignorance that all that is very beautiful or powerful and all that is below the standard of its ideal agitates it. This sensitiveness may increase to such an extent that all that does not bring any comfort or joy or happiness to the ego may become repugnant to it. It is this ignorant stage of the ego which in the Sanskrit language is called by the wise *ahankar*, and the whole method that the wise have taught in any age and in any part of the world has been for recognizing and understanding this ignorance which is the primary nature of the ego, and then for purifying one's ego from this by gentleness, by humility, by self-control, by tolerance and by forgiveness.

Man can dissimulate this ignorance, but that is not enough. Often outward manner may become a mask over something ugly hidden behind. There is only one thing that can free the ego from this ignorance and that is the love of God, the contemplation of God and the knowledge of God.

Love of God comes from belief in God. Belief is the first thing necessary, but belief needs support. It can be kept up by the belief of others surrounding one or by learning or study which will strengthen it. But he to whom the love of humanity is unknown can never know the love of God. As you can see the painter in his picture, the poet in his poem, the musician in his music, so in humanity you can see God. (*See* Questions and Answers, p 298.)

II:8 THE TRAINING OF THE EGO: TRAINING IS A SCIENCE AS WELL AS AN ART

It is a science and an art to understand the nature of the human ego and to train it. One can understand the nature of the human ego by a study of human nature, but one can learn the way of training by training one's own ego. Man can train his ego by being patient with all around him that has a jarring effect upon him, for every jar upon the soul irritates the ego. When man expresses his irritation he develops a disagreeable nature; when he controls it and does not express it, then he becomes crushed inwardly. The idea is to rise above all such irritations.

Life, as its nature, has a jarring effect which every sensitive soul can feel. When a person wishes to keep away from all jarring influences he had better not try to live, for life is a constant jar. Life is motion, and it is the nature of motion to strike against something. It does not require strength to stand against the jarring influences of life – there is no wall of stone or of iron that can always stand against the waves of the ocean – but it is a small piece of wood, little and light, that can always rise and fall with the waves, but always above them, uninjured and safe. The lighter and the littler man's ego becomes, the more power of endurance he has. It is two strong egos that strike against one another. The little ego, the light ego just slips over when a powerful wave of a strong ego comes forward, knocking itself over against a stronger wall that may throw it over.

The art of dealing with egos of different grades of evolution is to learn gentleness, tolerance and forgiveness which all come from charity of heart. When man stands on the same plane as the other, then he is subject to the influence of another ego, but if he rises above it, then every effort of the ego falls flat. There is a poem in Hindustani, the verse of Ghalib,

The world seems to me as a playground of children.
How constantly the infants seem busy with their toys!

Verily, the secret of peace is hidden in the cover of the ego.

II:9 THE TRAINING OF THE EGO: FORGIVENESS

In order to learn forgiveness man must learn tolerance first, and there are people whom man cannot forgive. It is not that he must not forgive, but it is difficult, beyond his power to forgive, and in that case the first thing he can do is to forget. The first step towards forgiveness is to forget.

It is true that the finer the man is, the more he is subject to being hurt by the smallest disturbance that can produce irritation and inharmony in the atmosphere. A person who gives and takes hurts is capable of living an easy and comfortable life in the world. Life is difficult for the fine person, for he cannot give back what he receives in the way of hurt, and he can feel it more than an average person.

Many seek protection from all hurting influences by building some wall around themselves, but the canopy over the earth is so high that a wall cannot be built high enough, and the only thing one can do is to live in the midst of all inharmonious influences, to strengthen one's will-power and to bear all things, and yet keeping the fineness of character and a nobleness of manner together with an ever-living heart. To become cold with the coldness of the world is weakness, and to become broken by the hardness of the world is feebleness, but to live in the world and yet to keep above the world is like walking on the water.

There are two essential duties for the man of wisdom and love: that is to keep the love in our nature ever increasing and expanding, and to strengthen the will so that the heart may not be easily broken. Balance is ideal in life. Man must be fine and yet strong, man must be loving and yet powerful.

II:10 THE TRAINING OF THE EGO: TRAINING BY REFRAINING FROM FREE IMPULSES

The wise, knowing the nature of the ego is to rise and to move and to disturb the atmosphere, practise in their lives to restrain the ego from its free impulses. The tendency of the ego to rise shows itself in the desire of standing when others are sitting, and running when others are walking, and dancing when others are standing. In the mental plane the desire to be proud, the desire to be vain, to show conceit, to show one's superiority over others, all come from the ego. The wise therefore, by learning the lesson of humility, of gentleness, of mildness, make their spirit, as it is called in the Bible, poor – 'Blessed are the poor in spirit.'

These manners are sometimes taught, but if one does not feel them within oneself they become forms and conventions without spirit or life or effect in them. It is only love which can teach these manners that keep the ego under control. If one does not learn them from love, then one learns them from suffering. Pain naturally crushes the ego, and if one has had much pain in one's life it has a softening influence on the ego.

Wisdom is a great teacher. It shows man what he is when he lets the ego be free and uncontrolled, and what one gains by control of the ego. Imagine a rider sitting on a horse without reins in his hand, letting the horse go free wherever it likes. He risks his life at every moment. The happiness is his who rides on the horse and controls it and has the reins in his hand. And he is the master of his journey.

GATHA III

The manner of friendliness is considered as the main part in the study of Sufism, for the Sufi in all ages has given great importance to the art of personality. As Sufism is the religious philosophy of love, harmony and beauty, it is most necessary for a Sufi to express the same through his personality.

No doubt in the East manner is given great predominance in life. The courts in the East were schools of good manner, though a great deal of artificiality was combined with it. But in the path of Sufism the same manners which are used at court were learned with sincerity. According to the Sufi idea all beauty comes from God; so a beautiful manner is a divine expression.

In these modern times people seem to be against manner because of their agitation against aristocracy, as there are many who are against religion because they are cross with the priests. When man agitates against beauty he cannot be on the right way, and the movement of today against all beauty that exists in the form of culture and manner is a battle with civilization.

The Sufi calls the manner that comes from the knowledge of unity, from the realization of truth, from the love of God, *akhlaq Allah*, meaning the manner of God. In other words God, expressed in man, shows in the action of that man the manner of God. The following are the different aspects of the manner, known by the Sufis as *ilmi adab*:

adab	respect
khatir	consideration
tawazu'	hospitality or welcome
inkisar	humility or selflessness
khulq	graciousness
matanat	seriousness

189

halim	tenderness of feeling
salim	harmony
wafah	fidelity, loyalty, constancy
dilazari	sympathy
kotah kalam	moderation in speech
kam sukhun	sparing of words
mu'tabar	self-respect, keeping one's word, proving trustworthy in dealings
buzurgi	venerability
ghairat	honour or pride
haya	modesty

Also: bravery – experience – generosity – forgiveness – large-mindedness – tolerance – to take the side of the weak – to hide the faults of others as one would one's own out of sympathy and respect for another.

III:2 THE MANNER OF FRIENDLINESS:
RESPECT – ADAB (1)

There is no one in the world who does not deserve some respect and he who pays respect to another, by so doing, respects himself, for respect creates respect, disrespect re-echoes in disrespect. The greatest education that can be given to a child is that of respect, not only for his friends, parents and relations, but also for the servants in the house. Once the Prophet hearing his grandson call a slave by his name, told him, 'Call him uncle, for he is advanced in years.' If one wishes to respect someone, one will surely find something to respect in him, and if there were nothing at all to be found, then the very fact that he is a human being quite entitles him to respect.

One form of respect is to consider another person as better than oneself; even if one did not hold that he is so, to regard another person as better than oneself by reason of humility, also from graciousness. No person is respected who has no respect for another.

There is another form of respect which is to recognize another person's superiority in age, experience, learning, goodness, birth, rank, position, personality, morality or spirituality. And if one has been mistaken in recognizing another person's superiority it is no loss, for respect given to man in reality is respect given to God. He who deserves respect is entitled to it, but when someone does not deserve it and yet you respect him, it shows your graciousness. To a fine person it is a matter of great regret to have lost the opportunity of paying respect when there was an occasion; an unrefined person does not mind.

There are many who out of cleverness wrap their disrespectful attitude in an ironical form of speech and make sarcastic but polite remarks in order to insult. In that way seemingly they have not shown any disrespect and yet they have satisfied their desire of being disrespectful. In some people there is a spirit of injury which feeds on hurting by a disrespectful attitude shown in thought, word or action. If man only knew that in life what he gives he receives. Only sometimes the return does not come immediately; it takes time.

He is really respectful who gives respect, but he who looks for respect from another is greedy; he will always be disappointed. Even to pay respect in order to get respect in return is a kind of trade. Those who reach a spiritual realization will only give respect generously without thinking for one moment of receiving it in return. When one sincerely gives respect to anyone, not for show but from the feeling of one's heart, a happiness rises together with that, which is the product only of the respectful attitude; and nothing else can give it.

There are many to whom one is indebted for their help, kindness, protection, support, for their service or assistance, and there is nothing material in the world in the form of gold or silver, which can express the gratitude so fully as a real respect. Remember therefore that for something that you cannot pay back in silver or gold you can make return only in one way, and that is by humbly offering respect.

III:3 THE MANNER OF FRIENDLINESS:
RESPECT – ADAB (2)

A respectful attitude is the first and principal thing in the development of personality; not only respect towards someone whom one considers superior, but respect for everyone one meets in life in proportion to what is due to him. It is through conceit that man gives less honour where more honour is due, and it is by ignorance that man gives more honour than what is due. Respecting someone does not require only a desire to respect but an art of respecting. One ignorant of this art may express respect wrongly. It is self-respect which makes one inclined to respect another. The one who has no respect for himself cares little if he respects another or if respect is at all necessary in life.

To respect means to honour. It is not only bowing and bending or external action which expresses respect. A disrespectful person may bow his head before a person and strike him on the face by his word. True respect is from the attitude which comes from the sincere feeling of respect. The outward expression of respect has no value without inner feeling. Inspired by a respectful attitude man expresses his feeling in thought, speech or action which is a true expression of respect. A sincere feeling of respect needs no words, even the silence can speak of one's respectful attitude.

There are three different expressions of respect. One is that when the position or rank of a person commands one to respect whether one be willing or unwilling, and under the circumstances one cannot help but respect – which is nothing but an outer expression of respect. The second expression of respect is that when a person wishes to please another by his respectful manner; to let another feel how respectful he is and what a good manner he knows. By this expression one has two objects in view: one, to please another, and the other, to please oneself by one's way of pleasing.

The third way is the true feeling of respect which rises from one's heart, and if one tried to express it, one could not express it enough. If one were not able to express it fully it can always be felt, because it is a living spirit of respect.

The mark of people having tradition behind them by birth, nation or race, shows in their respectful tendency. To them disrespect either on their part or on the part of another means absence of beauty. Life has many beautiful things, flowers, jewels, beauty of nature, of form, of line, of colour, but beauty of manner excels all, and all good manner is rooted in a respectful tendency.

It is a great pity that this subject is not regarded as the most important to be considered and to be developed today, when the stream of the whole world is running in the direction of commercialism which values the beauty of matter in gold and silver instead of beauty of character and personality.

III:4 RESPECT – ADAB

The highest expression of love is respect. Respect is not only due to one's superior or elder, but even to a child. Only, one should know to what extent it should be given and in what form it should be expressed. In loving one's mate, one's friend or relation, one's parents, one's teacher, one's priest, the best expression of love that can be shown is a sincere respectful attitude. No love-offering can be more precious than a word, an act of respect.

Very often conflicts between religions have arisen because people who respected their own religion looked with contempt at the religion of another. If one did not respect one's friend's religion, one could at least respect one's friend, and out of respect for one's friend one would regard one's friend's religion respectfully. Very often with all love and devotion and sincerity friendship breaks, only owing to disregard on the part of one or the other of the law of respect.

What is worship? Worship is not dancing before God, worship is an act of respect offered to God, to whom all respect is due. The man who worships God and does not respect man worships in vain; his piety is his mania. A true worshipper of God sees His presence in all forms and thus, in respecting others, he respects God.

It may even develop to such an extent that the true worshipper of God, the Omnipresent, walks gently on the earth, bowing in his heart even to every tree and plant. And it is then that the worshipper forms a communion with the divine Beloved at all times, when he is awake and when he is asleep.

III:5 HONOUR – GHAIRAT

Ghairat, protection or defence of honour, is considered by the wise a great quality, a chivalry which is found as a rule in rare souls. The man regardless of this sense is no better than a domestic animal, a dog or a cat. When their master does not want them he can scold them, drive them away, and they can come again wagging their tail, for there is no sense of pride in them to be hurt; they only feel the discomfort of having to move from a comfortable place. They could also feel their master's displeasure, but there is no soreness about it. In man the sense of honour is developed, with his evolution it develops more. It is not only necessary that man should be humble, but it is also necessary that man must be proud. Pride is the sign of evolution, honour comes out of pride. If there were no pride nor honour, virtue would not exist.

Very often people confuse *ghairat*, this sense of honour, with conceit, sometimes with jealousy. But even the spirit of jealousy which stands to defend one's honour can be no other than a virtue. People call it conceit, but they do not know the meaning of honour: that in the sense of honour there is a divine spark hidden, for it is the perfection of honour which is the Logos, the Ego whom the Sufis call *kibria*.

No doubt when this sense of honour is developed without wisdom, a person could become foolishly sensitive and not only defend his honour but die for nothing, in illusion, just as the story of Othello suggests. For a man whose sense is developed in *ghairat* his honour is not only in his person, but in his friend, in his beloved, in his mother, his sister or wife, in someone whom he respects or whom he loves or with whom he connects himself.

This sense of *ghairat* has its lights and shades in dealing with friends, in the give-and-take, and very often people prefer death to dishonour, and according to a final point of view they have their reason. Those who cause difficulties in life, who are a burden to their relations, a trouble to their friends, an annoyance to their acquaintances, a disgust to strangers, are the ones who are lacking in this sense. This shows that the sense of *ghairat* developed makes one's life more harmonious, for an honourable man minds his own business and keeps himself out of the way, troubles anybody less, even if he has to suffer more trouble for it.

There is a story that four persons were arrested for the same crime and were taken to be judged before the wise king. He saw the first person and said, 'Hang him.' He saw the next person and sentenced him for his whole life. He saw the third person and said, 'He must be banished.' He saw the fourth person and said, 'I could never have expected you to do such a crime.' The first three underwent their punishments, but this last one went home and the next morning was found dead. That one word of the king was worse than death to him.

Ghairat is a sign of noble birth in whatever condition man may be. He may be in rags, yet his spirit of *ghairat* will shine out through all conditions, proving him to be noble.

Humility has its place, pride has its place in life. In the place of pride humility cannot be fitted. Once the Nizam of Hyderabad was walking in the country and a knight happened to see a thorn stuck in his shoe. He rushed before the attendant had seen it and took out that thorn from the king's shoe. The king looked back and said, 'Were there no attendants present? It was for them, not for you, and since you have taken this work you can no longer continue to be my knight. Please retire.' It is not by the humbleness of the surroundings that the king is exalted, it is the sense of honour expressed by his surroundings that makes a king a true ruler.

For a Sufi the sense of honour is not for his personality, for him who does not give his person a greater place than dust, and the central theme of whose life is simplicity, and whose moral is humility. Yet remember that the Sufi breathes the breath of God. So he is conscious of the honour of God. His pride is greater therefore than the pride of every man. It is in the intoxication of this pride that he proves to be God-conscious.

III:6 THE MANNER OF FRIENDLINESS: CONSIDERATION – *KHATIR*

*K*hatir means consideration for someone which is shown in the form of respect, help or service. Very often it wants a sacrifice, it may even need self-denial. However, consideration is the highest quality that can be found in human nature. Consideration of age, of experience, of knowledge, of position, consideration of some good done by a person, also consideration of somebody's feebleness, weakness – all is included in the word *khatir*.

This spirit of consideration, when developed, extends not only to the person for whom one has consideration, but as far as, for that person's sake, having consideration for another who is related or connected with the person in some way or other. When a king is respected and not his ambassador, that means lack of respect to the king.

For a Sufi this quality becomes his moral. The Sufi learns consideration beginning with his *murshid*, but this culminates in consideration for God. When one arrives at that tenderness of feeling, every person in the world one considers. To the Sufi the missing of an opportunity of considering another is a great disappointment, for he does not consider it to be a fault towards a human being, but to God. Verily, he is pious who considers human feeling.

No doubt it needs no end of endurance to consider everybody and to be considerate always. It wants no end of patience. However, by being considerate nothing is lost, if seemingly nothing is gained. The reward of this virtue is always in store. Consideration is the sign of the wise.

III:7 SHARING WITH OTHERS – *TAWAZU'*

Tawazu' in the Sufic terms means something more than hospitality. It is laying before one's friend willingly what one has; in other words, sharing with one's friend all the good one has in life, and with it enjoying life better.

When this tendency to *tawazu'* is developed, things that give one joy and pleasure become more enjoyable by sharing with another. This tendency comes from the aristocracy of the heart. It is generosity and even more than generosity, for the limit of generosity is to see another pleased in his pleasure. But to share one's own pleasure with another is greater than generosity. It is a quality which is foreign to a selfish person, and the one who shows this quality is on the path of saintliness.

Tawazu' does not cost, it is the attitude of mind. If by nature man is not hospitable, the hospitality he gives is of no use. The one who has experienced the joy of this quality feels a greater satisfaction in sharing his only piece of bread than in eating it by himself. Duality in nature keeps all such beautiful qualities of the soul away from man. The thought of unity is productive of all good qualities in man. It is not only in giving or sharing pleasures that one shows hospitality to another; even in word, manner or action one can show this feeling. A desire to welcome someone, to greet, to respect, to offer a seat to someone, to treat with courtesy, to see someone off with respect – all these things show the sign of *tawazu'*.

III:8 MODESTY – HAYA (1)

Haya is the finest feeling in human nature. Modesty is not necessarily meekness or humility or selflessness or pride. Modesty is a beauty in itself and its action is to veil itself. And in that veiling it shows the vanity of its nature, and yet that vanity is a beauty itself.

Modesty is the life of the artist, the theme of the poet and the soul of the musician. In thought, speech, action, in one's manner, in one's movement, modesty stands as the central theme of grace. Without modesty beauty is dead, for modesty is the spirit of beauty. Silence in modesty speaks louder than bold words. The lack of modesty can destroy art, poetry, music, and all that is beautiful.

And if one asks, 'What is modesty?', it is difficult to explain it in words. It is a feeling which rises from a living heart; the heart which is dead has not the taste of it. The modest person compared to the immodest one is like a plant standing by the side of a rock. If the heart of the immodest is like the earth, the heart of the modest one is like the water. Modesty is life itself. A life which is conscious of its beauty, inclined to veil it in all its forms, is modesty.

At the same time modesty is the proof of sincerity and of prudence. The firecracker cries aloud, 'I am the light!', and is finished in a moment. The diamond, shining in its light constantly, never says a word about its light.

III:9 MODESTY – HAYA (2)

Modesty is not necessarily timidity or cowardice. The bravest can be modest, and it is modesty which completes bravery. Modesty is the veil over the face of the great, for the most modest is God Himself, who is not seen by anyone except those intimate with Him. Beauty in all its forms and colours, in all its phases and spheres, doubles itself, enriches itself by modesty. Modesty is not something that is learned. It is in nature, for it is natural.

Modesty does not only cover what is beautiful and amplifies its beauty, but covers all that is void of beauty, in this manner fitting it into all that which is beautiful. A noble heart can even rise to such a degree of modesty that he would plead for another person's fault, trying to make out of it no fault – even knowing that it is a fault.

Yes, a modest person very often will not raise his voice out of dignity or say a thing out of consideration and respect, will not argue and pull his own way when dealing with someone who has no thought of modesty. In this case he may often lose his battle. However, one cannot hope always to ascend and descend at the same time. One should ascend sacrificing all that those who descend will get, or else one must descend, sacrificing all that those who ascend will achieve. Life always demands sacrifices. In every walk of life there is a battle to be fought. And in that case, the one who loves to ascend, he may just as well ascend rather than want to descend.

The Prophet has said, '*Al haya wa'l iman* – Verily, modesty is a great piety.'

III:10 SELFLESSNESS – *INKISAR*

Inkisar in the terms of the Sufis means selflessness. The psychology of human nature is such that man feels inclined to hit every head that is raised. Not only man, but all living creatures have that tendency. To protect themselves from that, many intelligent creatures in the lower creation make holes in the earth to live there, hiding themselves from the beasts and birds of prey. No sooner do they raise their head from their hole than they are caught by their enemy who thirsts for their blood. As humankind is evolved, man does not immediately hit the raised head, but he cannot keep from being agitated at the sight of it.

Understanding this mystery of human nature and studying the secret of the whole life, the Sufi has traced that spirit in its essence belonging to the source of all things. He calls that spirit *kabir* or *kibria*, the ego or egoistic. It has taught the Sufi a moral: that not only man, but even God is displeased by self-assertion. And the manner that he adopts in order not to arouse that agitating spirit he calls *inkisar*, meaning selflessness.

In theory it is a small thing, in practice it is a great art. It is an art which wants a great deal of study of human nature; it requires careful observation and constant practice. This art teaches to take precautions before every activity in speech or in actions so as to cause least disturbance to human feeling. It is the thorough study of human susceptibility and practice of delicate manner which teaches man *inkisar*.

The further he progresses the more his sense becomes keen; therefore he finds more and more mistakes in his own life as he goes forward in this path. This subject is so delicate that one does not only commit a fault by showing pride or conceit, but even in expressing modesty or humility. *Inkisar* wants a great delicacy of sense. One must be able to see the lights and shades produced by every action and word one says or does. And once a person has mastered this art he has mastered the same art which Christ promised to the fishermen saying, 'Come hither, I will make you fishers of men.'

The Sufi gives more importance to this subject than a Yogi, for the way of the Yogi is asceticism, the way of the Sufi is the development of humanity in nature. But according to the prophetic point of view the only way of pleasing God is *inkisar*, which is greater than so-called goodness. A good person, proud of his goodness, turns his pearls into pebbles. A bad person, full of remorse for his faults, may make jewels of his pebbles.

Selflessness is not only pleasing to man but it is pleasing to God. There is not one moment in life when God is unaware of man's word or action; and beyond his word or action God is aware of man's attitude which very often man hides in his words or actions. Nothing is hidden before God who is a perfect Judge and a Forgiver, and upon whose pleasure or displeasure depends the happiness or unhappiness of man's life. Therefore man has not only the task of considering the pleasure or displeasure of his fellow man, but also a duty to God of considering what is pleasant to God and what is unpleasant. To Him to whom all the beauty and riches, glory and greatness belong, man can take no offering which is worth anything, except one thing and that is selflessness.

Life may be pictured as a building in which there are several doors that one has to go through in moving about, and the frame of every door is smaller than one's size. And as man's natural inclination is to rise straight, at every attempt he makes to rise, his head is knocked against the frame of the door; and the only thing that can save him from knocking his head against the doors is to bend. It is this logical lesson which the wise turn into good manner.

Verily, all that leads to happiness is good.

PART SIX

◆

EVERYDAY LIFE
Taqwa Taharat

Gatha I

It is a very necessary thing in the life of an adept to make his mind and body adaptable to the spiritual life. In other words, it is necessary for a man to become his natural self before he begins his journey in a spiritual path. It is this naturalness which is called by the orthodox purity. Pure water or pure milk means water or milk in its own essence; when another element is mixed with it the object then loses its purity. To become spiritual means to purify one's spirit from the foreign elements which take away the natural feeling of the spirit.

Concentration, contemplation, meditation, all these help to make the spirit its natural self again, but the vehicles that the spirit uses to experience life must help the spirit to become natural. These vehicles are the mind and the body. However great the musician, if the instrument is not in tune he cannot do anything with it. It is not right to say that only the spirit matters and the body does not count. Therefore it is necessary that first the mind and body be made fit vehicles for the spirit to use.

The difference between a pious person and a spiritual person is this, that the pious person makes the mind and body ready for his own spirit to use and the spiritual person, after making the mind and body ready, gives them to God. Piety is the first step and spirituality the next. There is no exaggeration in the saying that cleanliness is next to godliness. The body must be considered as the temple of God, and this sacred house of God must be made pure in every way. Then the light of God is reflected in it.

Beasts and birds all have a tendency to be clean and pure, and on the part of man it is necessary to develop this tendency. It helps not only on the spiritual path but also in the development of mind. To the artist in his art, to the scientist in his science, in all aspects of life it gives happiness. When man neglects it, it does not mean that he does not like it; it is only out of negligence that he overlooks things which are of the first importance. One's body is of all things in the world the closest to oneself, and its influence has a great effect and an immediate effect upon one's mind and soul. A great many illnesses are caused by lack of consideration of the necessary cleanliness of the body, which is a science and an art in itself.

On the soul and mind one's own body makes the first impression; all other things come afterwards. Yes, there are souls who have arrived at such a plane of spirituality that the condition of the body does not matter to them, but they are not to be followed as examples. It is the normal path which is safe and is for all.

The question: 'Would this not give one too much the thought of self?' can be answered: 'The thought of oneself exists when the light of God is absent. In the presence of every beautiful thing man forgets himself.'

I:2 THE INSTRUMENT OF OUR BODY

The body is an instrument for experiencing life. Both the worlds, that within and that without, are reflected in this instrument. Therefore purity of the body is the first essential thing and the most essential in the path of spiritual attainment. Every civilization has a peculiar method of cleanliness, but the mystic is not satisfied with the customary manner.

Mystics have two views: one view is that external cleanliness matters nothing to them, and the other that it is most important. As the work of an astronomer depends upon a telescope, and as it is necessary for him to keep the telescope as clean as possible, so it is necessary in the life of the mystic to keep the body in a fit condition.

All the passages in the body are connected with the centres which are most important in spiritual development, and it is upon the cleanliness and purity of these passages that spiritual development depends. Besides these nine passages it is necessary to keep the skin in a proper condition for spiritual purposes. It is from the mystical conception that humanity first learned the idea of clothes. There have been times when certain races painted their skin, and by certain Yogis the body was covered with ashes. In ancient times the body was covered with the bark of trees. But behind all this there was always an inclination to keep the skin in a proper condition.

It is upon the cleanliness of the body that sensitiveness depends. Therefore people who have no regard to the cleanliness of the body are less sensitive than those who have regard to it.

Besides the cleanliness of the outer part of the body it is equally important, perhaps more important, to consider the cleanliness of the inner part of the body. Mystics therefore take precaution about what they eat and drink and have methods of cleansing the inner part of the body also. No mystic in the East guides a pupil who has not first prepared his body for the spiritual purpose.

Cleanliness of the body, besides its importance for spiritual and moral development, also prevents serious disease.

I:3 THE BREATH

It is necessary that the breath should flow freely through the lungs, tubes and veins of the body, and things that one eats and drinks often block the channels through which the breath passes, invigorating and vivifying every particle of the body. All skin diseases are caused by want of breath in the skin. The mystic feels not only the vibrations of music but even the vibrations of another person's breath. The skin of the mystic in time becomes sensitive and feels even the vibrations of the breath of another. Music, so to speak, touches every particle of his being.

Breathing exercises will not give proper results if the channels of the breath are not cleared. The spine, the lungs, the tubes and veins of the body, the intestines, should be kept clear. When the channels of the breath are blocked, man feels heavy, depressed, lazy, drowsy and confused, the expression becomes dull and the voice harsh. Then the movements become void of grace and beauty; when sitting or standing or walking or moving, in every action one expresses a weakness, a lack of spirit.

Feebleness is different from lack of spirit. A person may be strong bodily but may lack spirit, and the teaching of Christ is that it is the spirit that quickeneth, the flesh profiteth nothing.

I:4 OUTER AND INNER ABLUTIONS

The vehicle which is made of earth can be cleansed with water and by air. Therefore besides external ablutions inner ablutions are necessary to make the body a proper vehicle for the working of the spirit. In many different religions different ways of ablution are taught. They are not only for the cleanliness of the body, but are also helpful in making the body a fitting instrument for the spirit to experience life.

The external organs of the body are used for external activities, but the inner ones are the instruments of the mind. The factors which are closer to the mind, and which are more important for man than the physical organs, are the centres which are located in the body. And the cleaner the channels of the breath are, the more active do the centres become. The breath is to these centres as the air is to the plants. Besides inner ablutions, the breathing practice itself cleanses the channels of the body.

1:5 INNER ABLUTIONS

Besides making ablutions it is necessary that the channels of the breath be kept clean, and for this consideration is necessary about what one eats and drinks. Food that is raw and indigestible and stale food, stale and decayed vegetables, rotten fruits, meat that has been preserved for a long time and all such things, not only block the channels of the breath, but their influence on the breath makes it impure. Naturally when a person cannot digest food or when his lungs are not open and free, the breath is not pure.

The Sufi takes great care in his life as to what he should eat and what he should drink. Alcoholic drinks and drinks made from decayed fruits naturally make the breath impure. Smoking tobacco has a bad effect on the breath. Those who observe the mystical rules carefully even refrain from all flesh food, even from eggs. White meat is preferable to red meat, for red meat has particles which block the channels of the breath.

This was the reason why the eating of pork was prohibited by the prophets of Beni Israel. No doubt to the pure all things are pure, but in order to become pure it is necessary to observe the rules of purity.

One must not judge of another person's spiritual evolution by seeing what he eats and drinks, because this has nothing to do with a man's evolution. Shiva, the great Lord of the Yogis, had fish for his food, and wine was given in the church of Christ as a sacrament. Therefore no one has the power to estimate his fellow men from what they eat or drink, but everyone who wishes to tread the spiritual path may observe the mystical law, which certainly enables one to progress speedily. It must be remembered that it is the spiritual ideal which is the first thing to be held fast. What to eat and drink and what not to eat and drink is a secondary thing. Any dispute about this proves to be unnecessary.

I:6 VEGETARIAN DIET

The question of vegetarian diet is often discussed among seekers after philosophical truth. Some people give no importance to what they eat or drink, and there are some who give more importance to it than necessary.

There are two things which speak against flesh-eating. One thing is that meat as a substance hinders spiritual progress, and the other is that the unkindness towards animals is a breach of moral law. Considering the first question, it is no doubt true that meat causes two kinds of harm to an adept. One is that it produces in man to a certain extent the animal nature; also it has an influence on the character of man. The nature of the animal he eats certainly has an influence upon a man's character. It was therefore that the prophets of Beni Israel forbade their followers to eat the flesh of certain kinds of animals and birds. Mystically speaking, it clogs the channels of the breath and the important psychical centres which work in man as the instruments of wireless telegraphy.

Morally there is no doubt that it has a hardening effect upon the heart of man which is meant to sympathize, not only with his fellow man but with every living creature. There is no doubt that if all the people in the world became vegetarians there would be no more wars. A person who refrained from killing the lower creatures would surely not be inclined to kill his fellow man.

Of course there is another side to the question: life exists in all aspects of the creation, even in plants; and if one does not see the harm done to the plants it is because they cannot express it. Looking from this point of view one can observe that life lives on life. At the same time the creation is a process by which the lower form of life evolves to a higher form, and the life used in this process of evolution is not really lost. On the contrary, it is raised to a higher consciousness. It would not be an exaggeration to say that the animal which is used as the food of man has been transformed from the animal kingdom to the human, which is really a natural process of evolution, the human kingdom being the goal of the lower creation. However this point of view does not help man morally or physically in his individual evolution. He has not gained by eating flesh; on the contrary, he has allowed himself to evolve more slowly than he could otherwise have evolved.

The impression on the consciousness of man of having done harm to another creature which can feel pain as he himself can is not a good one. It blunts the fine, tender and sympathetic feeling towards all living beings. At the same time not every person who eats meat is capable of considering the subject philosophically, and therefore of giving an answer to his conscience or to another one as an explanation of having caused harm to a living creature for his enjoyment.

For many thousands of years the human race has lived on flesh food, especially in the cold countries, and the bodies made with that essence for thousands of years are so dependent upon flesh food that they cannot abstain from it without causing some harm to their health. Man feeds on things of which he is made, and it is not in every case easy for a man to give up flesh food, even if he realized its disadvantages. There are countries where there are deserts – no trees to be found for miles – and the inhabitants could not live if they did not live on flesh food.

For the evolution of humanity in general uniformity is necessary. If some ate flesh and others lived on vegetables, it would be as if carnivorous and herbivorous animals were living in the same forest. Certainly, people living different lives cannot live together harmoniously and the strong must in every case have the upper hand. Tenderness of heart will not answer the same purpose as strength and power. Therefore it is a question how vegetarian diet can be introduced in the world.

There is another side to this question. If animals were left alone they would multiply and the herbivorous would become a prey to the carnivorous animals. The tigers and lions and bears and wolves would increase and would be in search of man. So the human kingdom would diminish and the animal's increase.

For those who strive in the spiritual path it is most essential to be thoughtful and considerate and to be kind to the whole creation; and if they can manage to live a vegetarian life it is no doubt very helpful to them. It is not right however for a vegetarian to look at the flesh-eater with contempt and regard his own harmless attitude with pride. There are many vegetarians who will prove selfish and unkind to their fellow man, whereas there are many non-vegetarians who will prove to be otherwise.

Verily, charity of heart must begin at home and then expand, so that it may reach the very lowest of the creation.

1:7 THE FIVE ELEMENTS OF THE BODY

The body is made of five elements according to the mystical view: earth, water, fire, air and ether. Yet these terms must not be compared with the scientific terms; these are mystical conceptions and they should be understood in a mystical sense. These five elements form the sustenance of the body, at the same time these elements purify the body.

For instance, no ablution with water only is sufficient, earth is required also. In the East the Brahmins used pure earth, some used ashes. In the East gram flour is still used in the place of soap. The scientist can never deny the fact that there is no better disinfectant than earth itself. The use of water for every kind of ablution has been taught by all religions in some form or other. That shows that it is not only of use for cleanliness, but it helps in spiritual development. The scientist today admits that there is no better tonic than pure water. This has always been held to be so by the mystic who called the rivers sacred rivers and gave water in healing.

As the use of earth and water cleanses and purifies the body externally, so it has a purifying influence on the internal part of the body. By eating wholesome food and drinking pure water not only does one receive nourishment, but this cleanses and purifies every particle of the body. It is therefore that an adept must avoid eating and drinking anything unwholesome. This does not mean an absolute restriction to certain food and drink, but just that care in eating and drinking is necessary.

Once a person has advanced in spirituality nothing matters to him, neither what he eats and drinks, for he lives in the spirit the most part of his life. For him the body is a coat and he does not care if it is full of holes or if it is patched, but for a person who has yet to develop spiritually and who follows a process, consideration is necessary. It is most necessary that the body should be kept pure outwardly and inwardly, that it may become a suitable vehicle for the manifestation of the spirit.

1:8 PURIFICATION

Man's health and inspiration both depend upon purity of breath, and to preserve this purity the nostrils and all the tubes of the breath must be kept clear. They can be kept clear by proper breathing and by proper ablutions. If one cleanses the nostrils twice or oftener during twenty-four hours it is not too much, for a Muslim is taught to make this ablution five times – before each prayer. The cleansing not only of the nostrils but also of the ears is necessary, for part of the breath works through the ears and if the ears are not protected and cleansed, sometimes one hears a sound which often is that of the breath which does not find its way smoothly through the regions of the ear.

The throat and palate are also important factors for the flow of the breath. The palate and throat are kept clean by the adept by gargling. The adept drinks water at fixed hours for the purpose of cleansing the veins and tubes in the chest, so that the breath may find pure channels for its passage.

An adept drinks water before going to bed and after rising from sleep. It is necessary that these laws of ablutions should be practised by the student of thought first, in order that others may follow. Hygienic consideration is the first principle which is necessary for the health and happiness of the generality.

I:9 SOBRIETY

Sobriety is most necessary in the path of spiritual evolution, especially in the first stage when the body must be made pure for spiritual revelation. Everything intoxicating deadens the nerves more or less, and the centres which are the factors for spiritual realization become dead. Although at times they may seem more active, too abnormal an activity is always exhausting. The centres which show sensitiveness during the time of intoxication, after its influence become weary and lifeless. Fakirs or Yogis who take intoxicants in order to excite the centres become dependent for their spiritual experience on material objects. In the end they find their seeming advancement fatal.

Heavy smoking may block not only the channels of the breath but even the centres, and thereby intuition is confused. No doubt smoking gives a momentary comfort because it brings a kind of repose to the smoker, but it is only a passing comfort. Smoking not only has an effect upon the throat or lungs, but by it the two important centres, the heart and brain, upon which the whole spiritual progress depends, will become blocked.

The principal thing in spiritual attainment is to be self-sufficient, and the first step to self-sufficiency is to make one's body independent of all such things upon which its comfort and enjoyment depend. The sages of all times and the mystics of every cult have observed the value of continence and fasting for the very reason that the body, upon which the experience of the whole life depends, must first be made fit by purity.

I:10 FASTING

The reason why fasting is observed by those who live in retreat is to let the breath pass through every vein and tube of the body, which can be made possible only when there is no outer substance such as food or even drink in the body to block the channels.

When breath has touched every particle of the body, the body naturally becomes more sensitive and the pores of the skin open, making the centres transparent so as to feel outwardly and inwardly all that is to be felt. This can be understood by seeing the difference between the intelligence and the intuitive faculty of a fine person and of a dense person.

Continence also helps, not only to keep the channels clear, but it conserves all the energy in every particle of the body and especially in the centres where it is most needed. Another thing is that continence keeps every outer element away. By this the adept is better able to keep his body and centres free from every foreign element, becoming at the same time a reservoir of energy, which expresses itself as radiance and magnetism.

Professed celibacy is an assumption of chastity which must sooner or later break by nature, together with man's profession of the same. The true celibacy therefore can be practised, without profession and without outward appearance or attributing it to any religious rank, only for a certain time and for a certain purpose.

GATHA II

The purity of the body is more desirable than bodily strength. Purity of body consists of three things: pure blood, sound muscles, and skin in proper condition. One might ask, 'How can one be strong without a pure body?' But I should say one can be. There are many strong and vigorous looking people with something wrong in their flesh, blood or skin. Health from a spiritual point of view does not mean a strong muscular body; health means a body sound in all its aspects.

The standard of normal health is different for a mystic from what a scientist today thinks. To the scientist the emotional side of man is not of interest; if the body is perfect according to his idea, he thinks man is healthy. But from a mystical point of view, if bodily man is strong but his emotional nature is buried beneath, he is not healthy, there is something wrong with him. Therefore a physician will find many not in proper health, but still more a mystic will find not in proper health. The person who is healthy to a physician is not necessarily healthy before a mystic, but good health from the point of view of a mystic is good health from the point of view of a physician.

The illness that humanity has today is lack of that emotional nature which is productive of sentiment. In the East, though times are changed, still there is a recognition of that health-iness which is recognized by a mystic as good health. They name these qualities by beautiful names as considerate, thoughtful, mild, gentle, sympathy, harmonious, selfless. When these things lack in a person the mystic considers it lack of health. Even an animal can be materially strong. If man were strong he would be no better than an animal. It is purity which is necessary – in the body first, in the mind afterwards – which produces in a person a state of health which alone can be truly called good health.

II:2 PURIFICATION

The nature of the memory is to hold an impression, agreeable or disagreeable. And therefore a person holds a thought in mind whether it is beneficial to him or not, without knowing the result which will come from it. It is like a child who holds a rattle in his hand and hits his head with the rattle and cries with the pain, and yet does not throw the rattle away. There are many who keep in their mind a thought of illness or a thought of unkindness done to them by someone and suffer from it, yet not knowing what it is that makes them suffer so, nor understanding the reason of their suffering. They go on suffering and yet hold on in memory the very source of suffering.

Memory must be one's obedient servant; when it is master then life becomes difficult. A person who cannot throw away from his memory what he does not desire to keep in mind is like a person who has a safe – but the key of that safe he has lost. He can put in money, but he cannot take it out. All faculties in man become invaluable when a person is able to use them at will, but when the faculties use the person, then he is no longer master of himself.

Concentration is taught by the mystics in order to exercise the will, making it capable of making use of all faculties. A person with will-power can remember what he wishes to remember and can forget what he wishes to forget. All things that deprive one of one's freedom in life are undesirable. The mind must be free from all bad impressions of life which take away the rest and peace of life. By concentration one is able to hold a certain thought one desires and to keep away all other thoughts. And when one is able to keep away all the thoughts one does not wish to think about, it becomes easy to throw away the impressions of years, if one wishes to forget them. Bad impressions, however old and intimate, are like rubbish accumulated which should be removed in order to make the house clean.

The human heart is the home of the soul, and upon this home the comfort and peace of the soul depends.

II:3 PURITY OF MIND (1)

Purity of mind requires the destroying of all bad impressions which are already collected there or which the mind receives at the instant. One can destroy those impressions by different ways, and the way is adopted according to the impression one has to destroy. Some impressions want to be washed off from the mind. Some require to be erased from the surface of the mind. Some want to be shaken off like dust from the clothes. Some require burning like the wood in the fire, which after its test through fire turns into ashes, and some impressions must be drowned so that they will never come up again. Bury certain impressions like a corpse, find every way of annihilation which is suited for that particular impression, so that your mind may be clear.

The mind is not only a means of thinking or reasoning, but it is the king of one's being, and upon the condition of mind one's health, happiness and peace of life depend.

Now the question is what to destroy and what to keep in mind. Collect and keep all that is beautiful and destroy all that is void of beauty. Collect and keep all that is agreeable and destroy all that has a disagreeable effect upon you. Collect and keep all that is harmonious and destroy all that creates inharmony in yourself. Collect and keep all that is restful and destroy all that disturbs the peace of your life. As some dust gets into the works of a clock and stops it from going, so the effects produced by all impressions which are void of beauty and harmony and which disturb your peace keep you from progress.

The mind cannot act properly when it is hindered by impressions which have a paralysing effect upon it. Life is progress and stopping from progress is death. Failure does not matter in life for a progressive person. Even a thousand failures do not matter; he has before his view success, and success is his even after a thousand failures. The greatest pity in life is the standstill when life does not matter further. A sensible person prefers death to such a life. It is as a paralysis of the soul, of the spirit, and is always caused by holding bad impressions in mind.

No soul is deprived of happiness in reality. The soul's very being is happiness. Man brings unhappiness upon himself by holding in his hands the clouds of bad impressions which fall as a shadow upon his soul. Once a person is able to clear from his mind, by whatever process, the undesirable impressions, a new power begins to spring from his heart, opening a way before him to accomplish all he wishes, attracting to him all he requires, clearing his path of all obstacles, and making his atmosphere clear for him to live and move and to accomplish all he wishes to accomplish.

II:4 PURITY OF MIND (2)

It is upon the purity of the mind that the health, both of body and of mind, chiefly depends. The process of purifying the mind does not differ very much from the process of cleaning or washing any object. Water poured upon any object washes it, and if there is a spot which cannot be washed away by the water, some substance which can take away that spot is applied to wash it thoroughly. The water which washes the heart is the continual running of the love-stream. When that stream is stopped, when its way is blocked by some object which closes the heart and when the love-stream is no longer running, then the mind cannot keep pure. As water is the cleansing and purifying substance in the physical world, so love is on the higher plane.

Sometimes when it is difficult for love to take away some impressions that are disagreeable, which block the way of the love-stream, they may be washed away by some element that can destroy them. The whole life is a chemical process and knowledge of its chemistry helps man to make life happy. An unhappy person, being unhappy himself, cannot make others happy. It is a wealthy person who can help the one who is hard up, not a poor person, however much desire he may have to help. It is the same with happiness which is a great wealth, and a happy person can take away the unhappiness of another, for he has enough for himself and more besides for the others.

Earthly pleasures are the shadows of happiness because of their transitoriness. True happiness is in love, which is the stream that springs from one's soul, and he who will allow this stream to run continually in all conditions of life, in all situations, however difficult, will have a happiness which truly belongs to him, whose source is not without but within. If there is a constant outpouring of love one becomes a divine fountain, for from the depth of the fountain the stream rises and on its return it pours upon the fountain, bathing it continually. It is a divine bath, the true bath in the Ganges, the sacred river. When once one has the key of this fountain, one is always purified, every moment of one's life, nothing can stay in the mind causing unhappiness. Happiness alone is natural and it is attained by knowing and by living naturally. (*See* Questions and Answers, p 298.)

II:5 PURIFICATION OF THE MIND

The principal thing to attain happiness is to purify one's mind from all things that disturb it and create inharmony. There are not only bad impressions which disturb the tranquillity of mind, but there are many feelings of resentment and resistance against things which do not agree with one's own idea which disturb one's mind.

The person who has some business to carry out, some profession to attend to, requires a tranquil mind, but especially the one who journeys on the spiritual path needs tranquillity of mind most. Prayers, concentrations, meditations have no effect if the mind is not purified from all disturbances. Therefore for an adept no cost and no sacrifice is great enough to keep harmony within himself.

A Sufi tries to keep harmony in his surroundings, the harmony which demands many sacrifices. It makes one endure what one is not willing to endure; it makes one overlook what one is not inclined to overlook; it makes one tolerate what one is not accustomed to tolerate; and it makes one forgive and forget what one would never have forgotten if it were not for the sake of harmony. But at whatever cost harmony is attained, it is a good bargain, for harmony is the secret of happiness, and in absence of this a person living in palaces and rolling in gold can be most unhappy.

Harmony is brought about by attuning oneself to all beings, to all things, to all conditions, to all situations. And he who cannot tune himself – he tries to tune others, and while going to tune others he breaks the string. It is like a person who has a violin in his hands trying to tune the cello. If he wishes to be in tune with the cellist, he must tune his violin to the cellist's pitch. Every soul, as its nature, seeks constantly for harmony, but rarely there is to be found a soul who really knows how to create it. If one says, 'This noise which goes on always next to my ears makes me mad', he cannot stop the noise. He must know how to close himself from that noise; if he cannot, to accustom himself to that noise so as to bear it and eventually to rise above it, that it may no more create inharmony.

Very often at the sight of inharmony one tries to escape it. But inharmony has such a wonderful magic that if one avoids it in the East, one meets it in the West; it never leaves a person. Whom it loves it follows, and the best way to meet with inharmony is to try and harmonize with it. Knowing that the source and goal of all things is the perfection of harmony and bearing that idea in mind, if one meets with inharmony – which has no existence in reality, which is like a shadow – it must certainly disappear as the shadow disappears at the sight of the sun.

It is very difficult to evolve oneself and at the same time to keep in tune with the unevolved ones through life. It is like being drawn from above and at the same time pulled from below. And if there is anything that can save man from being torn to pieces in life – there is only one way and that is to resound, to respond to all that is asked of man. It is this principle which is

221

taught by Christ in the Sermon on the Mount. The Sermon on
the Mount may seem to teach a willing surrender to all, but
that is not the way to look at it. The real lesson that one can
learn from it is to try and harmonize with all instead of with one
note. Every note is fixed in its place, so is every man fixed in his
ideas and ways. But the one who treads the spiritual path – he
is all notes and he is no note in particular. Therefore he may
rightfully be called the key note, the note which makes a
consonant chord with every note that is played with it.

There is no beauty where there is no harmony; harmony is
the fruit of love. Therefore by attaining harmony in life one
reaches the perfection of all three: love, harmony and beauty.

II:6 THE POWER OF MIND

Anything that weighs upon the mind, such as a worry, a
fear or a feeling of remorse, keeps the mind below the
pitch at which it is meant to be. When the mind is weighed
down by anything, however learned a man may be, however
capable and efficient, he can work very little. Learning does
not help the mind which is not in its right place. So it is seen
to be with many learned people: most capable and efficient,
and yet incapable of accomplishing anything important in life.
This is mostly found in life, and rare is the case where it is
not so.

All the affairs of life are accomplished by the power of mind.
External conditions are nothing but mechanisms with which
the mind works as an engineer, producing from life all that is
desired. Therefore whatever be the condition in life, the principal
thing is to shake off all things that weigh upon the mind, thus
making the mind free to fulfil its task through life.

Often people find themselves helpless before a difficult
situation, but very few stop to think that it is not only
the situation that is difficult, but there is some difficulty in
one's own mind. One hardly gives a thought to this question,

for every man's eyes are fixed upon the difficulty of the situation alone. It is like seeing a wall standing before one and yet not realizing if one has a hammer in one's hand. If one realized the power that the mind has, not only the wall but even mountains, if they were standing before one, could be removed. Many seek for a power from without, ignorant of the fact that all power is hidden within. When, by freeing his own mind from all that weighs it down, man realizes the power he inherits from the source of all beings, he will realize in himself an enormous power. The mastermind is the master of life.

II:7 EVERY MIND HAS ITS OWN STANDARD OF GOOD AND BAD

Every mind has its particular standard of good and bad and of right and wrong. This standard is made of what one has experienced through life, by what one has seen or heard. It also depends upon one's belief in a certain religion, one's birth in a certain nation and origin from a certain race. But what can really be called good or bad, or right or wrong, is what comforts the mind and what causes it discomfort. It is not true, although it appears to be, that it is discomfort that causes wrong-doing. In reality it is wrong-doing which causes discomfort, and it is right-doing which gives comfort. And for the very reason that a certain thing gives comfort it is right, and what causes discomfort is wrong.

Very few in the world look at it in this way. If one who does well all his life is unhappy, I would rather he did not do well. His well-doing is neither well for him nor for another. The standard of right or wrong and good or bad, made rigidly on the action, is the artificial standard which seems outwardly a moral law, but causes degeneration in the end. The standard of action must be made natural, not artificial. The curse of the present day is the artificiality of life today. Man must be taught to consult his own spirit, and from his own feeling to find out and make a distinction between right and wrong and good and bad. When this natural principle is adopted by humanity, the greater part of the world misery will come to an end.

This wrong and artificial standard is taught today to children at home and to young people at school. They begin to learn that that is wrong which they have heard others call wrong, that that is right of which they have read in a book that it is right. Something is good because their parents have said it is good, something is bad because their friends have told them so. An artificial standard made in this way buries the spirit which alone has the right to discern between right and wrong, and good and bad. On that day when people will arrive at the freedom of making their own standard by their own feelings, a better condition will come.

For those searching after truth, journeying through the spiritual path, this is the first thing to learn: to find out for themselves under all conditions in life what is good and what is bad, what is right and what is wrong – not from what they are taught or told, but from their own feeling which can be perceived by a delicate sense of realizing through life what really gives comfort and what causes discomfort. Life is not made to be good and unhappy. Life is made to be happy, and therefore one has to be good – no happiness to be sacrificed to goodness, but that goodness must be considered the real goodness which in its result is happiness.

II:8 THE IMPRESSION OF ILLNESS AND WEAKNESS ON THE MIND

The action of every illness or weakness is more manifest in its impression on the mind. There are many people who after an illness that has lasted some time become so much impressed by it that even after their cure the impression remains. Therefore to those who suffer for many years from an illness, their illness becomes natural, becomes a part of themselves, and the obstacle to their cure is not the illness but the impression engraved on their mind.

So it is with weakness or a defect of any sort. Very often a person confesses, 'This is my defect, but I cannot help it.' If there is any weakness or defect, it is merely in the impression. When a person says, 'There are moments when I lose my temper', or when a person says, 'I would like to tolerate, but I cannot stand that person', his weakness in this is nowhere but in the impression he has in his mind. Therefore the best cure for every illness and weakness is denial of the same. Affirmation deepens the impression and contemplation of it makes it worse.

There is no harm in denying one's illness or weakness, for that is not telling a lie, as it does not exist in reality, it is merely a shadow. Truthful confession of something which is unreal is worse than a lie. One must first deny that to oneself, and then to others.

The Sufi whose ideal through life is the realization of God and His perfection, after realizing his ideal cannot say, 'I cannot "tolerate" – or "endure" – or "stand" anybody' and he cannot say that he cannot think, act or feel as he thinks right. The idea of the Sufi is always to suggest to oneself that which one wishes to be, that which one would like to be. And when he finds he failed to think, speak or act as he wished to, he must think the condition of the process is to fall several times before one gets one's balance, instead of thinking, 'It is my weakness, I cannot do otherwise.'

Those who walk toward the perfection of power and wisdom take every step forward with a new hope and new courage, and weakness to them is a story of the past, it does not exist any more. They do not recognize such a thing as existing, they cannot accept themselves being what they do not wish to be. They picture themselves as their ideal, what they would like to be. Some time or other in their lives, if not sooner, later, they certainly succeed in moulding their life to their ideal.

II:9 KEEPING THE MIND IN A PURE CONDITION

All that exists lives on its own element, springs from its own element, and returns to its own element. So earth to earth, water to water, fire to fire and air to air. Purification means to make a certain object itself: nothing added, nothing foreign attached to it which does not belong to it. These two rules make one understand the process by which the mind could be nourished and purified.

The mind is nourished by thoughts and impressions that are harmonious and productive of beauty and which result in satisfaction; for harmony is the nature of the soul, beauty is its source and goal, and by harmony and beauty the mind is nourished, as it is made of harmony and beauty. And the same elements are needed to purify the mind of all undesirable thoughts and impressions: harmony as water and beauty as soap, purifying the mind of all thoughts which are void of harmony and beauty.

The first thing in purifying the mind is to be able to discern the foreign element there. As all that is foreign to the body does not agree with the body, making it ill, so all that is foreign to the mind disturbs the peace of the mind, and it is that which proves that it does not belong to the mind. Such things are worry, anxiety, fear, sorrow, or any sort of disturbance that takes away the tranquillity of the mind, preventing it from experiencing that joy and peace for which it longs and in which alone is its satisfaction.

There are many who do not know the importance of keeping the mind in a pure and harmonious condition, and the few who know it find it difficult to bring about better conditions in practical life. In the first place it is difficult to accomplish outward duties, to answer the demands of life, and yet to keep the mind in perfect tranquillity. It needs the knowledge of purifying the mind of all external influences. And the way one can manage it can be said in a few words: to throw away inharmony by the power of harmony and to wash away all that lacks beauty by preserving the great power of beauty within oneself.

II:10 KEEPING THE MIND FREE
FROM ALL UNDESIRABLE IMPRESSIONS

The best way of keeping the mind free from all undesirable impressions is not to partake of them at the moment when they fall upon the mind. For instance, if someone is disagreeable, instantly his influence produces the same thing in another person with whom he is disagreeable. The best way to avoid it would be to stand on one's guard that one may not catch his infectious disagreeableness. All such things as pride, prejudice, jealousy, intolerance, coldness, have a great influence upon a person. When speaking, working or walking with someone, one can easily partake of one's companion's disagreeable impulses, because as a rule a person thinks there is justification for giving it back: a word for a word, a frown for a frown. A person feels satisfied in boasting, 'He said two words to me, but I gave him back the same in four words.' He feels very glad for the moment, thinking 'I have given back what I have received', but he does not know that, if he had not given it back, the same that the other person had thrown upon him would have returned to that person a thousandfold.

The psychological point of view therefore differs from the ordinary point of view, for in the psychological point of view there is a science; it teaches one not to take in one's mind what is disagreeable, inharmonious. By understanding this one can maintain the purity of mind; and it requires fortifying oneself with will-power, making the heart as a stone wall, for all that is thrown at it not to pierce through, but to fall down.

The psychological effect of every impression is such that each impression has a tendency to be held by the mind. All we see during the day has, consciously or unconsciously, an influence upon our life. All good or bad things, or things with beauty or ugliness, they remain with us and flourish in our minds. If it was an impression of beauty – that would flourish; if it was an impression of ugliness – that would flourish. This is the principal reason why dreams have effect upon our life. It is the impression that the dream has made upon us that works out its destiny in the waking state. Therefore if, by being on one's guard, instead of resisting evil one would only slide over it, it would run away by its own force.

However good a person, if he easily partakes of impressions he cannot be trustworthy. The one who has no will-power cannot even trust himself. There is no will-power in fighting with another; one shows will-power in fighting with self. The one who is strong enough to keep away from his mind all undesirable impressions, will in time radiate harmony and will create the atmosphere of peace. Thus, making himself happy, he will bring happiness to others.

Gatha III

The real purity is experienced not by means of the outer ablutions nor by keeping away evil thoughts, but by keeping the heart pure from feelings which disturb the rhythm of the mind, and thus upset the whole spirit. Feelings have a greater power than thoughts. If evil thoughts are monsters, evil feelings are as demons. Such feelings as the desire of robbing someone of his rights or his belongings have a very disturbing effect upon the spirit. Before such a feeling is put into action the effect is more; while it is being put into action it is less; but afterwards the effect is most. Life rightly and honestly lived has inner struggles, but by adding to it feelings that disturb life's tranquillity one only adds to one's troubles in life, which then become endless.

Purity of heart must not be considered a virtue but a necessity; a necessity not only to be considered for the good of others, but for one's own life. The feelings which produce that weakness in the heart take away strength from the eyelids; the glance drops instead of the eyes firmly gazing straight. Nothing in the world, however valuable or rare, can make up for this loss.

The main thing that must be remembered is that the soul is pure and the lack of purity it cannot bear without feeling restless. The spirit has a tune and a rhythm. When it is out of tune and out of rhythm, if the riches of the whole world be given to it, it is worth nothing. It is purity and peace which is the soul's constant seeking.

III:2 KEEPING THE HEART PURE

As the rust is natural to the iron and as the milk turns sour, so is the heart that becomes rusted, and its feeling which by nature is as pure as milk turns sour. Then nothing in the world is tasteful to that person, and life with all its beauty becomes worthless. It is this condition which must be avoided. An adept must keep his mind pure from rust.

The rust comes from allowing the heart to bear malice and spite against anyone, by having hatred and prejudice against anyone, by wanting to take revenge, by looking down upon another with contempt and by the feeling of jealousy, rivalry or envy. The heart wants a constant care to keep it from getting rusted, for the nature of this life of illusion is such that some little unimportant things, which are not of the least value, coming from the outer life, the heart may be affected by; and the rust may be produced, as the mere touch of water can produce rust upon the iron. Once the feeling has become soured it is as difficult, if not impossible, to turn it sweet again as to make the sour milk sweet.

A soul has brought from heaven its love for sweetness. It may after coming on earth develop a taste for salt, sour or bitter, but its innate longing is always for the sweet. And what its life needs most is not sugar, which is required in some degree for physical health, but the sweetness which is the original property of his heart and which is needed most for his true happiness and real well-being.

III:3 THE RADIANCE OF THE FACE

As the cleansing of a metal object produces a shine in it, so is the cleansing of the heart, especially from any feeling that produces humiliation. When a person thinks, 'I have been wrong by acting in a certain way, by saying a certain thing or by having thought something which should not have crossed my mind', he loses, so to speak, a radiance which even beams out through his countenance and which is called in Persian *ab-e-ru*, meaning the radiance of the face.

Every person shows from his expression his condition of heart. Therefore the innocence of the expression is the sign of the purity of heart. Man may be clever, learned, qualified, most able, he may be strong physically or even mentally, he may be wealthy, of high rank, but none of these outside things help him to retain that glow of the countenance which depends only upon purity of heart.

Many know and some say that the eyes can tell everything that is in the heart of man, but fewer there are who know the cause behind it. The eyes are like the thermometer of the centre in the head which is focused to the centre of the heart. Every impression that the heart bears, beautiful or ugly, is mirrored upon the centre of the head, and so it is reflected accordingly in man's visage; specially in his eyes which express the most.

There are many clever people, but so few there are who may be called wise. The clever ones plot and plan one against the other and exchange evil thoughts between themselves. So those deceitful and treacherous, intoxicated by their interest in life, cover their eyes with the cover of selfishness, thus keeping the heart from showing out its light which alone illuminates the path of every achievement in life.

It might seem hard work to empty one's heart of all bad impressions and ill feelings, of all bitterness and evil thoughts, and yet it is not nearly so hard as the task of earning one's daily bread. The work in one's everyday life takes most part of the day, the emptying the heart of all undesirable things takes but a few moments' silence. It is the desire of erasing from the heart every undesirable impression that enables one in time to purify one's heart.

III:4 INNOCENCE

Innocence is the real purity according to the mystic, for innocence is the sign of purity of heart. The intuitive faculties play a greater part in the life of the innocent. People call them simple ones. Nevertheless innocence proves often more beneficial in life than worldly cleverness. The innocent are oftener blessed by providence than those worldly wise always trying to get the best of everyone and to seize every opportunity that may seem to be advantageous in any way.

It is not easy for a clever person to try and become innocent; it is something natural and manifests with the blooming of the heart. Innocence is the sign of the thriving of a spiritual personality. If one can develop anything, it is only this, that one may abstain from trying to be clever, and know that a selfish and clever person, with all his qualification of getting the best of another, comes across, sooner or later, a person cleverer than he. Often a clever person finds his own chain tied around his legs.

No one has arrived at a higher degree of spirituality without innocence. Innocence does not mean not knowing; it only means knowing and yet not knowing. A stupid person must not be confused with an innocent person, for the former is blind, whereas the latter only closes his eyes when he wants to. It is the wise one, really, who becomes innocent on arriving at a stage of perfection in wisdom. It is two kinds of persons who shows childlike simplicity in their lives: the silly one who shows childish traits and the wise one who shows innocence.

III:5 REJECT THE IMPRESSION OF
ERRORS AND SHORTCOMINGS

There is generally a tendency seen in those treading the spiritual path to feel discouraged at having bad impressions upon their heart of their own faults and shortcomings. And they begin to feel that they are too unworthy to have anything to do with things of a sacred nature. But it is a great error, in spite of all the virtue humility has in it. When one acknowledges something wrong in oneself, one gives that wrong a soul out of one's own spirit, and by withdrawing from all that is good and beautiful, spiritual and sacred, instead of developing the spirit of rejecting all errors, in time one becomes a receptacle of what is wrong. One goes on disapproving and yet collecting errors, so producing within oneself a perpetual conflict that never ends. When man becomes helpless before his infirmities, he becomes a slave to his errors, he feels within himself an obedient servant to his adversary.

The greater the purity developed in the heart, the greater becomes the power of man. As great the power of man within himself, so great becomes his power on others. A hair's breadth can divide power from weakness, which appear to have as wide a gulf between them as between land and sky.

III:6 PURITY OF HEART (2)

He alone is capable of removing from the heart of another doubt, deceit, fear or malice whose heart is already pure from these things or who, at least, can empty his heart of these things. There is a weakness of the heart and there is a strength of the heart. The heart's weakness is caused by things it contains which enfeeble it, such as doubt, deceit, fear and malice. The absence of these things produces that purity of heart which in itself is a power. This power could be increased by faith, hope and righteousness.

Purity of the heart causes its expansion and the lack of purity makes it narrow. Asif, the mystic poet of Hyderabad, says:

If the heart is large
it can be largest of all things.

Besides, it is purity alone which opens the doors of the heart.

All that hinders that purity stands as a closed door of the heart.

The pure-hearted may seem to be thinking, saying or doing simple things, and yet there is a beauty and charm in all they do, for there is nothing more attractive than light itself. All that is besides light depends upon the light to show out its beauty; light is beauty in itself. Purity of the heart is the only condition that allows the inner stream to rise.

The pure-hearted see deeper, though they say little. There is no pretence about them. What they know they know, what they do not know they do not know. The pure ones make all pure, for to them all is pure. Their presence makes everything pure. As the pure water is the best tonic, so is the contact of the pure-hearted person. In the spiritual path when one is able to accomplish this thing, there is not much then that remains to be accomplished.

III:7 EXALTATION

Exaltation depends upon purity. The body cleansed gives an exaltation which is experienced by all living beings on the physical plane. The heart cleansed of all impurities gives a much greater exaltation, which is experienced in the inner plane and is reflected on the outer plane.

Most people little realize the meaning of exaltation. In point of fact all things man seeks for and becomes occupied with, are most often methods adopted to obtain an exaltation: through food, perfume, music or through the beauty of colour and line. No method however succeeds in giving the experience of a fuller exaltation in the absence of purity of heart. In plain words, it is the pure-hearted who enjoy the beauty of music, colour or perfume more fully than those without purity of heart; although the pure-hearted seem to need these things which bring about exaltation less, sometimes for the very reason that the very purity of the heart gives them that exaltation which others strive to achieve by different methods.

Amir, the mystic poet, says:

Their eyes refused the wine,
her generous offer, saying
'We do not need thee,
we are intoxicated perpetually.'

The reason behind the refusal of the pious, at times, of music, art, gaiety or merriment was that they already possessed the exaltation which others try to gain by these things. It does not at all mean that the pious are always against things of beauty and pleasure. It only means that they are rich by the feeling of exaltation which comes from within, without adopting for it any other methods. Nevertheless the pious are the ones who are capable of enjoying beauty in all its aspects fully. As Hafiz says:

If the pious ones would hear the song I sing
They would get up and dance unrestrainedly.

III:8 PURIFY THE MIND FROM FEAR

To purify the mind from fear is of great importance, and this can be best done by analysing what causes one fear. Fear is an outcome of long-standing problems unsolved. When once a person looks his own problem in the face, he gets an insight into the cause of fear, and as in the sun many germs are destroyed, so the germs of fear are destroyed by the light of intelligence. Fear comes from weakness to face the consequences of one's condition, attitude and deeds. Once a person has solved the problem as to how he will meet the consequences, the fear is done with. The best way of getting over the fear of swallowing a bitter pill is to swallow a bitter pill and to experience by it that it is not more bitter than it is.

Fear comes also by being too cautious for one's health, morals and reputation; also by being too considerate of the feelings of those one loves, and too regardful of those under whose influence one is; also by taking too much to heart what others say. Fear very often remains in the heart of man in the guise of virtues, and very often a timid one is taken for a righteous one. But the timorous well-doer is worse than a fearless sinner.

The best practice one can make is to speak with oneself, with one's own fear; to dispute with it and to root out the reasons on whose foundations it rests. What generally happens is that all things one fears, one fears even to think of them. But the solution of getting above fear lies in analysing the cause of the fear and so making it non-existent.

Man by nature possesses a tremendous power hidden in his heart, the power which waits constantly to become manifest. This power is hidden by fear. The day when fear disappears, this latent power manifests to view.

III:9 KEEP THE HEART FREE FROM POISON

Antipathy turns into malice, and malice culminates in bitterness. To possess it in one's heart is like possessing in one's heart a poison, a poison that clouds wit and produces obscurity. If one keeps one's heart free from malice, one has accomplished a great deal, for it is in the clear heart that the light from above is reflected.

Often without an intention on one's part malice enters, of which man is unconscious. Often the man who possesses malice is quite innocent, for his heart is reflecting the malice which is projected from another heart. It is therefore that care must be taken to keep one's heart free from the impressions and influences coming from others.

The question: how can one avoid this, is answered thus: that the heart will focus itself on a person or an influence which is akin to its own quality. That is the nature of the heart. Therefore, even if the impression came from another, for the influence of another the man who reflects it is responsible. To make the heart reflect good qualities, one must prepare it, one must train it, for it is the good quality of heart that will keep away undesirable impressions and thoughts, and will only reflect good impressions and desirable influences.

A method of purifying one's heart is to repeat every morning and every evening:

> My *thoughtful self!*
> *reproach no one,*
> *hold a grudge against no one,*
> *bear malice against no one;*
> *be wise, tolerant, considerate,*
> *polite and kind to all.*

III:10 THE REAL PURIFICATION OF MIND

The real purification of mind is in purifying it from thoughts and impressions which live in it as a germ of disease. The best way of cleansing the mind from all this is to be able to empty the mind of any thought, feeling or impression. To be pure means to be natural. The spirit in man in its natural condition is not a thought but mind, not love but heart; for as the thought is the outcome of mind, so is love the outcome of the heart. To attain to the purity which is the seeking of the mystic one must be able to purify one's spirit from every thought and feeling, however deeply impressed or engraved in one's heart.

The mystic goes as far as purifying himself from his identity by removing it for a certain time and by putting something else in its place. From beginning to end the whole process of spiritual development depends upon this.

PART SEVEN

◆

METAPHYSICS

Tasawwuf

GATHA I

Belief is a natural tendency to accept knowledge without doubt. Every soul is born with this tendency to accept every knowledge that is given to it in whatever way or form. Therefore no soul in the world is born an unbeliever. There is a saying of the Prophet, 'Every soul is born a believer, and it is others that make that soul unbeliever.' This unbelief comes by the conflict of one's knowledge with belief.

Belief has two tendencies. One is the tendency of water that runs and the other is that of water that becomes frozen. Some people who have a belief like to keep that belief unchanged as a rock and identify their ego with that belief. People of this temperament are steady in their belief, but often they lack progress. If they happen to have a right belief there is no danger of their giving it up, but if it is not right they are perplexed. Those whose belief is likened to the running water perhaps go from one belief to another and they may not seem steady in their belief. Still their life is progressive. The progressive soul can never hold one belief and must change and go on changing until it arrives at the ultimate truth. For a simple person steadiness of belief is more advantageous than change for change may lead him astray, but for an intelligent person it is natural and necessary that he must go from belief to belief until he arrives at his final convictions.

Belief is of four kinds. The first kind is a belief accepted because it is believed by all. The second is a belief accepted because it is believed by someone in whom the believer trusts. The third belief is the belief that reason helps one to believe. The fourth belief is conviction about which one is as sure as if one were an eye-witness. The four different kinds of belief are held by souls of different evolution in life and different temperaments.

There is a knowledge which one can perceive with the senses, and there is a knowledge which one can perceive with the mind alone, and a knowledge which can be realized by the soul. And it is for this reason that, when a person wishes to touch a thing which can only be perceived, and when a person wishes to feel a thing which can only be realized spiritually, he naturally becomes an unbeliever.

In point of fact one person's belief cannot be another person's belief; every belief is peculiar to the person. Even if two persons held one belief there would be the difference of the point of view – even though it be as small as the difference between two roses. Therefore it is unjust, no doubt, on the part of one person to try to press his own belief on another person. At the same time the person who refuses to try to understand the belief of another from bigotry or pride, closes the door of his heart that otherwise would have let the knowledge come in.

There are two tendencies that can be developed in a person: either constantly to try to believe in whatever comes before him, or to try to disbelieve whatever is presented to him. And there is the use and abuse of both these tendencies. The use of the believing tendency is the taking of every chance of acquiring knowledge. The disadvantage is that one takes the chance of readily falling into error. But the use of the disbelieving tendency is only a protection from error, and its abuse is preventing every chance of further acquisition of knowledge.

Nature is full of covers; its activity covers and uncovers it. At every covering and uncovering it is natural that the belief of the individual should change. Therefore when a Sufi is asked, 'Do you believe in this or that?' he says, 'My belief is for me, yours is for you. There is no faith to which I give my unchanging belief, nor any belief that I reject without having investigated it.' If you are asked, 'What belief does the Sufi teach?', you may say, 'No belief, but he helps the pupil to seek and find within himself his own belief.'

I:2 FAITH

Faith can be defined by two words: self-confidence and certainty in expectation. Faith does not mean expectation without certainty or self-confidence. All things in life are appointed from eternity for a certain time; every experience and every knowledge comes in its own time. No doubt in this free will plays a certain part, as destiny plays a great part. We make our road in life by our expectations. Things that we have not attained to we look forward to and hope to attain; ideals that we wish to reach we expect to reach some day. And that which determines our success in attaining our ideal is faith.

It is faith that uncovers things veiled with a thousand covers. It is faith that attracts things almost out of reach. The distance between heaven and earth, the difference between life and death can be bridged by faith.

There is blind faith and there is faith which is not blind. Faith is blind when its power is small and reason does not support it – then faith may be called blind. But in fact the mind has all power. Every expectation that it has will certainly be fulfilled sooner or later. It may not be in a certain limited time, but in eternity its fulfilment will come. Faith is the power of the mind; without faith the mind is powerless.

When faith leads and reason follows, success is sure, but when reason leads and faith follows, success is doubtful. Faith causes the attitude of mind, the influence of the attitude of mind works psychically upon every affair. The belief 'my friend is faithful to me and is helping me', by itself influences the helper, and when there is a doubting attitude, 'perhaps my friend or my agent is faithful to me, perhaps not,' then the fact is made doubtful.

Faith can bring a surer and speedier cure than medicine, and both success and failure in life depend very much upon faith. Man rides upon the elephant and controls tigers by the power of faith. The great people of the world, the greatest people, are great more by their faith than by anything else, because mostly great people have been adventurous and at the back of a venture is faith, nothing else.

Reason can strengthen faith, but things that are beyond reason can be reached by faith alone. If faith is limited by reason, it is held down so that it cannot rise, but when faith is independent of reason it is raised by the force of the ideal, and then reason has scope to advance and reach the ideal.

Both those who believe in an ideal and those who do not have arrived at their conviction by faith; in the former it is positive, in the latter negative. An unbeliever asked a believer, 'If there were no God then would not all your prayers and expectations be in vain?' The believer answered, 'If there be no God and if my prayers are vain and all that I have done for God is lost, then I am in the same case as you; but if He exists then I have the advantage.' Faith is natural and its negative unnatural.

As all things in this artificial world are made by faith, so the whole creation is made by the faith of the divine Mind. Therefore as the divine Mind has been able to create all by faith, so man by this divine attribute can rise to the source of his being.

Thought, speech and action without faith are as body without life. All things by faith are made alive, for faith is the life of all things. Think what joy trust brings, and what a feeling of suffocation doubt brings! When a person does not trust another that means that he has no confidence in himself. He is not happy through this. It would be no exaggeration to say that loss resulting from misplaced confidence is better than all gain resulting from unjustified suspicion.

I:3 HOPE

Hope is a quality sometimes dependent on its object, sometimes independent of it, and these two different aspects of hope cause two different natures, the optimistic and the pessimistic. When the dependent nature is developed it makes man a pessimist, and when hope stands alone without dependence, this develops optimism. The optimistic person compared with the pessimistic may seem blind, and no doubt he is at times blind. But without doubt, as blind people develop a faculty of doing things without sight which people with seeing eyes cannot do, so the optimist can accomplish things without knowing how or why.

Hope cannot be called sureness or certainty, but it is a feeling which almost by its own force may bring sureness and certainty. Hope dependent upon reason is weak, and the more dependent the weaker it is. No doubt hope together with reason is strong, perhaps stronger than hope alone, but in proportion as reason supports hope so hope depends on reason, and as in many cases in life reason cannot reach the object of hope, hope then sinks.

In fact hope is more than a faculty or a quality; hope may be called the substance of life. Wise and foolish, rich and poor, strong and weak, all live in some hope. Hope can prolong life and lack of hope can shorten it. The joy that one gets from hope is greater than the joy that comes from possession of the object hoped for. Therefore there is a Sanskrit saying that Brahma in the creation took honey from all the flowers, and that this honey was hope. The interpretation is that out of all things that are beautiful and that give joy and happiness the essence is taken, and that essence is hope.

Hope is strengthened by reason but it stands on the foundation of patience, for it is possible that in spite of all reasons a person may completely give up hope if patience is lacking. If I used the poetical expression that the rocks and trees are standing in the deserts and forests resting in hope, that would be no exaggeration, because to the eyes of the mystic every aspect of life shows that it is standing in hope. This can be better seen in the life of human beings, because every person seems to be waiting from day to day and from hour to hour for something to come that he is hoping for.

The loss of hope is worse than the loss of life, and provided that hope stands by man's side – though no one else stands by him, it does not matter.

I:4 PATIENCE

Patience in other words is control, and one can say that the will should control the activity of the mind and hold it in check. To be patient is sometimes extremely difficult, for great energy is required to control the activity of the mind. We may picture patience as a wall against which the tides beat. The wall must be strong to resist the waves, and so it is with patience.

There are four different kinds of patience: patience in action, in thought, in word, in the manner of feeling. There are two different acts of patience: the first is to stand firm against the activity of another person, the second to stand firm against one's own activity. Not to resist the activity of another person is an act of patience of the former sort, and to control oneself when one wishes to do or say a certain thing is an act of patience of the latter sort. The most difficult test of patience is to have to wait for something which one wants at once.

The symbol of patience is the cross. The vertical line indicates activity, the horizontal line control. Patience is for the saint and the sage the first lesson and the last. The more one learns to bear the more one has to bear, such is the nature of life. Yet in reality patience is never wasted, patience always wins something great, even when to all appearance it loses. Sometimes a patient person seems a vanquished one, but in reality the victory is his. In the path of mastery as in the path of renunciation patience plays the greatest part.

Every faculty has a tendency to act more and more quickly. Every activity starts from a rhythm that is productive, and when the activity is increased the rhythm becomes progressive, and if it is increased still more the rhythm becomes destructive. These three rhythms are called in Sanskrit *satva, rajas* and *tamas*. It is only by control that one can keep the productive and progressive nature; lack of control allows destruction to set it. Will alone has the power to control each activity, either of the body or of the mind. When a person walks he wishes to walk faster, when he speaks to speak more quickly. It is the nature of activity to tend to increase its speed, and if this increase is permitted, very soon the destructive element comes about. The stronger this faculty of control becomes in a person the stronger the person becomes, and the more one loses the power of control the weaker one becomes.

There is no doubt that patience often seems a crucifixion, but one must remember that resurrection is always reached through crucifixion. Patience often seems like the effacement of self, and it is true that it is self-effacement. And yet nothing is lost, for by this practice of control a far greater power is attained. The Persian poets have called patience death. Doubtless it is to all appearance death, for it causes activity to cease, but in reality it is a greater life.

1:5 FEAR

Fear is considered by the mystics to come from the intervention of the earth element, and its effect is to make the body stiff at the moment when a person is afraid. According to metaphysics fear is caused by the lack of light. Therefore the more light there is in the heart, the more fearless the heart becomes. There is a *surah* of the *Qur'an* which supports this, where it is said, 'There is no fear in the master-mind.'

Fear arises from the strangeness of an object or from ignorance on the part of the person who fears. A Marathi poet says:

It is the self that creates before itself the object of fear.
One's fear comes from oneself.

Every attitude towards life has a re-echo and the attitude is formed by expectation. When one expects one's fellow man to love one, he does love one; and when one expects harm from another, then harm comes. When a person is afraid of a dog, he instils in the dog a tendency to bite him. This can be seen very plainly in the lower creation. Each animal fears another animal, and the expectation of harm makes it fear more than does the idea of the hugeness of the form or the bodily strength of another animal. Many things in life can be brought about not only by wanting them and thinking of them, but by fearing them – both objects and conditions.

To clear one's mind of fear is like bringing light into a dark room, and as light is needed to illuminate a dark room so the light of the soul is necessary to clear away the thought of fear. Man is more impressionable than any other living being, owing to the fineness and sensitiveness of his nature, but at the same time man alone is capable of rising above all fear, for in him there is a torch that can show him a way through the darkness.

Man fears all that is hurtful and harmful in any form, and more than all man fears what he calls death. As with every object and condition that arouses fear the fear is caused by ignorance, so even the fear of death is due to ignorance. Man is afraid if he is in the water where so helpless a creature as a fish feels safe. It is not only the fact that man is incapable of remaining in the water that arouses fear in him, but the water is a strange world to him, he does not know what is in it. Many have died in the water of fright of the water before having actually sunk.

This life of names and forms is therefore called by the mystics *maya*, an illusion which is subject to being made into that which one would like to make it. When one fears, it frightens one, but when one clears one's heart of all fear, the whole world of illusion turns into one single vision of the sublime immanence of God.

I:6 JUSTICE

Justice is a faculty of mind which weighs things. There is also a faculty attached to it which sees whether things are in their true places and sees the fitness of things. This is also the power to view two sides of a subject or of a thing: the side where it is complete and the side where it is incomplete. This faculty is kindled by the light of intelligence; the more intelligence the greater justice. It is generally the lack of intelligence that produces injustice.

The development of the ego often obscures this faculty, in the same way that clouds eclipse the sun. Therefore a selfish person, however clever, lacks pure intelligence and therefore is deficient in the true sense of justice. It is often personal feeling, a personal like or dislike, that disposes the weights in the scales of justice to suit the personal fancy. Therefore often a person who boasts of his sense of justice is really more unjust than one who makes no such claim. A just person is one who can decide against his own interest if necessary. Only when personal bias is absent can a decision be called just.

Into the scales of justice a person throws weights from his store of knowledge, and it is his own ideas about the value of things that weigh and balance them. But as opinions change at every step in evolution, what may seem just or unjust today is not likely to seem so tomorrow. What a person calls wrong at one time will seem at another time in his life to be right, and it is the same with regard to what at one period of his evolution he considers right.

No wonder that the prophets, reformers and poets have so often contradicted themselves in their writings! One can find contradictions in all the scriptures of the world, and it needs a perfect development of the faculty to look at this idea with a perfect view. (*See* Questions and Answers, p 299.)

I:7 REASON

Reason is a faculty that raises out of itself an answer to every question one asks. There is a store of knowledge of names and forms, of principles, of feelings. From that store of knowledge an answer rises; it is that which is called reason.

This store of knowledge is different in every individual and it is for this reason that two people may disagree, and at the same time both may have reason for what they say. This shows that reason is not outside oneself; it is within oneself and at each stage towards evolution reason changes. The answer that a person may get from within to a certain question in one month may change in the next month.

Every object and condition suggests a reason, but the more one penetrates through the object or condition, the more one realizes that there is reason under reason, and one condition may suggest numerous further reasons, according to the depths one may touch. When there is a discourse about justice or injustice, right or wrong, one applies one's own reason, and when one cannot understand the reason of another, one's knowledge is incomplete.

The effect that different names and forms produce is an illusion, and so is reason which is the creation of mind, when it is compared with the ultimate reality. Reality is above reason. When reason follows reality it is helpful, but when reality is covered under reason it is an illusion.

The one who penetrates through the numerous covers of reason comes to the depth of knowledge, but the one who clings to the first reason he has touched remains there. For him there is no progress.

I:8 LOGIC

Logic is a support that reason takes to strengthen itself. It may be called a fortification of reason. The analytical faculty of the mind seeks for something substantial to make reason cut and dry. In other words logic may be called authorized reason, or reason supported by the reason of others.

Logic has a larger field than reason, because the scope of reason is only the mind of one individual. The scope of logic is vaster; it represents the minds of many individuals who have thought on the same subject. Logic is a degree higher in knowledge than reason. When one person gives a reason and another person says there is no logic in it, that means that there is no support for this reason from other minds which have thought about the subject.

In one sense logic may be said to be concrete and realistic knowledge, and yet in another sense it is most limited and poor knowledge. It is limited to names and forms that are forever changing. It is poor because it is founded on a substance that is subject to destruction.

When logic helps to strengthen the knowledge of names and forms and of conditions it is of great help, but when it confines the progress of the soul which is made on a different path, it is a great hindrance. In other words it may be said that the possessor of logic is a learned man, but he who is possessed by logic is lost.

I:9 TEMPTATION

Temptation is a momentary illusion. The beauty of some object covers the eyes of reason and man is drawn back or pushed aside from the track which he follows in order to arrive at his desired destination, whatever it be. Therefore what is a temptation to one person is not necessarily a temptation to another. The same object which is a temptation to one may be a goal to another. One cannot wisely point out 'this is a temptation, and that is not'. In reality all is a temptation and nothing is. It is not the object or the action which forms the temptation but the situation. In order to be aware of the temptation one has to meet with, it is well to keep before one the goal one wishes to attain and always to reason out, before taking a step toward anything, whether it will help or hinder the attainment of one's desired end.

There are three forms of temptation. The first is that which cries aloud what it is, which shows itself clearly. The second form is that in which the temptation disguises itself and hides the goal from the eyes of man, so that man may at once forget his destination. In the third form the temptation appears for the moment a greater gain than the desired object. In such a case reason no doubt helps, and yet it cannot help altogether, for as the temptation belongs to the external world, so does reason also belong to the external world. There is only one thing that can counterbalance it, and that is the faculty of intuition. If this faculty is really developed it comes to man's rescue in all his difficulties.

If one desires to reach the goal one must make a great fortification against temptation. One should keep before one the object to be attained and feel behind one the strength of intuition to push one forward. The further we go the greater will be our temptations. Even after the attainment of an object temptations still persist, ready to snatch away the object attained, which is very well explained in the myth of Orpheus.

It is not necessary to be so careful as to become timid, nor should we be so bold as to commit ourselves to follies at every step we take. We must keep the balance and keep on the straight path with our gaze fixed on the desired goal.

I:10 TOLERANCE

Tolerance is the first lesson of morality, and the next is forgiveness. A person who tolerates another through fear, through pride, from honour or by the force of circumstances does not know tolerance. Tolerance is the control of the impulse of resistance by will. There is no virtue in tolerance which one may practise because one is compelled by the circumstances to tolerate, but tolerance is a consideration by which one overlooks the fault of another and gives no way in oneself to the impulse of resistance.

A thoughtless person is naturally intolerant, but if a thoughtful person is intolerant it shows his weakness; he has thought, but no self-control. In the case of the thoughtless, he is not conscious of his fault, so it does not matter much to him.

But a thoughtful person is to be pitied if he cannot control himself owing to the lack of will.

The activities in the worldly life cause many disturbances and they have a constantly jarring effect upon a sensitive soul. And if one does not develop tolerance in nature one is always subject to constant disturbance in life. To wish to live in the world and to be annoyed with its activities, is like wanting to live in the sea and be constantly resisting its waves. This life of the world, full of different activities constantly working, has much in it to be despised if one has a tendency to despise. But at the same time there is much to admire if one turns one's face from left to right!

It is in our power to choose the view of imperfection or the vision of perfection, and the difference is only in looking down or looking upwards. By a slight change of attitude in one's outlook on life one can make the world into heaven or hell.

The more one tolerates, the stronger one becomes in this way. It is the tolerant one who is thoughtful, and as thought becomes greater, one becomes more tolerant. The words of Christ, 'Resist not evil', teach tolerance.

GATHA II

They say, 'Forgive and forget', and that is very expressive of the process of forgiveness. It is impossible to forgive unless you can forget. What keeps man from forgiving his fellow man is that he holds the fault of another constantly before his view. It is just like sticking a little thorn in one's own heart and keeping it there and suffering the pain. It may also be pictured as putting a drop of poison in one's own heart and retaining it until the whole heart becomes poison.

Verily, blessed are the innocent who do not notice anybody's fault. And the greater credit is to be given to the mature souls who, recognizing a fault, forget it and so forgive. How true are the words of Christ, 'Let those throw a stone who have not sinned.' The limitations of human life make man subject to faults; some have more faults, some have fewer, but there is no soul without fault. As Christ says, 'Call me not good.'

Forgiveness is a stream of love which washes away all impurities wherever it flows. By keeping this spring of love which is in the heart of man running, man is able to forgive, however great the fault of his fellow man may seem. One who cannot forgive closes his heart. The sign of spirituality is that there is nothing you cannot forgive, there is no fault you cannot forget. Do not think that he who has committed a fault yesterday must do the same today, for life teaches continually and it is possible that in one moment a sinner may turn into a saint.

At times it is hard to forgive, as it is hard to take away the thorn that has gone deep into one's heart. But the pain that one feels in taking away the thorn deep set in the heart is preferable to keeping the thorn in the heart constantly. The greater pain of a moment is better than the mild pricking going on constantly. Ask him who forgives what relief there is in forgiveness. Words can never explain the feeling of the heart at the moment when one has cast out the bitter feeling from one's heart by forgiving, and when love spreads all over within oneself, circulating like warm blood through one's whole being.

II:2 ENDURANCE (1)

The human being is physically and mentally so constructed that he can endure only a certain degree of vibrations, audible or visible. Therefore noise distracts his mind and strong colours also make an uncomfortable effect. All that is called noise is beyond the range of his power of endurance. Generally soft colours appeal to him more, for the vibrations of soft colours are soothing and do not need endurance on the part of man.

But atmosphere demands the greatest strength of endurance. One can endure colour or sound, but it is difficult to endure atmosphere which is not congenial. Man prefers to endure colour or sound which is difficult to endure rather than the personality of another person, because human activity has a more jarring effect than colour or sound. Man does not need to speak or act in order to create a jarring effect upon another. If his mind is in that state, he has a jarring effect upon others without having to speak or act.

If there is a thing most difficult to endure it is man, and yet the soul most longs for the association of mankind. If a person were in a forest where he did not see a human being, after a few months, when his fancy were satisfied to some extent, he would long to see the face of a human being; the trees and plants and animals and birds are not sufficient. This shows that it is not only that like attracts like, but like needs like. The position of man is a strange position in life; man is uncomfortable with his kind and unhappy without his kind, and he does not know what best course there is to take.

The Sufi therefore learns the lesson of endurance, to take the right course, for if one does not endure a devil one cannot endure an angel. If man is not happy on earth he cannot be happy in heaven. A person who has no endurance, his need will not be answered even in paradise. Although it is difficult at times to endure, yet if one will not make an effort to endure, one will have to endure then at all times. The world is what it is, it cannot be changed.

If we want it to be different we must change ourselves. If we become susceptible to jarring effects, jarring influences, not only human activities around us but even the moving of the leaves will make us uncomfortable. To a miserable person the midsummer day is worse than a dark night, all seems gloomy, everything seems wretched, and he himself melancholy. This tendency is developed by not making an effort to endure but avoiding situations which ask for one's endurance. In all walks of life success is assured for an enduring man, and with the lack of this quality, whatever be man's qualification, he is kept back from success.

By endurance I do not mean to love and admire all things and beings whom one likes or dislikes. Endurance means to be able to stand, to be able to tolerate, to be able to overlook all that is not in accordance with one's own way of thinking. All the troubles caused among friends, families, among nations are the result of lack of endurance. And if this spirit of endurance would spread from individuals, in time it would become the spirit of the multitude, and the conditions would become much better than they are at present.

II:3 ENDURANCE (2)

It is endurance that makes things valuable and men great. Gold and silver are not more beautiful than the delicate and fragrant flowers which are much superior in colour, fragrance and delicacy to gold and silver. Why then are the flowers the slaves of gold and silver coins? Because gold and silver are durable and the flowers have not that quality. In this ever-changing world full of sensitiveness, endurance is very rarely to be found.

A person without endurance is in torture night and day, for life can be pictured as the waves of the sea, always slapping and knocking against what is standing firm. One who is susceptible of being moved by this continual motion of life has no rest for a single moment. 'There is no peace for the wicked.' It is really not the wicked but the weak, because wickedness is the extension of weakness.

Endurance is an exercise of strengthening the will-power. The nature of life will always remain the same. It is man who can change himself, but what generally people do is that they wish life to become still, because they are disturbed. It is just like travelling on the sea: man wants the sea to stay calm instead of building his boat strong enough that it may travel on the waves and stand all storms.

All the great persons of the world, whatever had been their mission in life, proved their greatness by this one quality: endurance. The enduring personality is like a ship that can stand storms and winds under all conditions, the ship that saves itself and others. Such blessed personalities, showing the strength of God, have been called the saviours of humanity.

II:4 WILL-POWER

Will-power is not mental power, but it appears in the form of a mental power: the mind, as a globe, gives out the light of the will. Will-power, plainly speaking, is soul-power. Therefore the more one realizes its source, the more one develops the power of will. No doubt the mind is an instrument, also the senses are instruments of the will-power, and if these instruments are not sound and well developed, the will-power cannot work properly; it is like a blunted sword in the hand of a skilful warrior. Therefore in the Sufi cult practices are given to make the mind as well as the senses proper tools for the use of will-power.

As the plant is sprung from the earth, but is nourished by the rain falling from the sky, so the will-power springs from within, but is developed by external activities. It must be remembered that the inner life reflects on the outer life and the outer life reflects on the inner life; both parts of life are interdependent.

Will-power is like a battery of life and as difficult as it is to deal with a strange mechanism, and as dangerous as it is to work with a battery of enormous power, so difficult and dangerous it is to develop and to work with the will-power. In the first place power is blinding – beauty is revealing. Wrong and unjust and unreasonable tendencies may rise from power, and one may destroy oneself in its expression. Christ teaches us on this subject where he says, 'He who taketh the sword shall perish by the sword.' But by this it is not meant that one must not develop will-power. It only means that, before developing will-power, one prepares knowledge and strength to control it when it is once developed, and the knowledge and the clearness of vision to utilize it rightfully.

Will-power in man is the secret of God and in this secret the mighty power of God is hidden. Therefore in the East where mystical ideas are known to people, they always say, 'We do not know, behind this limited human form, what is hidden.' This makes them know and consider what is hidden in every person they meet. Hafiz says:

Do not let yourself be befooled
by the patched sleeve of the dervish.
You do not know if under this patched sleeve
a mighty arm is not hidden.

What we call miracle is the outcome of the same power, except that what is above the human limitation cannot be called natural, it is supernatural. Therefore the miracle is not done by man, but by the superman, who in the religious term is called the divine man. Man is inferior in his selfishness; when he rises above self he is superior. Therefore the right to develop will-power is the right of the superior man. The difference between what is called white magic and black magic is only the use made by the inferior man or by the superior man of the same will-power. Just as by the strength of arm you can take man's life or you can save man's life; both things are accomplished by the same power.

No better use of will-power can be made than for self-control, for the control of the body, for the control of the mind. One who controls his body will control his mind; the one who controls his mind will control his body. The best use one can make of will-power is to use the power for self-discipline, on passion, on anger, on all things which abide in man's nature as his great enemies. In other words, by will-power one must build up a force to fight oneself, with that part of oneself which offends us. It is rarely that a man lives on earth who thinks, speaks and acts as he wishes to. If he does so he is no doubt a master. Doing a miracle apart, if one can make oneself obey one's own will one would surely rise to a great exaltation.

In the spiritual path the development of will-power is the college education, the moral education is the school education which comes before. But after the development of the will-power, then there comes a work, a duty that one has to perform toward God and toward humanity by the expenditure of thus developed power of will. (*See* Questions and Answers, p 299.)

II:5 KEEPING A SECRET

The power of keeping a secret is the digestive power of the mind, and one who cannot keep a secret is like a person who cannot digest his food. As indigestion is the malady of the body, so giving out of the secret is the disease of the mind. The mind is a fertile ground and it is the product of the mind which is all we see before us created and produced. Therefore the mind which conceives a secret will prove to be a fertile land, and the mind which cannot assimilate a secret is like a barren desert. Those who have accomplished something in life have accomplished it by this power, the power of keeping a secret. Those who have wasted their lives have wasted them by the lack of this power; with all their intelligence, learning and goodness they have proved to be shallow. The more one knows the secret of the world, the more one feels inclined to keep it secret. And the more one keeps what one knows secret, the more life unfolds to one its secret.

One naturally keeps secret all that is bad, ugly and undesirable, and one feels naturally inclined to expose all that is good, deserving, worthwhile and beautiful. Yet even that, if kept secret, will show the phenomenon in time of a seed hidden in the ground which will spring up, when the hour comes, with its leaves, fruits and flowers. Therefore sometimes Sufis have taken a contrary way: to keep secret all the good one does and to let one's faults be known. There exists in Persia a sect of Sufis who are called *Rind* who still practise the same principle. There is a saying of a *Rind*, 'Be a lover from within and become indifferent outwardly.' This is a becoming manner rarely seen in the world.

When a person arrives at such a stage of spiritual advancement, when the fault or weakness of another he regards as his own fault, when he sees himself standing in the position of another, when he sees in another his own self, then he feels inclined to cover the fault of another as he would his own.

In all ages there has been talk about the sacred word and it has always been considered a great secret: that secret is the tendency of keeping secret. It is not in everybody's power to keep a secret, for the secret is heavier than an elephant to lift. The weak-minded is weighed down by the heavy weight of the secret. The person who has not developed this power feels as a congestion of heart, from which relief can only come when he has given out the secret; till then he is in pain.

Also it must be remembered that the power of body can stand nowhere in comparison with the power of mind, and the power of the one who keeps a secret is greater than the power of the giant who lifts a mountain. All that one holds is conserved, all that one lets go is dispersed.

II:6 MIND

Mind develops to its fullness in man, although it exists in its primitive stage in all the different aspects of creation. Man therefore is so called from *manas*, which in Sanskrit means 'mind'. Many psychologists have thought that mind is the possession of man only, that the animal has no mind, but it is not so. Even the plants have a mind; where there is feeling there is mind.

There is no difference between heart and mind, although 'heart' expresses more than 'mind'. The heart is the depth and mind is the surface. The mind is a receptacle of all to which it is exposed; it is like the photographic plate. And therefore all conditions, happy or unhappy, all actions, good or bad, all that is beautiful or void of beauty, become impressed upon the mind. The first impression is upon the surface, and as the impression is retained in the mind so it reaches the depth of the heart. It is like the photographic plate; once it is developed, the impression becomes clear and deeply engraved. But the photographic plate is not creative and the heart is creative. Therefore every impression which once reaches the heart becomes as a seed in a fertile ground. The heart reproduces all it has received.

Therefore it is greatly to the disadvantage of the fault-finding man that he wishes to find fault with all he sees, for if he is not able to throw away immediately the undesirable impression received – which is not always so easy – in due time he begins to reproduce what he has received. Human nature is such that all the bad things he sees in another seem to man worse than they are, but when he himself does the same, he always has a reason to defend his fault. It is like partaking in all that one dislikes in another only by the habit of fault-finding.

For the wise who have risen above the ordinary faults of human life it matters little if they find fault, but they are the ones who do not find fault. They as a rule overlook all that seems undesirable, and that action of overlooking itself prevents all the undesirable impressions from penetrating through their hearts. There is a natural tendency in man as in the animal to protect his heart from all hurt or harm, but that is the external heart. If man only knew what harm is brought to one's being by letting any undesirable impression enter the heart, he also would adopt the above-said policy of the wise: to overlook. (*See* Questions and Answers, p 300.)

II:7 THOUGHT

Thought is a wave of the mind. The difference between thought and imagination is that the former is an activity of the mind directed with intention, and imagination is an activity which is not directed intentionally, but rises mechanically like the wave of the sea. Therefore imagination has less power than thought. No doubt the imagination of a man with a powerful mind also will have an influence and an outcome; but thought intentionally directed has strength of will with it, and therefore its power is great.

A clear mind can have a clear thought, and therefore clearness of thought depends upon the cleanliness and the awakening of the centres. When the organs of the body, and especially the centres, are not in a clean and normal condition, then one's own thought is unclear to oneself, the thought of others still less clear. Man in reality is by nature a mind-reader, and the state of body and mind is abnormal when he cannot read thought. To him to whom his own thought is clear, the thought of another person will be clear. It is he who does not know himself who does not know others.

Man's thought may be likened to an indiarubber ball. It can be directed to any point one wishes to hit, but there is a likelihood that the thought so directed will rebound and hit the sender. A thought of love sent to another must rebound and bring love to oneself, and likewise the thought of hate.

Thought depends upon mind, as the plants depend upon the ground in which they are sown. Fruits and flowers grown in one kind of ground are sweet and fragrant, in another kind of ground they lack that sweetness and fragrance. Therefore the wise know the mentality of a person by his thought, they know from which soil that thought comes.

As water is found in the depths of the ground, so love is hidden beneath every heart; only the difference is that in one part of the earth the water is far down below the earth, in another part of the ground it can be found quite near. It is that water that makes the earth flourish, and so it is the love element which makes the ground which we call the mind a fertile ground. Every thought coming from a fertile and flourishing ground must bear some fruit; a loving person's life is itself a garden. But otherwise, if it is a barren soil, from there you expect nothing but volcanic eruptions, the volcano that destroys itself and its surroundings. And every element, in the form of a thing or being which is destructive, must of necessity destroy itself first.

In order to make thought fruitful mental culture is necessary. First the digging of the ground; the inner culture of the Sufis begins with the digging of the ground. What is meant by *zikar* is this digging process. But it is not only the exercise, it is living the life. Digging the ground is what may be called consideration. It is constant consideration which cultivates the mental ground. Then one must water this ground, and this water is the love element – to give and to receive love. Give more and take little is the principle. And when in a ground so cultivated and so watered the thought-plants spring, they must necessarily bring forth sweet fruits and fragrant flowers.

II:8 DEPENDENCE UPON GOD – *TAWAKKUL*

Dependence is nature and independence is the spirit. The independent spirit becomes dependent through manifestation. When One becomes many then each part of the One, being limited, strives to be helped by the other part, for each part finds itself imperfect. Therefore we human beings, however rich with the treasures of heaven and earth, are poor in reality because of our dependence upon others. The spiritual view makes one conscious of this, and the material view blinds man, who then shows independence and indifference to his fellow man. Pride, conceit and vanity are the outcome of this ignorance. There come moments when even the king has to depend upon a most insignificant person. Often one needs the help of someone before whom one has always been proud and upon whom one has always looked with contempt.

As individuals depend upon individuals so the nations and races depend upon one another. As no individual can say, 'I can get on without another person', so no nation can say, 'We can be happy while another nation is unhappy.'

But an individual or a multitude depends most upon God in whom we all unite. Those who depend upon the things of the earth certainly depend upon things that are transitory, and they must some day or other lose them. Therefore there remains only one object of dependence – that is God who is not transitory and who always is and will be. Sa'di has said, 'He who depends upon Thee will never be disappointed.'

No doubt it is the most difficult thing to depend upon God. For an average person who has not known or seen, who has never had any idea of such a personality existing as God, but has only heard in church that there exists someone in the heavens who is called God and has believed it, it is difficult to depend entirely upon Him. A person can hope that there is a God, that by depending upon Him he will have his desire fulfilled, a person can imagine that there can be some being whom people call God, but for him also it is difficult to depend entirely upon God. It is for them that the Prophet has said, 'Tie your camel and trust in God.' It was not said to Daniel, 'Take your sword and go among the lions.' One imagines God, another realizes God. There is a difference between these two persons.

The one who imagines can hope, but he cannot be certain. The one who realizes God – he is face to face with his Lord, and it is he who depends upon God with certainty. It is a matter either of struggling along on the surface of the water or courageously diving deep, touching the bottom of the sea.

There is no greater trial for a person than dependence upon God. What patience it needs, besides the amount of faith it requires, to be in the midst of this world of illusion and yet to be conscious of the existence of God! To do this man must be able to turn all what is called life into death, and to realize in what is generally called death – in that death, the true life. This solves the problem of false and real. (*See* Questions and Answers, p 301.)

II:9 PIETY

People very often mean by piety orthodoxy, a religious appearance or a great goodness. Really, piety means purity. Piety is the healthy state of mind; the person of healthy mind is really pious. That mind is pious that fears not, which is above reproaches, which by its innermost joy makes even the body feel light. The pious feel exalted, for piety is purity from all things and conditions of earthly life which pull man down to the earth. When man feels light in his body and joyful in his heart, his soul becomes exalted and that is the sign of piety. If there is not this feeling in man, however much good there be in him, it is of no use, his learning of no value, his religion, his prayer all in vain.

Religion, prayer or meditation are all methods by which the joy, which is within man, which is man's divine heritage, may be brought to the surface. Sufis have used different words from those of the orthodox in expressing their spiritual ideas. Therefore instead of calling man 'pious' they call him *khwanda peshani*, the smiling forehead. It means that if his lips do not smile his forehead smiles. How true it is that before man weeps or laughs his eyebrows give warning of what is coming. That is what is meant by the word 'expression' in the English language. There is an inner joy, a divine feeling which rises up as water from a fountain and shows itself in many forms: in smiles, in tears, in words, in silence. Man expresses it in dancing, in singing; his voice, his word, his gesture, all express piety.

Hafiz has said in sarcasm to the long-faced pious, who have become so out of orthodoxy, and look at singing or dancing with contempt:

If the heads of the pious would hear my words sung,
they would get up and begin to dance.

Then he goes on to say:

Hafiz says things sometimes through drunkenness
which he ought not to say.
O pious one, I pray you will overlook it all.

The Sufi's piety is the divine joy which is the soul's real treasure, and it does not matter in what way it is achieved, religiously or irreligiously, as long as it is achieved. It is the thing the Sufi values most.

II:10 SPIRITUALITY

It is most amusing how many different meanings people give to the word 'spirituality'. Some call spirituality great goodness, some mean by it melancholy, some mean by it a miserable life, some think spirituality lies in communion with spirits, some consider wonder-working and the art of the conjuror spirituality. Every good or bad power, so long as it is a power, people often imagine to be a spiritual power. Many picture the idea of spirituality in a religious authority, whereas it is the simplest idea if one cares to understand it by rising above complexity. Spirituality is contrary to materiality. One who is conscious of matter alone, is material; one who becomes conscious of spirit also, is spiritual.

He who thinks, 'I am my body' and sees no further, is material. He may as well say, 'I am my coat', and when the coat is worn out he may say, 'I am dead'. The one who is conscious of the spirit, to him his body is a coat and as by taking off one's coat one does not die, so even by the death of this body the spiritualized soul does not die. It is the spiritual person who will attain in time immortality. He does not need to study much to prove to himself that he is spirit, for study will never convince him. It is the spirit itself which must realize itself. The soul is its own evidence, nothing else will make the soul realize its own being.

The whole work of the Sufi which he calls inner cult is towards soul-realization. It is realized by rising above matter, and yet the condition is that one can only realize it by getting through matter. As the fountain is necessary for water to rise, so the material body is necessary for the soul to realize itself. The water which remains still in the depth of the fountain sees itself rising and falling within itself, and there lies its joy. The same picture illustrates the condition of spirit and soul. The spirit which rises upwards is the soul; it falls again in its own being, and the realization of the spirit of this joy can alone be called spirituality. (*See* Questions and Answers, p 301.)

GATHA III

III:1 ATTITUDE

Attitude is the principal thing in life. It is not the conditions in life which change life for us, but mostly it is our attitude toward life and its conditions upon which depends our happiness or unhappiness. With a sympathetic attitude one is able to sympathize with those who deserve sympathy and even with those who do not deserve sympathy; it is not the deserving or undeserving persons, but mostly it is the attitude with which they are seen.

A person who is impressed by wrong, to him there is much wrong in the world and less right. The more he looks at life with this attitude, the more wrong he sees; in the end to him everything becomes wrong. It is a kind of mental agitation against one thing a person met with in life which was wrong, which makes him see wrong in everything. A person who has once burned his lips drinking hot milk blows the buttermilk to cool it before he drinks. The human mind is like a compass. If it is once made to point wrongly, whatever way you may take, it will seek its own point all the time. So it is with the doubting person. A person who begins to doubt his enemy, next doubts his friend; then he comes to doubt his nearest and dearest friends in life. He cannot make his mind trust anybody in the world. With the best motive one may approach him, in every way one may show him sympathy, he will still think, 'Perhaps in this sympathy there is hidden an enmity.' It is generally the case with human beings that their attitude becomes fixed, it is not a rare thing seldom met with. But the one who trusts will trust everyone and under all conditions, and the one who idealizes and sees good, will see good in and will idealize even undeserving ones.

No doubt a better fixed attitude is preferable to a bad one, but the most desirable thing is to have the attitude unfixed, moveable. One must be free to form an opinion about a person and to adopt a method of working under certain conditions without one's attitude being subjected to some preconceived ideas one has, to be able to approve or disapprove, to be able to like or dislike, to be able to choose or give up. Goodness is better than wickedness, but freedom is higher than goodness. By freedom is meant not only freedom from outer influences but freedom from certain inner influences which obsess one's life, often making it wretched and miserable in all conditions.

The attitude becomes high and broad when one looks at life from a higher point of view. When the point of view is not high the range of man's sight becomes limited, he becomes narrow in his outlook on life; in his feelings, thought, speech and action the same is expressed. Why is God pointed out on high toward the sky? Why not toward the earth – for God is everywhere? The reason is that within the range of God's sight the whole universe stands as a little grain of corn, as to one who flies in the balloon and looks down from high the whole city comes within the range of his sight. When he stands on earth he sees no further than the four walls which keep the whole world covered from his sight.

What does it mean to become spiritual or godly? It means to have a higher view of life, to look at life from a higher point of view. It is the high viewpoint in life which ennobles the soul; it is by the broad outlook on life that spiritual aristocracy is realized.

III:2 SYMPATHY

Sympathy is an awakening of the love element, which comes on seeing another in the same situation in which one has been at some time in one's life. A person who has never experienced pain cannot sympathize with those suffering pain. In the same way a person sympathizes with someone whose honour or reputation has been harmed. The one who has no honour or reputation himself would not mind, for he does not know what it is and what it is to lose it. A rich person who has lost his money may be laughed at by somebody who has never had it. He can sympathize with him who has wealth, and still more can he sympathize with him who had wealth and lost it.

Very often the young imagine they love their mother and think they sympathize with their parents, but the young cannot come to the full realization of their love until they reach that situation. Very often people think it cruel and unkind of their friends when they do not receive sympathy from them, but they do not know that to have sympathy does not only mean having a warm heart, but it means having that experience which reminds them, making them sympathetic. Sympathy is something more than love and affection, for it is the knowledge of a certain suffering which moves the living heart to sympathy.

That person is living whose heart is living, and that heart is living which has wakened to sympathy. The heart void of sympathy is worse than a rock, for the rock is useful, but the heart void of sympathy produces antipathy. Man is most active physically and mentally, and when his heart is not tuned to sympathy, his mental and physical activity takes quite a contrary direction, which leads to inharmony and destruction.

No doubt love, affection or sympathy without wisdom may seem profitless, as for instance if a person was crying with pain and his sympathetic friend, hearing his cry, began to weep with him, doubling his pain. Sympathy can be useful only when man does not make the condition of the person with whom he sympathizes worse, but makes things better. The feeling of sympathy must be within; it need not manifest itself purely as sympathy but as an action to better the condition of the one with whom one has sympathy.

There are many attributes found in the human heart which are called divine, but among them there is no greater and better attribute than sympathy, by which man shows, in human form, God manifested.

III:3 THE WORD 'SIN'

Many wonder if sin is an attitude or an action or a situation or a result. And the answer is that all these combined together make either a virtue or a sin. The absence of one from it makes it incomplete, but all these together make it a complete virtue or sin.

Now the question is, what is the source of it? And the answer is that its origin is in wrong thinking. Wrong-doing comes from wrong thinking and wrong thinking comes from wrong feeling. And yet it is difficult to distinguish between feeling right and wrong. In short, as a definition of the word I would give this: every attitude, word or action that deprives one of the expected result – the result which is expected not only by the mind but by the soul – may be called sin. That which deprives one of peace, freedom, happiness, tranquillity of mind and ever-increasing power of will may be called sin, whatever the action. It may be an action which all the orthodox call virtuous, and yet it cannot be a virtue. Why is a virtue called a virtue? Because it brings happiness. It is not because it is a particular kind of action, it is because it brings to one what one's whole being is desiring. It brings freedom, it brings the air of happiness, it gives by its pressure upon one's mind an increase of will-power. That is why it is called virtue. Therefore no person in the world can judge another person, whether superior to him in evolution or inferior. The person himself is the best judge of his action.

In the Messages of the past it was necessary that a standard of virtue should be given to the world as a law given from the prophets of God, but at this period it is not necessary. The Sufi Message does not bring to the world a law made so plain as to say which is which, but the principle of the Message is to waken in the spirit of those who receive this Message that spirit that they may recognize what is right and what is wrong, that they may become masters of their destiny. And by their realization of this their progress on the spiritual path may become much higher as compared to those who during the period of the prophets depended to be directed in their lives by the law made by the prophets and carried out by the priests. The Sufi Message does not bring this. It brings the spirit of freedom, the air of happiness, that which gives happiness with increased will-power, which opens up freedom for those who can recognize for themselves the difference between right and wrong. And in that the evolution of humanity is brought a step forward from what it was before.

After a certain time the same principle that the Sufi Message has brought to the world will culminate and will appear as a law among nations, because the Message is the throwing of the seed. Just now you do not see the fruit and leaves, just now you see the seed which is hidden under the dust and on the ground. But time will bring the tree with its fruit and its leaves. When the nations recognize the divine law and the law of the time, then humanity will no longer be ruled by the laws made by a few favoured people for their convenience and as they think right. But the law will recognize the divine indication which is constantly working through every soul, guiding it on the path, showing it the way of its destiny. And when such a time comes, there will not be a necessity for so many laws, so many lawyers, so many law courts, and no end of prisons and no limit to the prisoners! These will cease to exist. There will no longer be the necessity of strict laws and severe punishments.

If one could only see that among one hundred people who are sentenced by the courts there is hardly one to be blamed, to be held responsible for his fault. And if there is anyone to be held responsible it is all we human beings. Why do we not all work, why do we not all help them to kindle the light in their soul that would show them their path plainly? It is not necessary that the clergyman, the priest only should be responsible for the evolution of each individual. We must work in the capacity of brother and sister to everyone. In the realization of the brotherhood in the Fatherhood of God we must hold it as our duty, our sacred task, to waken in our brother with love, with respect, with modesty, with humility, that power of understanding what is really for his best, what can really benefit him. It is not the mission of one person, it is the mission of every person. And if we each considered our share of work in the message and showed it by our own example in the world, we should be doing a great duty toward God and humanity.

III:4 THE WILL, HUMAN AND DIVINE –
QADR AND QAZA

The question of the will human and divine may be seen from two points of view, from the point of view of wisdom and from the point of view of the ultimate truth. If words can explain anything, it is from the former point of view; the latter point of view allows no word to be spoken in the matter, for in the absolute truth two do not exist, there is no such thing as two, there is One alone.

From the wisdom point of view one sees one weaker, one stronger, and one has to give in to the power of the other. This one sees in all aspects of creation. The little fish is eaten by the larger fish, but the little fish lives upon smaller fishes. So there is no one in this world so strong that there is not another stronger still, and there is no one in this world so weak that there is not another who is weaker still.

The other thing to consider is the opposing conditions and situations which stand before a willing mind and a striving person like a stone wall, so that with every wish to do something and to accomplish he cannot find his way. It is this experience which has made man say, 'Man proposes, God disposes'.

The Hindu philosophers have called these two great powers, one of which is as a creator and the other the power of destruction, by the names Brahma, the Creator, and Shiva, the Destroyer. And the most wonderful part in this creation and destruction is that what Brahma creates in a thousand years, Shiva destroys in one moment. Since God is almighty, the wise see the hand of God in the greater power, manifesting either through an individual or by a certain condition or situation, and instead of struggling too much against the difficulties in life and despairing over those losses which cannot be helped, they are resigned to the will of God.

In short, every plan that a person makes and his desire to accomplish that plan are often an outcome of his personal will, and when his will is helped by every other will that he comes in contact with in the path of the attainment of a certain object, then he is helped by God, as every will goes in the direction of his will, and so his will becomes strengthened; and often one person accomplishes something which perhaps a thousand people could not have been able to accomplish. Then there is another person who has a thought, a desire, and finds opposition from every side; everything seems to go wrong, and yet he has the inner urge which prompts him to continue in the path of attainment. There also is the hand of God behind his back pushing him forwards in his path, even though there might seem opposition in the beginning of his work. But all is well that ends well.

The saintly souls who consider it as their religion to seek the pleasure of God and to be resigned to His will, are really blessed, for their manner is pleasing to everyone, for they are scrupulous lest they may hurt the feeling of anyone. And if by some mistake they happen to hurt someone's feelings, they feel they have hurt God whose pleasure they must constantly seek, for the happiness of their life is only in seeking the pleasure of God. They watch each person and every situation and condition, and their heart becomes trained by constantly observing life keenly. As a lover of music whose ears become trained over time, who distinguishes between the correct and the false note, so they begin to see in every desire that springs in their heart whether it is in accordance with the will of God. Sometimes they know the moment the desire has sprung, sometimes they know when they have gone halfway in the path of its pursuit, and sometimes they know at the end of strife. But even then, at the end of it, their willingness to resign to the will of God becomes their consolation even in the face of disappointment.

The secret of seeking the will of God is in cultivating the faculty of sensing harmony, for harmony is beauty and beauty is harmony. The lover of beauty in his further progress becomes the seeker of harmony, and by trying always to maintain harmony man will tune his heart to the will of God. (*See* Questions and Answers, p 302.)

III:5 OPINION

Opinion is an outcome of mind. It is an outburst of its reasoning and judging faculty, and so an opinion accords with the evolution of a particular mind. Opinions clash when two people of different stages of evolution express themselves. Therefore the wise are reluctant to express their opinion, whereas for the unwise it is easy; the simpleton is only too glad to express his opinion uninvited. In the ancient education of children that was the one thing that was taught from childhood in good families: that the child must not be too ready to express his opinion.

Very often in expressing one's opinion – rather in giving one's idea about another – one places oneself before others for examination. As soon as a person has expressed his opinion, all others know what note of life he strikes – those, that is, who have the knowledge to know it. This does not mean that one must not have an opinion. It would be like saying one must not have a mind. Where there is a mind there will be an opinion.

Does it not very often happen to an intelligent person that immediately after having expressed his opinion he finds how foolish he has been in expressing his opinion? Often through nervousness, through lack of control over oneself or lack of patience, one expresses one's opinion. That opinion is especially valuable which comes by invitation. When someone has asked, 'Please, tell me, what do you think of it?', then the opinion becomes the answer to a demand.

Sometimes an opinion is nothing but the voice of pride, and sometimes one's opinion is coloured by one's favour or disfavour. Sometimes an opinion lacks knowledge of the object on which it is formed. The wise person therefore asks himself the question whether he has thorough knowledge on the subject upon which he expresses his opinion. If one took into consideration that very often one does not know what effect the expression of opinion may produce in the mind of the hearer, what reaction it will have, desirable or undesirable, one would certainly think much before expressing an opinion.

In the terms of the Sufis there is a phrase, *dakhl dar ma'qulat*, interference with the expert. For a nurse to attempt to direct the surgeon who is busy doing his work, for the clerk to advise the Justice while he is taking a case, for a student of the violin to tell the composer what he must do in a certain composition, all these things are meant by that phrase. If one considered what study, practice and experience are required in order to acquire a thorough knowledge in any line of work, and if one would consider, by the time a person has reached a certain age, what he has had to pass through and what he has had to learn, one would certainly have consideration for the expert and for age before expressing an opinion.

No doubt there are minds which show from childhood that brilliance which another person may not acquire in a whole lifetime, and again there is a genius who might show from youth an exceptional capability. But even such gifted souls need consideration, none the less. I have seen those who promised to be really something in life, who promised to accomplish something worthwhile in their lives, yet, and in spite of all their energy, enthusiasm and knowledge, taking gentle steps in the path of life and halting at every other step lest they do a wrong thing instead of the right.

What is Sufism? It is wisdom; to learn wisdom at every step in the path of life is the only work of the Sufi.

III:6 Conscience

Conscience is not only a record of one's experiences and impressions gained in life, but it is a living voice of the heart which makes all that is in the heart, so to speak, dance in the light of justice. Therefore conscience is a world in man, a world as living as the world in which we live; and even more living than this, for the world of conscience is durable, whereas the outer world is subject to destruction. The idea of 'hiding' or 'covering' a certain thing is for our limited understanding. In point of fact nothing can be covered, nothing can be hidden, since the nature of life is action and reaction. Every outer experience has a reaction within, every inner experience has its reaction in the outside of the life. In the *Qur'an* it is said, 'Their hands and feet will give evidence of their action.' The idea, from the point of view of metaphysics, may be explained thus – that there is no action which has not a reaction; every outer action has a reaction inwardly, and every inner action has a reaction outwardly.

The finer the person, the finer his conscience, and grossness makes the conscience gross. Therefore one person is more conscientious about his doing than the other person; one person repents more for his mistakes and failures than another person. But the most interesting thing in the law of life which one might watch is that the scheme of nature is so made that a conscientious person is taken to task more seriously by the scheme of nature for his evil doing than an ordinary person, who never thinks what he says or does. It might seem as if even God did not take notice of his wrong-doing. According to the metaphysical point of view, in the soul of the conscientious God is more awake; in the soul of the other, God slumbers, He does not take serious notice of things.

If one were to watch one's own conscience one would no longer have a thirst for phenomena, for there is no greater phenomenon than what is going on within oneself, and the action and reaction of every experience in life which materializes and manifests to one's view in various ways and forms.

A clear conscience gives the strength of a lion, but a guilty conscience might turn a lion into a rabbit.

But who is it in the conscience who judges? In the spheres of conscience the soul of man and the spirit of God both meet and become one. Therefore to a soul wide-awakened Judgement Day does not come after death, for him every day is Judgement Day.

No doubt the sense of right and wrong is different in every mind. The right of one may be wrong to another, and for another the wrong of one may be right. The law of action is too complex to be put in words, for every step advanced gives a certain amount of freedom of action; and as one goes along further and further in the path of truth, one's freedom is greater and greater at every step.

And yet no individual lives a life between the four walls of his individual self; every person is related and connected with a thousand ties with all others, known and unknown even to himself. Therefore the souls do not need regard for themselves only, but for the Whole Being, since every soul is a part in the whole scheme of Nature. And conscience is the test which can voice that inner harmony in everything one thinks, says or does, thus keeping the soul tuned to its proper note. (*See* Questions and Answers, p 304.)

III:7 CONVENTIONALITY

Conventionality is no doubt man-made, as art is man-made. But as in art there is the finishing of nature, so in conventionality there is the finishing of civilization. No doubt conventionality is acquired, not inherited, but at the same time the love of conventionality is inherited also. Children born into families in which conventionality has existed for a long time are born with a tendency towards it, and it becomes natural for them to learn it; while learning it they do not feel it to be foreign to their nature.

The extremes of all things good and bad are to be avoided. Nature has helped as far as that the soul is born on earth, and then comes education in which is the fulfilment of the purpose of life. Conventionality is not the goal, and yet this which makes civilization is a bridge which is connected with the goal of life. Conventionality loses its virtue, as do all things, when it becomes void of sincerity, for sincerity is the soul of every virtue.

We come now to the question: what is conventionality? It is a law of behaviour which is used in life for the convenience and comfort of man. All that is man-made is as imperfect as man. Therefore if one would try to find out the mistakes of conventionality one could find them in every civilization existing at any period of history. Nevertheless the most civilized at any period have been the most conventional people of the time.

During the age of aristocracy conventionality increased in every part of the world and became the main part of education for that time. And when revolt arose against the spirit of aristocracy everything good and bad that aristocracy stood for was condemned. Whatever line of reform the people in the world may adopt, they cannot be free from conventionality and yet progress. These two things cannot be separated. The only thing that can be done is to break one form of conventionality and build another form; call the first form conventionality and the next Bohemian life – it all comes to the same.

There is one thing that must be considered, that freedom is the soul's purpose and if, without hindering the conventionalities, one can rise above them so as to breathe the breath of freedom, that will be the true democracy. Democracy void of culture and refinement can very well be called anarchy.

But there are two laws which, if one considers them deeply, will become useful in living the right life. One thing is to strive to achieve beauty, comfort, happiness and peace for oneself. The other is sharing these same things with others; hence the necessity of conventionalities. The one who is a slave to conventionality is a captive, the one who is the master of conventionality is the possessor of that kingdom of which it is said in the Bible, 'Blessed are the meek, for they shall inherit the Earth.' (*See* Questions and Answers, p 306.)

III:8 LIFE

The life which we know is from our own life; therefore the nature and character of that life which is eternal is beyond man's comprehension. By this it is not meant that man is incapable of knowing the deeper life, but only that what man knows of life is from the knowledge of his own life. The difference between the life known to the generality and the life which is unknown is that of the illusion and the reality. Man mocks at the idea if he be told that all this is illusion, until he dives deep and finds out by comparison that this life which is subject to birth and death and subject to changes is a life, and yet no life. This life is like a bubble in the sea. The bubble is existent, and yet in reality non-existent when compared with the sea. And yet we cannot say that the bubble is non-existent, for it merges in the same sea in which it once appeared. So nothing takes it away but its own source and its original being.

The nature of this life of ours can be better understood by knowing its secret, and the knowledge of its secret will certainly enable us to live it to the best advantage. What happens is this: man, eager and anxious to get the best out of life, owing to his ignorance becomes a loser in the end. In order to know the secret of life one must understand the law of creation, the law of sustenance and the law of destruction. We must understand that destruction awaits every created thing, and to save it from destruction there is one mystery to be solved and that is the mystery of sustenance. What happens is that in every activity which is directed toward a certain result, owing to anxiety and eagerness one draws that result closer, before its time, and in this way very often one brings about that very destruction that could, with correct knowledge, be put off to a later time. Through this knowledge one develops patience, for it is very often the lack of patience which is the cause of destruction. An impatient person tries to reach too soon that culmination which causes destruction. By patience the one who is able to control his activities in life will become the sustainer of life and will make the best of life. In Hindu mythology Vishnu is the sustainer, in other words, the ruler of life.

Today, science, wakened to the same mystery, has been able to control matter to man's advantage, more than ever before in the history of the world. If this same mystery were used from a spiritual point of view in everything one does and one tries to accomplish in life, success would surely be the outcome.

In every little thing one does in life this must be understood. Even in such things as eating and drinking, if one does not sustain the rhythm, one cannot take the real benefit of the food one eats and the water that one drinks. The person who reaches before the time that culmination of appetite in eating will always complain of lack of digestion. So in business, industry, the professions, in study, meditation, in all affairs of life, whether of the heart or of the head, the need is to control one's activity and guide it and proceed gradually towards a culmination. (*See* Questions and Answers, p 309.)

III:9 THE WORD 'SHAME'

The word 'shame' is used in all different languages and the meaning of the word, as understood by different people, is more or less the same. But the question as to the real meaning of the word could be answered by saying that shame means want. A feeling in oneself of wanting something to make up one's ideal gives that feeling which one calls shame or, when one sees in another person something wanting, it is that which brings to one's mind that sense of want, and one expresses that sense by the word shame. It is interesting that in the Persian language there is a word *kham*, which can also be pronounced as 'shame', the meaning of which is 'foolish'; but the true meaning is 'wanting'.

The question arises whether the conception of shame is inherent or acquired. That is where the point of view of the mystic differs from the answers of modern psychology. While modern psychology says that all this is acquired, the Sufi will say it is inherent. The appearance of this sense in a child is worth noticing and it is of very great interest to a seer. When one sees it from a metaphysical point of view, from a spiritual point of view, it opens up a vast field of thought. One learns, by thinking about this sense of wanting, that the human soul by nature is perfect – and the life of limitation on earth is imperfection; therefore the soul continually sees wanting in itself and want in others and becomes unhappy over it.

The soul who sees the want in others becomes unhappy over others; therefore there will be no end to the unhappiness of that soul, for there will always be the want in this life of limitation. But the soul who sees the want in itself no doubt has a chance to gain all that which is wanting, although the more a soul will advance, the more it will find itself wanting.

Therefore the nobler the soul, the more sense of shame it has, for that sense is wakened in it; and the lack of nobleness of spirit is signified by the lack of that sense. There is one person who fights against that sense, which in time becomes blunted, and he might feel happier for the moment having that sense in him blunted. However, the limitation is there. The sense of shame is a channel which leads to that goal which is called perfection, but no doubt the more it is wakened, the more one is subject to unhappiness. And yet true happiness is in the realization of perfection, and therefore in the end he does not lose much in spite of the apparent gains that come to the one who is shameless. In practical life in the midst of the world the shameless has apparently more ease of action and of movement likewise. The one who has the sense of shame awakened, for him life is difficult.

But the sense of shame living in the heart of man is like a pearl in the shell, and as long as it is in the shell it may not fetch its price, but there is a pearl just the same. Whatever price the pearl fetches, the marketplace is not the place for it; its real place is the crown of the king. So a person with real, living quality may not always be appreciated, may have troubles in life, and yet sometimes his qualities will fetch their proper price. And if they do not fetch the proper price still there is no loss, for beauty in all its aspects is beyond price.

Where does man learn virtue? He learns it from that sense of shame. And what develops virtue in man? It is again the same sense. Often this sense works as a sharp knife upon a feeling heart, but it only makes it a cut diamond. By this we come to a realization that what is most precious in life is feeling. And if the feeling sense loses its sharpness, it is as if man who is the salt of the earth has lost savour, and there is nothing else which can supply it. Through all the times of the world's history, whenever a civilization has touched its summit, this sense has developed in the generality, for the heights of every civilization show the fineness of human feeling, which is the highest of all aspects of culture.

The manner of the saints has been to approach God with this feeling. It is this feeling which made the Prophet Mohammed cover himself with a mantle every time the thought of God came. It is the same feeling which gives a person modesty. And all the different forms of prayer have come from this inner tendency of man in the presence of the God of perfection. (*See* Questions and Answers, p 312.)

III:10 TOLERANCE

Tolerance is the sign of an evolved soul, for a soul shows the proof of its evolution in the degree of the tolerance it shows. The life of the lower creation shows the lack of tolerance. The tendency of fighting one with another which one sees among beasts and birds shows the reason at the back of it: that intolerance is inherent in their nature. By a psychological study of the nature of the lower creation one will find that as evolution takes place among birds and animals this tendency of intolerance becomes less and less. It is the love element developing in their nature which brings them together to form flocks and herds. The same tendency towards intolerance sometimes manifests in a more distinct and pronounced form in man. The reason is that man's responsibility in life is greater, his difficulties are many, and he lives in a community which is larger than a flock or a herd.

At the back of this tendency there is a most wonderful secret hidden, the depths of which are fathomed by the mystic. The mystic who sees God both within and without, who recognizes God both in unity and in variety, this mystic realizes that it is the One who has known Himself to be One, who does not know of two, who feels uncomfortable and agitated and revolts on knowing that 'there exists another besides Me'. And this is why the birds have a tendency to fight with their own kind, and so one finds the same thing among the beasts; among men, man is the enemy of man and woman of woman. The rivalry that exists between professions, and between people of the same position, shows the same thing, the principle that the nature of the ego revolts against another, especially of the same name and form in some way or other.

One may give a thousand reasons for intolerance, but the inner reason is one and the same in all aspects of intolerance. The Sufis have called it *kibria* which means vanity; vanity of the One to whom alone it belongs.

As a person evolves spiritually so he seems to rise above this natural tendency of intolerance, for the reason that he begins to see besides himself and the second person God, and he unites himself with the other person in God. It is the third person whose love or devotion makes two people unite. For instance, the children of the same parents love one another in realization of the idea that they are of the same parents; the people of one nation love one another in the thought that they belong to one nation. And when two people tolerate one another with the thought of God as their Creator and as their support, then they are more evolved, because then they can tolerate anyone of any country or race, of whatever name or form.

But when a soul has evolved still more, tolerance becomes the natural thing for him, because the highly evolved soul then begins to realize 'another person is not separate from me, but the other person is myself; the separation is on the surface of life, but in the depth of life I and the other person are one.'

Therefore tolerance is not learned fully by trying to follow it as a good principle. It is learned by having the love of God, by attaining the knowledge of self, and by understanding the truth of life. There is no need to ask further about a person who you think is spiritual. Once he says, 'I tolerate all', this is certainly the proof of his spirituality. (*See* Questions and Answers, p 313.)

Questions
and
Answers

SUPERSTITIONS, CUSTOMS AND BELIEFS
Etekad, Rasm u Ravaj

III: 1

Question: Would we receive the curses of people as well as the blessings?

Answer: Yes. One should always think that life is an opportunity. Every moment is an opportunity. Sometimes one can do good by not troubling oneself, just by seizing the opportunity. If one is attentive and brings some pleasure and happiness, it is not always that it costs. What it costs is attention: if one keeps one's attention fixed upon that idea and one is constantly seeking where one can do some little good to another, by giving one's place in a bus or tram, by just having a little consideration for the aged, a little consideration for someone who is perhaps not honoured or respected. If one can offer what a person is lacking in his life without him knowing, that is always a great thing.

To do good is the work of the sage. Sometimes people are over-enthusiastic, which does harm. It is a spell, a fit of goodness that does no good. The real goodness is that which comes spontaneously. A thief is always on the look-out to rob something. So a good person who is always looking for an opportunity to do good, will always find it.

Question: Will you tell something more of the time when God grants wishes?

Answer: God grants wishes at two times. One time is when your heart is free from every thought or feeling or emotion, in the most peaceful and tranquil condition. At that time every wish that is sown is just like a seed sown in fertile soil. If one had the patience to wait in the great power of God, whatever be the wish, it will certainly be granted.

Question: Has one the right to wish for oneself?

Answer: Yes, as long as the consciousness says that the wish is right. But there is another stage when a person has so advanced spiritually that he thinks, 'God's wish is my wish. God knows better than me. I may wish something wrong.' The one who gives his life in that way in the hands of God is greater still.

The other time when the wish is granted is when somebody is satisfied, has been made happy by you. Naturally out of his heart springs a kind of fountain which pours upon you a kind of blessing. It will be just like rain from above which in time will bring its fruits and flowers.

III:3

Question: Hindus practise cremation; the Bible considers it as a crime. Who is right?

Answer: I should like to give a personal idea on this subject, apart from the Bible and Hindus. There may be advantages and according to another point of view disadvantages. I look at it that a person has always had of horror of being burned by fire. No doubt in a cold country one wishes to draw near to the fire, but in tropical countries, except at the time of cooking meals, one keeps away from it. Religious descriptions of agonies have always been pictured by fire and may well be expressed by the picture of fire, because that is a most horrible experience. One knows how one feels on being burned by fire. One knows that it is agony, and even the agony of pain and wounds cannot be compared with fire.

I do not mean to say that it may not do good to a person who wishes to purify himself from his worst enemy, so to speak, from fire; for the one who knows how to profit by things can find profit in anything, in the worst thing in the world. But for the average person I should think that merely the thought of the body which one has loved all through life being burned by fire would give him a great shock. Although he may not experience the tortures of the body, yet the remaining part of his being would have a terrible trauma even at the thought of it.

There is another way of looking at it. According to the words of Jesus Christ, 'Give all to Caesar that is due to Caesar, and give all to God that is due to God', we must return all to the origin to which it belongs. There is fire, heat, in us; it departs to the region of heat. There is a part of air; after death it departs by itself to the air element. The consciousness of the highest regions departs to the regions to which it belongs. What remains, this body of clay, this body of the earth, 'falls flat in the arms of the earth', as says Omar Khayyam. So naturally all that the soul has borrowed throughout the manifestation returns to its origin. And the physical body is earth's due: if it is paid back to the earth, it is like giving the child in its mother's arms. It seems to me a most natural process. There may perhaps be much against it, but it seems to me a most harmonious idea.

III:10

Question: Will you explain to us the meaning of the different signs of the zodiac and the special influence of each of them?

Answer: In order to know the meaning of the signs of the zodiac and the special influence each one has, one must study astrology. It is a science itself. But if I must say anything about it, I shall only say that the soul is light, the mind is light, the body is light. It is the light of different grades, and it is this realization which connects man with the stars and planets. The influence of the stars and planets works upon the person for the reason that the person is connected with that planet by the reason of the time and its influence upon the planets and the souls. To put it more plainly, there are certain times when a certain planet has its influence; at that time a child is born; then the child is born under that planet, then the child has that character.

The signs of the zodiac are expressive of the symbolical meaning of the influence of that. There is a science of astrology known to the Sufis, a science which is called *raml,* and the study of it gives one insight into that question.

Question: What is the effect of the signs of the zodiac upon a person who does not believe in their influence?

Answer: The effect is the same as the effect of heat and cold upon the one who believes it and upon the one who does not believe in heat or cold.

INSIGHT

Kashf

III:9

Question: Suppose a person has had for years some interest very near to his heart which has developed his power of concentration. When that interest ceases is that person more capable of strong concentration on a new interest because of his previous experience?

Answer: Yes, certainly. All our experiences are nothing but preparations for something else. Nothing that belongs to this world, however precious, must hinder one's path of progress. For every step in the direction to that spiritual gain must be the aim of every soul, and the concentration upon the object is just a step.

Question: A feeling of deadness seems to come ...

Answer: Here is the question of concentration and not of its effect. The question of effect is quite a different subject again.

Then the question comes: of what object? Something to steady the mind. It may be a tree, a flower, the sun or a star. Of course according to the object a reaction is produced, and according to the reaction an object is produced. According to the nature of the object reaction is produced.

Every belief and every experience for a wise person is a step of a staircase. He has taken this step, there is another step for him to take. The steps of the staircase are not made for one to stand there, they are just made for one to pass, to go further, because life is progress. Where there is no progress there is no life. One should go on. Death and disappointment, the two things are one, and if there is a hereafter then the death was a passing stage. And so is disappointment, it only has made one more steady, more wise.

Question: Does the staircase never end?
Answer: The end is not very desirable. The interest is in the staircase, in going on.

Question: And when a soul is perfection?
Answer: After perfection there is no interest. If there is no self, there is no interest. There is perfection.

III:10

Question: What do you mean by 'The will has to become like ebb and flow'?
Answer: I have not said that the will has to become like ebb and flow. I have said, 'We have to become like ebb and flow'. It is a symbolical expression. A certain thing is accomplished at one time by sympathy, something is accomplished at a certain time by indifference. With one situation we must meet by taking interest in it, in another situation we must become disinterested, not concerned with it. If the sea is always ebb and not flow or always flow and not ebb, then it is a dead sea. The living sea is inhaling and exhaling, both. Therefore in everything we do in life, in every manner we must have both things, ebb and flow. We must train in life and we must be able to meet every situation and event with the manner that situation demands.

Question: To keep a tranquil mind in the presence of an angry person, is deep beathing before answering any help?
Answer: One does not need to breathe deeply. The only thing is that when there is disturbance in the rhythm of one's being it shows first in the disturbance in the rhythm of the breath, for the person in a temper first loses power over his breath. Therefore breath is the result, not the cause in this case. What is necessary is will-power.

SYMBOLOGY

Naqsh Bandi

I:1

Question: If one would ask you if the message is given in plain words, in symbols or something else, what would you answer?
Answer: In all things in all manner.

Question: Is the Roman Catholic Church with its knowledge of symbols nearer to the truth than the Protestant Church?
Answer: I think that the knower of the truth will find the same truth in the symbols of the Catholic Church and will find the same truth in the absence of symbols in the Church of the Protestants.

II:10

Question: What is the meaning in the worship of the Brahmins of putting rice at the feet of the deity?
Answer: That all the love and light they will gain from the deity will spread in the world as seeds thrown in a furrow.

The name of the red powder symbolizes eternal life.

Question: Do the followers of Vishnu and Shiva and the worshippers of all the different deities worship in the same way?
Answer: It is almost the same. There may be small differences, not great. Just some differences which will perhaps distinguish one from the other. But at the same time mostly this is the form.

Question: Have they all the same sacred words and breathing exercises?
Answer: No, perhaps the words of the followers of Vishnu differ from those of the followers of Shiva. Of course, the meaning is the same. And breathing exercises do not differ much for the reason that the Yoga is one Yoga for all the Hindus. There are four different Yogas but only one system.

Question: Who gives them the words and breathing exercises? Priests? Are they *murshids*?

Answer: First of all the Brahmin is a priest by birth, the Brahmin is a born priest. Therefore the first lesson of the sacred word he receives is in his own family. But when he takes an esoteric path, at that time he needs the guidance of a *murshid*, whom the Brahmin calls a *guru*. It may be the same word perhaps which he has learned from his parents, still when that word is given by the *guru* that has a different value again. Perhaps he has repeated that word in his life, but when it is given by the *guru* the value of the word is different.

It is the spiritual effect of the word. At the time when the *guru* gives it, at that time the *guru* has charged this word with his own spiritual power. It is the same in Sufism.

Question: And for the not-Brahmins?

Answer: The manner of their worship is the same, but the worship of the other persons is done by the mediumship of a Brahmin, because only the Brahmin is entitled to perform the service. Brahmins are a community of priests. For *kshatrias* and *vaishas* and *shudras*, which are three different castes of the Hindus, the Brahmins have to perform services. The others have no power to perform the service anywhere.

Hindus, all those who live in India, have to take a Brahmin as medium. Through the Brahmin they are entitled to have a service. The Brahmin is the one who will perform the service, and they will stand there and partake of the service.

Question: Do they know the meaning of all the different actions they perform?

Answer: Not everybody. An advanced Brahmin knows it.

Question: Has it not changed the customs of the other classes?

Answer: Yes, they do prostrate. But going near the deity and putting the red powder and the ointment, that they do not do. Sometimes they bring for the Brahmin the red powder and the oil and leave it there. But then that is the Brahmin's work.

They have many different marks of caste. This caste mark denotes the third eye, the inner sense.

One thing is very admirable in the Hindu religion. It is so very diffuse in its ways of worship and in its doctrines and ideals and forms of philosophy that it gives a scope for a person of every grade of evolution. He has an answer in the religion of the Hindus whatever grade of evolution he has reached. For every person Hinduism will give an answer because it is so vast. If a person will try through philosophy he will find an answer. In worship, in symbology he will find an answer. Therefore it is something which answers the demands of every individual's life. If one takes the whole religion of the Hindus from the beginning to the end, it is so vast and deep and yet so simple that it answers the need of every person. Hinduism is not one religion, Hinduism is many religions in itself. There is no direction of life that is not expressed.

Question: Is that the reason that the Jains and the Sikhs have grown?
Answer: The religion of the Jains is Buddhism, and of the Sikhs is a modern reform of Hinduism.

III:6

Question: What is the meaning of the peacock feathers?
Answer: Peacock feathers are considered by the poets and mystics as a sign of beauty and a sign of vanity, and they are included in all the kingly grandeurs. Also the peacock is the bird upon which rode the goddess of music and literature, Saraswati.

Peacock feathers are used at the tombs of the Sufis by the guardians of the tomb and also by the healers, that by the pass of the peacock feathers, which is the pass of harmony and beauty, the bad influences may be taken away.

In India they use peacock feathers in the necklace of a child, and that is a little psychological trick. A child who is susceptible to evil eye is saved from its severe influence, because it is natural that the first glance of a person, instead of falling upon the child, will fall upon the peacock feathers, because these attract the curiosity of everybody. In that way the first severe glance is shielded by the peacock feathers. The same thing is done by the lion's nails which are put in the necklace of a little child.

BREATH
Pasi Anfas

II:10

Question: If through breath one can come in contact with another being, can one also come in contact with the dead?
Answer: Yes.

Question: Which is the most important part of breath, the inhalation or the exhalation?
Answer: Both.

Question: What is the link between the breath and the will?
Answer: The will is as the rider and the breath the rein in his hand.

Question: If breath is the vehicle of will, in what way is the will the link between men?
Answer: As one has to live in the midst of the world, so one has no other place to breathe between sky and earth. In this way, however much one wishes, one cannot fully escape being connected with others. This is why I have often said that we are interdependent upon one another. One cannot avoid this situation. The action of speaking, hearing, seeing and being seen, they all have their medium of breath. No sooner has the breath ceased to hold the organs of the body in perfect condition than man is no longer alive.

Question: What is the rôle of the will in the interdependence of men?

Answer: The will plays a most important part. By the power of will we master life – only if wisdom is at our side; if not, the same will may become injurious and harmful to us.

Question: In healing, is not most of the work done by the breath?

Answer: Yes.

MORALS

Suluk

II:7

Question: Can we blame those who do not see the wonder and mystery of life because of their ignorance?

Answer: We can blame no one, blameless or blameworthy.

EVERYDAY LIFE

Taqwa Taharat

II:4

Question: What is the process of drowning impressions in the ocean of the consciousness of eternal now?

Answer: The one who does not know the love of an individual does not know universal love. But if one stands there, one stands there without going forward. The love of an individual in love's path is a doll's play which is learned for the time to come. So the love of an individual is the first step, but when one progresses then one advances towards the love of a cause, a community, a nation, or even the whole universe. Man as a human being is capable of loving one, but his soul, as the light of God, is capable of loving not only one world, but even a thousand worlds, if there were so many. For the heart of man is larger than the whole universe.

METAPHYSICS
Tasawwuf

1:6

Question: Why are holy and wise people called high and the foolish called low?

Answer: The person whose intelligence is fully developed distinguishes high and low, but when his intelligence has gone back near to its original source, he distinguishes much less high from low. When he is dazzled by that light he does not distinguish differences. This is why great sinners are often tolerated near great sages. A small child whose intelligence is as yet undeveloped does not distinguish high and low. The intelligence is like the water of a fountain. When it has reached its highest point it goes back again to its starting point.

II:4

Question: What is the difference between soul and will?

Answer: The will is the action of the soul, the soul is the self of the will. The difference between soul and will is as the difference between the person and his action.

Question: Why is the expression used when a person is mad, that he is out of his mind?

Answer: 'He is out of his mind' means that he does not possess his mind, he does not have it under his control. It means that his mind is working mechanically, the will has no control over it. For the will is the ruler and reason is the minister. When both work together the mind is under control. When reason does not help, when the will has lost control, then the mind is not one's own. Therefore that expression is used.

II:6

Question: Why is it that we can only have the knowledge of God through the heart? What part of the mind does the heart represent?

Answer: Heart is the principal centre. Not the heart in the body, but the heart which is the depth of mind, for the mind is the surface of the heart. The heart and mind are one, as one tree; the root is the heart and the branches and the fruits and the flowers and the leaves represent the mind.

The heart is at the bottom of thought and imagination. All feelings always belong to the heart, thought to the mind. So what belongs to the mind can be expressed by words, but what belongs to the heart cannot. Everything in mind is intelligible, but what is beyond what is intelligible or cannot be expressed, that is heart. Deeper feelings with kindness, sympathy, all finer feelings which cannot be expressed in words are all activities of the heart. The heart is like the sea and the waves are its emotions.

The brain pervades the body. This fact is admitted by modern science. Brain is that susceptibility which is sensitive, such as nerves which are the sensitive feelers of the brain.

Question: Is intellectual knowledge located in the brain and wisdom located in the heart?

Answer: Neither is located in the brain or heart. Only, intellectual knowledge has much to do with the brain and wisdom comes from within the heart. But in wisdom the heart and the head both work. One may call the brain the seat of the intellect and the heart the throne of wisdom. Wisdom certainly may be called spiritual knowledge, but the best explanation of wisdom would be: perfect knowledge, the knowledge of life within and without.

II:8

Question: When a man is poor but can just manage to live with the means he has, is it good when he gives away material things and so makes himself dependent upon others?

Answer: The question what is good is a very difficult question to decide, because good is peculiar to every person. It all depends upon what that person thinks. When he thinks it is right, it is good. That is the only question.

There is the story of St Alias. He was an ascetic and for his food a loaf of bread was enough. He would not keep anything for tomorrow. If he was given enough food for four people in one day he would distribute it. If he had still more he shared it all. Next day he was without. If one said, why did he make himself dependent upon people for the next day, he would say, 'We live in this life interdependent. As long as I do not go to anybody, do not force upon anybody, as long as people only bring it, what does it matter? It is from Him. It is not depending upon others. It all comes from God, it all goes to the creatures of God. What does it matter?'

So it all depends upon the individual and how he looks at it.

II:10

Question: Those great creative spirits which at this moment are so necessary to work in the world, if they have in their soul a longing for spirituality, how can they keep a balance between their busy life and the concentration which is a necessity for the spiritual path? What must they sacrifice?

Answer: In the first place I should say that if one object is the seeking of one's soul and the other object is life's necessity, and if one object is to be sacrificed, it is better to sacrifice the one which is necessary but to keep to the soul's seeking.

There is another point of view. In order to become spiritual we should not become unworldly. We can just as well be in the world and yet not be of the world. We can be active in our everyday life and yet be concentrated. A person who can concentrate well can manage the affairs of the world better.

Those who have attained success in business, in worldly affairs, they had a better concentration. Therefore concentration is in no way a hindrance. A success gained through the power of spirituality is more secure and has a stronger foundation.

Furthermore there is one rule of life which must be understood: that success is gained by two ways, by the right way and by the wrong way. The wrong way means that which is against the spiritual idea, and when a person has started by one path he must keep to that path in order to be successful. If he finds that perhaps the other path might be better for success he will lose. A person who is going the wrong way, if he thinks that the right way will be better for success, he will lose. The person who is going the right way will not lose. His success will perhaps be slow, but it is secure and he will all through be successful. For the other one the greatest danger of losing success is going into the right path; that will be his loss.

III:4

Question: Is there in relation to *qaza* and *qadr* a difference in the path of the saint and the master?
Answer: Certainly. The saint is resigned to *qaza* and the master has regard for *qadr*. *Qaza* is the will of God and *qadr* the free will of an individual.

Question: What is free will? Can man in reality do a thing contrary to the will of God?
Answer: The answer is expressed in the first part of the Gatha. From the point of view of the absolute truth all is the will of God, there is no such thing as free will. But from the wisdom point of view there is a greater will, a mightier will and a smaller will. That shows on one side perfection of God, on the other side limitation, the fate of man.

Question: What is getting one's own will-power in hand?
Answer: There are two paths which lead to the goal, the saintly path and the masterly path. In one path the will is used most in outward things, in the other path the will is mostly

used to control one's own self; in other words, for the time being, against oneself. This is the saintly path.

It is wise, before one knows of the will of God, first to take one's own will in one's hand and to use it knowing that it is given for some great purpose in life.

Question: Will you please explain more about the two paths, the one that leads to saintliness and the one that leads to mastership?
Answer: One is the path of renunciation, abnegation, resignation, self-denial from the beginning to the end. And by doing this one arrives at that meeting ground where one touches that divine perfection.

Then there is the path of the master. The path of firmness and obstinacy, breaking and penetrating through every difficult situation that comes before him, and so fighting all along from the beginning to the end. In this he has to fight with himself and with the life outside. Therefore the struggle is both sides. And there is all the time the work of the will-power, and all through there is a battle, and in this battle all the conditions that he has to go through are of the same character and nature as of warfare: to be wounded and to cause wounds, to be hurt and to hurt another also. And in this way it is a constant struggle, but still for the higher aim and for the greater gain. In the end he strikes the same note which the saint has struck. Neither the path of the saint is easy nor that of the master. At the place where they meet both become one, for the resignation brings the saint to the same realization of harmony with the Infinite as the struggle brings the master to the same conviction in the end.

There is a third temperament and that is the middle temperament. In this temperament there is the saintly temperament and the temperament of the master, and that is the prophetic temperament. For the prophet begins his life with struggle and resignation; one moment struggle and another moment resignation, gain and resignation continiually going on. And therefore in the prophet one sees the saint and the master both in one.

Question: How to explain that 'creating is more difficult than destroying' and 'the power of Shiva, the Destroyer, is considered greater than that of Brahma, the Creator'?

Answer: Creation is difficult. Creation takes a great deal of patience and persistence. In order to make a building so many people are busy to make all perfect. For destruction what is needed? Just a little fire, just to put it on and burn it up. But at the same time all the courage and the strength and the power of all the people who have been building – that much power is necessary to destroy. So destroying is power. Therefore the power of Shiva is greater.

III:6

Question: Is not the disapproval of the conscience due to the soul's knowledge of certain consequences in the past?[1]

Answer: The whole life of the world is built on conventionality and accepted ideas, and conscience is made on this edifice. Conscience is not necessarily truth. Of absolute truth there is no word to be said; all else is *maya*, illusion. And when one looks from that point of view nothing is wrong, nothing right. If we accept right we must accept wrong. The German-born scientist Einstein's theory is what the Hindus have called *maya*, illusion, illusion caused by relativity.

The existence of everything is by our acceptance of it. We accept a certain thing to be right, good, beautiful, and once accepted that becomes part of our life. We have accepted it to be, so it becomes. A mistake cannot be a mistake unless we accept it as such. Our conscience tells us, but we have first told our conscience and our conscience has accepted it. Dervishes prove this by saying that fire will not burn us. Hell-fire is created in the conscience and when in the objective world we can prove that there is no such thing as fire, certainly in the conscience it cannot exist either. The dervish jumps into

1 Questions and answers about 'conscience' can also be found in Volume XIV, *Sufi Teachings: The Smiling Forehead*, where the subject is more extensively treated.

the fire and comes out unburned and so proves his case. The best way of testing life is to have conscience as a testing instrument to test and see if there is harmony or disharmony.

Question: Must we in order to create a harmonious atmosphere consider other people's opinion?
Answer: The more one takes notice of the feelings of another the more harmony one can create.

The work of reformation is fighting for a certain idea. The fight gives strength and the conscience does not take part.

Question: The rôle of conscience is very difficult.
Answer: Yes, but the best thing is always to take conscience as a testing instrument and to develop the sense of striking a more harmonious path at every step one goes; it is always looking for harmony and avoiding as far as possible, sometimes by pain and difficulties, anything unharmonious. Conscience is like everything else: by use it can become greater and a greater master of one's life. The conscience is the faculty of the heart as a whole.

Question: In what manner do the soul of man and the Spirit of God meet in the conscience and become one?
Answer: The heart in its depth is linked up with the divine Mind. So in the depth of the heart there is a greater justice than on the surface of our mind. So in the conscience is the court of God where God Himself sits on the throne of justice. In short, a person condemned by his conscience is more miserable than a person condemned by the court. Though in prison, he is even a lion, though in a cage, for him there is inner happiness. Sa'di said in a Persian verse:

Let me confess my faults to Him alone,
that I may not have to go before any one in the world
to humiliate myself.

III:7

Question: Will you tell us which has the most influence on the individual, heredity or environment?
Answer: The heredity is the foundation of the house and the environment is the building. And from this you can understand what is more useful and what less, what has greater influence and what less.

Question: The most civilized have been the most conventional people. How does it come that the artist generally is not conventional at all?
Answer: The artist lives in his own world. The greater the artist the more he has his own world; he does not live in the world. All those who live in their own world, they are out of the world, they have a civilization of their own. But when it comes to the question of the worldly life, life in the midst of the world, there comes the question of conventionality. One cannot ignore conventionality and at the same time live in the midst of the world.

The pianist Paderewski did not have time enough to comb his hair. That is another thing. But I do not think that he could have become President without brushing his hair. As an artist it is all right, but as a man in the midst of the world he has a world to face.

Question: Is not conventionality very often the result of personal taste and habits? How would it be possible to know what to change and what to keep, when the conventionality of each person depends upon his environment? There would certainly always be people who disagreed with this?
Answer: Of course this necessitates the exclusion of environments. Also this is the cause of divisions of humanity, and yet no civilization can avoid it very well, however greatly advanced in its thoughts. The progress will create necessities of such kind. People will not admit it, but they will live it just the same.

But I should think that the best way of understanding conventionality is the spiritual way. Once a person understands the spiritual moral he does not need to learn the man-made refinement; it will come by itself. As soon as man begins to regard the pleasure and displeasure of God in the feeling of every person he meets, he cannot but be most refined, whatever be the position of his life. He may live in a cottage, but his manner will surpass the manner of palaces.

Another thing is that when man has begun to judge his own action, fairness will develop in his nature and therefore everything he will do will be just and fair. He does not need very much the study of outer conventionalities, he naturally will become conventional.

And the third thing is that Sufi conception of God as the Beloved. When this conception is practised in everyday life and one regards it in dealing with everyone – that in everyone there is the divine Spirit more or less – one would regard everyone with that devotion and respect, with that thought and consideration which one would give to the Beloved God.

In these three ways this spiritual life teaches man the very depth of conventionalities, and if a civilization was built – which no doubt will be built one day – on a spiritual basis, the conventionalities of the world will become genuine and worth having.

Question: Do you think that conventionalities are fundamentally based on common sense?
Answer: Sometimes based on common sense, sometimes on the super-sense and sometimes beneath it.

Question: How can one make people who were lacking education see a thing that does not exist in their eyes, where they think there is no such thing as what aristocratic people feel is necessary for their happiness?
Answer: Civilization means progress. Those who are not educated, they must be educated to understand life better.

There are only two things, either go forward or go backward; either begin to think as everybody else without education thinks, or take the one who is not educated with you and go forward – one thing or the other. As the inner inclination is to go forward, take the one who cannot understand just now gently with you, showing him that all beautiful things are for the benefit of humanity. I should think that an ordinary man, if he is neglected, an educated man turns his back on him. If he would be brought closer to oneself, if he would be taught with simplicity and goodwill, not showing him that he is ignorant of beauty and culture, but showing him that in this is his real benefit, I am sure that the conditions, as bad as they are now, will become better, and there will be a better understanding between the classes as they are just now.

I will give you a litle example. When travelling in India I was staying in a place near a Hindu temple, and there were two porters who took care of that temple. They were Afghans, proud and stiff, rough and rigid in their manner, and yet in their expression there was honesty and goodness. As I passed through that way I saw them ignoring my entering and going out lest they might have the trouble of observing the conventions. One day one of them came to me with a message from his master. I got up from my seat and I received him most cordially. Since that time every time I passed, even if five times in a day, I was very well received with smiles and with a very warm welcome and I was no more ignored, because education had been given to that person without hurting his feeling. That gave him pleasure and certainly he thought that could give pleasure to another also.

To force a virtue upon a person is pride, but to let him see the beauty of good manners, that is education. Conditions today would become much better if we would take that to heart and know it as our sacred task to approach the people who need ripening in such a gentle way, with sympathy and love and to develop in their spirit that culture and beauty which will then be shared between us and them.

III:8

Question: How to regard the activity in life of the Shiva side of the deity?[2]

Answer: It is a subject which is very vast and it is difficult to explain it in two words. But that aspect of destruction and knowing about destruction can be easier understood again by something which we see in the modern science, by the medium of inoculation. By putting that destructive element in one's body one makes one's body disease-proof. That particular illness is no longer a disease, but the nature of the person.

That is the method of the mystic, it is destruction from a spiritual point of view. Death is a death so long as man is unacquainted with it. When man eats it up then he has eaten death; death cannot eat him. Then he knows the life eternal. That is the mystery of the message of Jesus Christ: to seek eternal life from the beginning to the end. The mystery of eternal life is that once a person has eaten death, then he is eternal.

In the little things of life, one person says, 'I do not like to touch vinegar, it hurts my health.' One person says, 'I cannot bear to eat cream, I cannot digest it.' Another person says, 'I cannot stand to have sugar in my tea, I do not like it.' For him the sugar is a poison. If he took the poison once, the same would become sugar for him. By all things that one thinks are foreign to one's nature one makes one's nature exclusive, and by becoming exclusive one makes oneself subject to them in a way. There comes a time when such things rule a person, a situation when he is under them. Such a person says, 'Bitter quinine – it is too bitter! I cannot stand it.' But when he is in a fever the doctor says he must have it. He dreads having it, at the same time he cannot help it.

Therefore the way of Shiva was always to work against one's weaknesses. He counted them as weaknesses, not as nature. What is nature? All is our nature, but what we cannot stand,

2 This question has also been treated, in another connection, in the revised Volume VIII, *Sufi Teachings: The Art of Being*.

that we make foreign to our nature. If we have separated it, there comes perhaps a time that we become so weak that we cannot help having it. Would you believe that among the snake charmers I have found some who, by making the snakes bite them time after time, have gradually developed so that poison does not hurt them. They just catch the snake in their hand; if the snake bites them, it does not hurt them. Shiva is pictured with a cobra round his neck. Out of death he has made a necklace, it is no more death to him.

One can take this to extremes, but still it is a law that must be studied and known. The only mystery it teaches is not to consider anything in nature as foreign to one's nature. If it was not in us one would not know it. By this one overcomes all the destruction which is the source of fear and pain and disappointment.

Question: Does this mean that if there is no poison there is no moral? That there is no good and no bad if there is no poison?
Answer: No, it does not mean that. Good is good and bad is bad. But at the same time one can rise above bad or one can be submissive to badness. One can become weak before the evil or become strong. The idea is to become strong before the evil instead of weak.

Question: What is the meaning of Moses raising the serpent's image to cure people from a plague?
Answer: The serpent is also the sign of death. When death is controlled, when the serpent is controlled, then one has risen above the plague. It is only a sign of conquering death.

Question: If one sees that one has begun a thing with haste, what should one do?
Answer: One should be sorry for having begun it too quickly and one should try to regulate the rhythm gradually. As in the beginning there is need of patience, so also in the end. Patience should be all along, patience is the secret of the whole thing. There are many virtues but no virtue can be

compared with patience, for it is not only a virtue, it is a power within itself.

Question: Is it perhaps God's way of making us immune to sorrow, when He sends us troubles and difficulties?

Answer: Every way is God's way. When He sends us troubles and difficulties, that is God's way. Neither is there a law of God to send us only sorrow and trouble nor to send us only joy and happiness. But if we are thankful and see the hand of God in all, we would certainly be grateful, even after a sorrow, and see in joy and sorrow both the way of God.

Very often there are people, more impressed by the doctrine of *karma*, who say if illness has come, 'Well now it is our *karma*, we have to pay the due. Then we must take it patiently.' I think there is a virtue in it also to see that it is from *karma*, but it is not sufficient. We must know that happiness is our birthright. In our happiness there is the happiness of God, in our sorrow there is not the pleasure of God. Therefore we must do everything in our power to get out of that illness, instead of thinking that *karma* has thrown that illness upon us, and that we must lie patiently as with a rock over us and not try to push it off because it is *karma*.

Question: Is it bad to be too impatient even for spiritual development?

Answer: 'Too' is always bad. If a person asked me, 'Is it right to be too good?', I would answer, 'It is enough to be good.' Impatience of every kind is to be avoided. One loses one's equilibrium. There is no gain out of impatience. Patience does not necessarily mean sloth, negligence and laziness!

Question: Is in our sorrow not God's sorrow reflected?

Answer: Certainly, as in our happiness God's happiness is reflected, so in our sorrow God's sorrow is reflected. If God would not sorrow, man would be greater than God, for man is capable of two things and God would only be capable of one.

Question: Why did you say then that God is not pleased in our sorrow?

Answer: I did not mean to say that in our sorrow there is not God's sorrow, but I meant to say that God is not pleased – as man is sometimes – in causing sorrow to another.

It is impossible to have no sorrow, but we want balance in sorrow and joy. When there is too much joy and no sorrow then life becomes monotonous.

Question: Is it a good plan for one to look for the cause of one's sorrow and gladness in one's own thought and action?

Answer: Sometimes it so happens that it is not the conditions which make sorrow. We allow them to make us sorrow. It is not only on them that it depends. It depends upon both things: a part of the sorrow comes from life and a part one makes oneself. Therefore if there is a response one helps life to give us a little joy, and then life will give a little joy. But if one prevents life to give a little joy then life becomes helpless. Out of a hundred things in everyday life there may be ninety-nine that we take too seriously. We might take perhaps one thing seriously and of the ninety-nine say, 'They matter little.'

III:9

Question: A false accusation fills a child with a sense of shame though there is no justification.

Answer: Anything wrongly suggested has always a wrong result. Sometimes a person carries a sense of shame too far, but it has its own value when it is used rightly.

Often people have done right things beyond their ordinary power, taken hold by their sense of shame. They get such a desire to amend that they are awakened from a sense of death. They make super-human efforts and they live again. Repentance is the outcome of shame

When the sense becomes more living the person feels the lack in himself and so he respects the lack in others. So what he does is to cover the lack of another instead of exposing it by criticism. When he develops further he sees other persons exposing their own lacking. So the pain of the wise and of the saintly souls is the pain they feel for others as if for themselves. They feel it like a knife. Spiritual life means to feel the life of another as one feels one's own life.

It looks so cruel on the part of man to expose the lack of another. It may satisfy his vanity or bring him a moment's pleasure, but from the spiritual point of view it looks very cruel. One can overcome this by feeling the oneness of life: 'The same life in him and in me, so his pain, his sorrow, his pleasure I share, because his life is my life.' So one cannot but be sympathetic to all in life and have more or less love, but the difficulty is that one does not know how to use it to one's best advantage.

Question: Will you please explain the words 'the sense of shame is like a pearl in a shell' and 'the price cannot be given in the marketplace, the place of that pearl is the crown of the king'?
Answer: That means that a virtue like this is appreciated and understood and rewarded fully in its right place. That is why it is said, 'in the crown of the king'. A person with this virtue is not appreciated by everybody. The person who has not got this virtue cannot appreciate it. For appreciation of this virtue a greater person is required. He who has no sense of shame cannot appeciate this virtue.

III:10

Question: Does the law of attraction work on a scientific basis according to the law of vibration?
Answer: Yes, there is a law hidden under every activity, and therefore there is certainly a law of vibration in every activity. No movement is free from the law of vibration. Therefore in attraction and repulsion also there is this law.

Mastery comes from the evolution of the soul. The sign of mastery is to conquer everything that revolts one, and that is by tolerance. The souls who have attained to some degree that spiritual mastery will see with me that, not only with people but even with food, where a person says, 'This I do not like, that I will not eat', the soul who has gained mastery rejects nothing; it may not approve of it, it may not be especially attracted to it. With the weather the masterly soul will not say, 'It is too hot or too damp or too dry.'

We do not tolerate what is before us. It is hard to tolerate, but we cannot help but meet it. The difference is in tolerating it. The whole system of the Yogis is based on making oneself acquainted with something that nature revolts against. In this way they could go too far in tormenting themselves. The extremity in all things is not right. At the same time that is the principle.

It is not the food, but how the person accepts it if he eats it. Thought works with simple food like medicine. If one says, 'It will do me good', it can cure. There are Yogis just now who will drink poison and not die or jump into the fire and not be burned. It is a practice to see that even an element such as fire does not hurt. You will find the intolerant souls most unhappy; everything hurts them, food, water, air, the change of weather, every person they see hurts them. Wherever they are, they are uncomfortable in the house and restless outside.

Question: What can one say to such a one?
Answer: It is very difficult. Therefore that tendency of rejecting, of having dislikes, prejudices – it is that tendency which must be conquered. It gives one such a mastery.

I remember my own experience when at school my teacher said that there was a tree the leaves of which were very good for a person, they purified the blood. That did not interest me, but he said, 'It is so bitter that you cannot drink it nor taste it nor touch it.' I thought, 'I can.' I did not care for the medicine, I only thought, 'Cannot, no one can!' I went home and gathered leaves and nobody could understand why I was gathering the leaves. It was more bitter than the water in the sea. I drank it and my satisfaction was that I did not even make a face. I was not tired of it, I continued for five or six days.

It is a demand on the part of a person if he wants to fight against all things. That gives the mastery. Mostly one does not fight. One always fights against things that prevent one getting what one wants. If one would fight with oneself then one would fight against the tendency of rejecting. That leads to mastery.

Question: I thought it was no use trying to force oneself.
Answer: As a general principle in life there is no use in force, but to train oneself is another thing. It is a method.

Sequential Order of the Gathas as Given in the Inner School Classes

Gatha I:1
Etekad, rasm u ravaj – Belief and superstition
Kashf – Pure – *safa*
Naqsh bandi – An ocean in a drop
Pasi anfas – The power of the breath
Suluk – The development of personality: the sense of beauty and
sincerity
Taqwa taharat – Everyday life
Tasawwuf – Belief

Gatha I:2
Etekad, rasm u ravaj – Belief
Kashf – As Thou art, so am I – *tat tvam asi*
Naqsh bandi – The symbol of the sun
Pasi anfas – The culture of the breath
Suluk – The development of personality: the jarring effect of the ego
of another
Taqwa taharat – The instrument of our body
Tasawwuf – Faith

Gatha I:3
Etekad, rasm u ravaj – Customs (1)
Kashf – The glance of the seer
Naqsh bandi – The symbol of the cross
Pasi anfas – Breath, the very life – *prana*
Suluk – The development of personality: what is the ego?
Taqwa taharat – The breath
Tasawwuf – Hope

Gatha I:4
Etekad, rasm u ravaj – Customs (2)
Kashf – Divine evidence
Naqsh bandi – The two forces

Pasi anfas – Five aspects of breath

Suluk – The training of the ego: what the ego needs and what it does not need

Taqwa taharat – Outer and inner ablutions

Tasawwuf – Patience

Gatha I:5

Etekad, rasm u ravaj – Hanuman

Kashf – Openness

Naqsh bandi – The symbol of the dove

Pasi anfas – The channel of the breath

Suluk – The training of the ego: constant battle with the ego

Taqwa taharat – Inner ablutions

Tasawwuf – Fear

Gatha I:6

Etekad, rasm u ravaj – Bells and gongs

Kashf – Movement (1)

Naqsh bandi – The symbol of the Sufi Order

Pasi anfas – The rhythm of the breath

Suluk – The training of the ego: the animal side of man's ego

Taqwa taharat – Vegetarian diet

Tasawwuf – Justice

Gatha I:7

Etekad, rasm u ravaj – The custom of drinking to the health of friends

Kashf – Movement (2)

Naqsh bandi – The symbolism of the dot and the circle

Pasi anfas – Dense and fine – *kasif* and *latif*

Suluk – The training of the ego: self-consciousness

Taqwa taharat – The five elements of the body

Tasawwuf – Reason

Gatha I:8

Etekad, rasm u ravaj – The origin of the custom of the seclusion of women

Kashf – The study of the whole

Naqsh bandi – The symbolism of lines
Pasi anfas – Breath, the vehicle of the self
Suluk – The training of the ego: vanity
Taqwa taharat – Purification
Tasawwuf – Logic

Gatha I:9

Etekad, rasm u ravaj – The custom of the seclusion of women (1)
Kashf – The mystery of expression
Naqsh bandi – The symbolism of the triangle
Pasi anfas – The mysticism of breath
Suluk – The training of the ego: the three parts of the ego
Taqwa taharat – Sobriety
Tasawwuf – Temptation

Gatha I:10

Etekad, rasm u ravaj – The custom of the seclusion of women (2)
Kashf – Different qualities of mind
Naqsh bandi – The symbology of the mushroom
Pasi anfas – Colour and sound
Suluk – The training of the ego: three stages through which the ego develops
Taqwa taharat – Fasting
Tasawwuf – Tolerance

Gatha II:1

Etekad, rasm u ravaj – 'Eat my flesh and drink my blood'
Kashf – The phenomenon of the mental record
Naqsh bandi – 'Die before death'
Pasi anfas – Fikar
Suluk – The training of the ego: necessity and avidity
Taqwa taharat – The purity of the body
Tasawwuf – Forgiveness

Gatha II:2

Etekad, rasm u ravaj – Customs of courtesy
Kashf – Impression

Naqsh bandi – Fruitfulness
Pasi anfas – Regularity of breath
Suluk – The training of the ego: training by abstinence
Taqwa taharat – Purification
Tasawwuf – Endurance (1)

Gatha II:3
Etekad, rasm u ravaj – Customs of the marriage ceremony
Kashf – The balance of life
Naqsh bandi – The symbol of the dragon
Pasi anfas – The life power
Suluk – The training of the ego: the two sides of the human ego
Taqwa taharat – Purity of mind (1)
Tasawwuf – Endurance (2)

Gatha II:4
Etekad, rasm u ravaj – The horse
Kashf – The language of the mind
Naqsh bandi – Water
Pasi anfas – Full breath
Suluk – The training of the ego: training is a science as well as an art
Taqwa taharat – Purity of mind (2)
Tasawwuf – Will-power

Gatha II:5
Etekad, rasm u ravaj – Oracles among the Ancient Greeks
Kashf – The influence of experience
Naqsh bandi – Wine
Pasi anfas – Thought and breath
Suluk – The training of the ego: training by refraining from free impulses
Taqwa taharat – Purification of the mind
Tasawwuf – Keeping a secret

Gatha II:6
Etekad, rasm u ravaj – The Greek mysteries (1)
Kashf – Intuition

Naqsh bandi – The curl of the Beloved
Pasi anfas – Be conscious of every breath
Suluk – The training of the ego: the ego is trained as a horse
Taqwa taharat – The power of mind
Tasawwuf – Mind

Gatha II:7

Etekad, rasm u ravaj – The Greek mysteries (2)
Kashf – Evidence of the thought
Naqsh bandi – The glance
Pasi anfas – Direction of breath
Suluk – The training of the ego: training by not gratifying vanity
Taqwa taharat – Every mind has its own standard of good and bad
Tasawwuf – Thought

Gatha II:8

Etekad, rasm u ravaj – The Greek mysteries (3)
Kashf – The activity of mind
Naqsh bandi – The myth of Balder
Pasi anfas – Breath in the development of mind
Suluk – The training of the ego: humility
Taqwa taharat – The impression of illness and weakness on
    the mind
Tasawwuf – Dependence upon God – *tawakkul*

Gatha II:9

Etekad, rasm u ravaj – The banshee
Kashf – Likes and dislikes
Naqsh bandi – The tree of wishes
Pasi anfas – Contraction and expansion
Suluk – The training of the ego: forgiveness
Taqwa taharat – Keeping the mind in a pure condition
Tasawwuf – Piety

Gatha II:10

Etekad, rasm u ravaj – The psychology of the shadow
Kashf – Acting contrary to one's nature – *viparit karna*

Naqsh bandi – The Hindu symbolical form of worship
Pasi anfas – Communication through the breath
Suluk – The training of the ego: 'blessed are the poor in spirit'
Taqwa taharat – Keeping the mind free from all undesirable
    impressions
Tasawwuf – Spirituality

Gatha III:1

Etekad, rasm u ravaj – Toasts
Kashf – Reason is earth-born
Naqsh bandi – Leili and Majnun
Pasi anfas – The length and breadth of breath
Suluk – The manner of friendliness
Taqwa taharat – Purity of heart (1)
Tasawwuf – Attitude

Gatha III:2

Etekad, rasm u ravaj – Wedding customs
Kashf – The word and the idea
Naqsh bandi – Leili and Majnun (conclusion)
Pasi anfas – Inspiration
Suluk – The manner of friendliness: respect – *adab* (1)
Taqwa taharat – Keeping the heart pure
Tasawwuf – Sympathy

Gatha III:3

Etekad, rasm u ravaj – Funeral customs
Kashf – The expression and the idea
Naqsh bandi – The symbology of religious ideas: Christ walking
    on the water
Pasi anfas – Thought-reading
Suluk – The manner of friendliness: respect – *adab* (2)
Taqwa taharat – The radiance of the face
Tasawwuf – The word 'sin'

Gatha III:4

Etekad, rasm u ravaj – The swansong

Kashf – The power of words

Naqsh bandi – The symbology of religious ideas: the opening
of the breast of the Prophet – *shaqq-e-sadr*

Pasi anfas – Lively breath – *nafsi garm*

Suluk – Respect – adab

Taqwa taharat – Innocence

Tasawwuf – The will, human and divine – *qadr* and *qaza*

Gatha III:5

Etekad, rasm u ravaj – Customs at the birth of a child in India

Kashf – The re-echo of the past

Naqsh bandi – The symbology of religious ideas: the dream of the
Prophet – *meraj*

Pasi anfas – The unknown dimension

Suluk – The manner of friendliness: consideration – *khatir*

Taqwa taharat – Reject the impression of errors and
shortcomings

Tasawwuf – Opinion

Gatha III:6

Etekad, rasm u ravaj – The superstition of the days, existing in the East

Kashf – Interest in all things

Naqsh bandi – The symbology of religious ideas: the flute
of Krishna

Pasi anfas – Breathing and meditation

Suluk – Sharing with others – *tawazu'*

Taqwa taharat – Purity of heart (2)

Tasawwuf – Conscience

Gatha III:7

Etekad, rasm u ravaj – Unlucky numbers

Kashf – Independence and indifference – *vairagya*

Naqsh bandi – The symbology of religious ideas: tongues of fire

Pasi anfas – Breath is likened to water

Suluk – Modesty – *haya* (1)

Taqwa taharat – Exaltation

Tasawwuf – Conventionality

Gatha III:8

Etekad, rasm u ravaj – The mysteries of omens
Kashf – A silent music
Naqsh bandi – The symbology of religious ideas: the story of Lot's wife
Pasi anfas – Breath and magnetism
Suluk – Modesty – *haya* (2)
Taqwa taharat – Purify the mind from fear
Tasawwuf – Life

Gatha III:9

Etekad, rasm u ravaj – The influence of time
Kashf – Three ways to develop insight
Naqsh bandi – The symbology of religious ideas
Pasi anfas – The subtle waves of breath
Suluk – The manner of friendliness: honour – *ghairat*
Taqwa taharat – Keep the heart free from poison
Tasawwuf – The word 'shame'

Gatha III:10

Etekad, rasm u ravaj – Planetary influences
Kashf – Tranquillity
Naqsh bandi – The symbology of religious ideas: the ten virgins
Pasi anfas – The mystery of breath
Suluk – Selflessness – *inkisar*
Taqwa taharat – The real purification of mind
Tasawwuf – Tolerance

GLOSSARY

ab-e-ruh	the radiance of the face
adab	respect
ahankar	the ignorant stage of the self
akasha	accommodation
akhlaq Allah	the manner of God
alif	the number '1'
Allah	God
ammarah	the lowest stage of the ego
andandamayakosh	the body of joy
annamayakosh	the body of earth
bast	expansion
bhavasagara	existence, ocean of life
bindu	the dot
bodhisattva	one who is to become a Buddha
buraq	animal of heaven
buzurgi	venerability
chakra	spiritual centre
chama	fan made of horse hair
dakhl dar ma'qulat	interference with the expert
dharma	sacred duty
dhikr	see *zikar*
dilazari	sympathy
fikar	a thought on the breath
garuda	bird on which Narayana the Godhead rode
ghairat	honour or pride
halim	tenderness of feeling
hatha yoga	physical training
hauz-e-kauthar	second fountain in heaven

haya	modesty
hosh ba dam	keep conscious of the breath; see also *nazar ba kadam*
hu	the eternal sound
ida	yogi term: the left side
ilmi adab	the science of *adab*, respect
ilm-e-rabbani	knowledge of the divine mystery
iman	faith
inkisar	humility
jelal	the right side: male, creative
jemal	the left side: female, receptive, responsive
kabir	great
kam sukhun	sparing of words
kamna kalpavriksha	a tree bearing all imaginable fruits
karma	the result of past actions
karobi	an Egyptian symbol
kashf	insight, opening
kasif	dense
kemal	perfection, the middle state between *jelal* and *jemal*
kham	raw, uninitiated, inexperienced
khwanda peshani	the smiling forehead
khatir	consideration
khulq	graciousness
kibria	the ego, vanity, pride
kotah kalam	moderation in speech
kumkum	red powder, applied to the forehead
kundalini	a serpent, cosmic energy
latif	fine
lawwamah	the ego, gratification of vanity
manas	mind
manomayakosh	the body of mind

mantra yoga	meditation, contemplation
mantram	a sacred word
matanat	seriousness
maya	cosmic illusion
meraj	the dream of the Prophet Mohammed
mithya	falsehood, untruth
miqna	veil
mureed	disciple
murshid	spiritual teacher
mu'tabar	self-respect, keeping one's word
mutmaina	the ego, having reached the human stage
nafs	the ego
nafsi garm	lively breath
nayat	meditation
nazr ba kadam	keep your eyes on your steps; see also *hosh ba dam*
nazr	influence of the evil eye
pani	water
pasi anfas	breath
pingala	yogi term: the right side
prana	breath vitality
pranamayakosh	the body of ether
puja	Hindu form of worship
qabz	contraction
qadr	free will
qaza	divine will
rajas	the active rhythm
raml	the science of astrology
Rind	sect of Sufis in Persia who keep secret all the good they perform
safa	pure

salim	harmony
sama	hearing, a music session
samadhi	meditation
sangam	coming together in unity
satva	spirit, constructive rhythm
saqi	the pourer of wine
shudra	lowest caste
sjaqq-e-sadr	the opening of the breast of the Prophet Mohammed
sushumna	the central ray of the sun
tamas	the destructive rhythm
taran	swimming
tat tvam asi	as Thou art, so am I
tawakkul	dependence on God
tawazu'	hospitality, sharing with others
trimurti	trinity
trishul	a trident
vairagya	indifference
vijnanamayakosh	the body of wisdom
viparit karna	acting contrary to one's nature
wafah	loyalty
wazifa	sacred word
yashmak	veil over the face
yima Jamsheid	bowl of wine from which Jamsheid drank deeply
zardash	gold disc behind the head of the king
zikar	a practice repeating the name of God

Index of Words
in Oriental Languages

halim	Mor III:1
hatha yoga	Mor I:4
hauz-e-kauthar	Sym II:5
haya	Mor III:1, 8
hosh ba dam	Brt II:6
hu	Mor I:8
ida	Sym I:4
ilmi adab	Mor III:1
ilm-e-rabbani	Scb II:7
iman	Ins I:3
inkisar	Mor III:1, 10
jelal	Sym I:4; Brt III:5, 7
kabir	Mor III:10
kam sukhun	Mor III:1
kamna kalpavriksha	Sym II:9
karma	QA Met III:8
karobi	Sym I:4
kashf	Ins I:5 (and passim)
kasif	Brt I:7
kemal	Sym I:4, 8; Scb III:9; Brt III:7
kham	Met III:9
khanda peshani	Met II:9
khatir	Mor III:1, 6
khulq	Mor III:1
kibria	Mor III, 5; Met III:10
kotah kalam	Mor III:1
kumkum	Sym II:10
kundalini	Brt I:5
latif	Brt I:7
lawwamah	Mor I:8
manas	Mor I:8; Ins II:2, Met II:6
manomayakosh	Sym III:8

GENERAL INDEX

Abbreviations

Scb Superstitions, Customs, Beliefs
Ins   Insight
Sym Symbology
Brt Breath
Mor Morals
Evd Everyday Life
Met Metaphysics
I   Series I
II   Series II
III   Series III
QA   Questions and Answers

Examples

Ins II:5   Gatha 5 of Insight series II
QA-Brt II:10   Question and Answer relating to Gatha 10 of
                Breath series II
Met II:7+QAs Gatha 7 of Metaphysics series II with its QAs

The mention '*also*' indicates that the same subject is treated in slightly different terms. For instance: 'Love, harmony and beauty' *also* in Met III:4, 'the lover of beauty ... becomes the seeker of harmony'.

References in **bold** are main entries.

Page numbers for each Gatha series and subjects are given at the end of the book.

attitude
>- should be moveable **Met III:1**
>- formed by expectation Met I:5

aura
>Sym I:4; Brt III:5

balance
>life is - Ins II:3
>- the ideal life Mor I:5; Mor II:9
>- necessary in life Brt I:6; Mor II:5
>- in exhaling and inhaling Brt III:9
>- in the organs of the body Ins I:4
>- in sorrow and joy QA-Met III:8

Balder
>the myth of - Sym II:8

banshee, the Scb II:9

beauty
>divine - Sym II:6
>- and harmony Evd II:9; Met III:4
>- harmony and love Mor III:1; Evd II:5; *also* Met III:4
>- and sincerity **Mor I:1**
>- of manner Mor III:3
>all - comes from God Mor III:1
>using the - of the earth Scb I:6
>turning ugliness into - Ins I:3
>- is modesty Scb I:9; Mor III:8, 9
>- is veiled Sym I:1

belief
>different kinds of - Met I:1
>- and customs Scb I:1
>- and superstition Scb I:1, 2
>-s are steps towards the goal Scb I:2; QA-Ins III:9
>- likened to running water Met I:1
>understanding - **Scb I:2**

Bible/Old Testament Sym I:3, 4, 6; Sym II:4; Sym III:10;
>Mor II:10; Met III:7

body
>the appetites of the - Mor II:3, 4
>cleanliness of the - **Evd I:1, 2**, 3, 4, 7
>the mechanism of the - **Brt I:1**, 3, 4, 6, 9; Brt II:1; Brt III:8
>the purification of the - Sym II:10; **Evd I:7**; Evd I:8, 9

conscience
- , a living voice of the heart **Met III:6**+QAs
also the thoughtless is not conscious of his fault
Met I:10; *and* God slumbers in the soul of the
unconscious one Met III:6
consideration
- in the form of respect, help, service **Mor III:6**
- for the expert Met III:5
conventionality
- the finishing of civilization **Met III:7**+QAs
conviction Scb I:2; Met I:1
Creator
the marvel of the - **Ins I:4**
Brahma the - Ins II:7; Sym I:9; Sym III:8; Met I:3;
Met III:4+QA
God the - Met III:10
cross
the symbol of the - Scb III:8; **Sym I:**2, 3, 8
the - symbol of patience, Met I:4
crucifixion
Sym I:3; Brt I:10; Met I:4
curl
the symbol of the - Sym II:6
customs
Scb I:1–10; Scb II:1–10; Scb III:1–10
- in greeting Scb I:3,4; *also* Scb II:2
- of veiling Scb I:8, 9
religious - **Scb I:6**

Day
the Last - Ins II:2,7
Judgement - Met III:6
the -s of the week **Scb III:6**
death
consciousness of - /mortality Scb II:8; Scb III:3
the fear of - Scb II:6, 8; Sym II:1; Met I:5
the influence of the - of one individual Scb II:9
warnings of - Scb II:9; Scb III:4; Sym III:8
- of the body Met II:10
- and patience Met I:4
conquering - Sym II:3; QA-Met III:8

ideal - Mor I:5
natural - Brt I:2, 4
a right - Met III:7
spiritual - Ins III:4
a vegetarian - **Evd I:6**
the three aspects of - Ins I:2; Sym I:9
the chemistry of - Evd II:4
the gradual development of - Sym II:1
the interdependence of inner and outer - Met II:4
the intoxication of - Sym I:7
the jarring effect of - Ins III:10; Mor II:8
the limitations of - Sym I:3; Mor I:3; Met III:9
the oneness of - QA-Met III:9
the purpose of - Scb III:4; Sym I:1; Mor II:5
the re-echo of - Mor I:1; Mor I:5; Met I:5; *also* Ins III:5
the tragedy of - Sym II:9; Mor I:7
- and death Scb II:6,8; Scb III:3; Ins I:3; Sym I:8; Sym II:3;
    Met II:8
- in the world a constant battle Scb I:10; Ins III:8; Mor III:9
- in the world an illusion Sym I:3; Mor I:3
- is action and reaction Met III:6
- is give and take Ins II:3; Mor I:1; *also* Mor III:2
- is a journey Sym II:10
- is motion Sym III:3; Mor II:8; Met II:3
- is an opportunity Sym III:10; QA-Scb III:1
- is progress Evd II:3
- is revealing Scb II:9
- lives on - Sym II,3; Evd I:6
- pictured as a building with several doors Mor III:10
- should be fruit-giving Sym II:2
seeing through - **Ins I:10**; Sym I:1; Ins III:9
likes and dislikes
Ins I:8; Ins II:3, 5, 9; Met I:6
light
the attraction of - Sym I:2
different grades of - QA-Sym III:10
an outpouring of - Scb I:8
the - of the breath Brt I:5, **9**, 10; **Brt III:5**
the - of the Christ-spirit Sym III:7
the - of intelligence Met I:6
the - of the Message Sym III:7

Prophet Muhammad
>the journey/dream of - Brt I:7; *also* Sym II:5; Sym III:5
>the opening of the breast of - Sym III:4
>teachings of - Scb I:9; Mor III:2
>'Die before death' Sym II:1
>'Every soul is born a believer' Met I:1
>'Tie your camel and trust in God' Met II:8
>'Verily, modesty is a great piety' Mor III:9
>- admired the horse Scb II:4
>- covered himself at the thought of God Met III:9

psychology
>the inner - of the mind Scb III:8; Ins II:1
>the - of shadow **Scb II:10**
>- the higher alchemy Ins II:1

purification *see* body, the purification of the; heart, the purification
>of the; mind, the purification of the

purity
>- is naturalness **Evd I:1**
>- of the channels of the breath Evd I:3, 5, 7, 8
>- of the heart Evd III:1, 2, 3, 4, 6, 7
>the rules of - Evd I:5
>- and piety Met II:9
>*see also* cleanliness

purpose
>the - of the creation Sym II:2
>the - of the idea of trinity Sym I:9
>the - of life Scb II:2; Sym I:1; Mor II:5
>ecstasy produces - Sym III:8
>every moment has its - Brt I:10

Qur'an
>Scb II:8; Ins I:9; Ins II:7; Sym I:3; Sym II:2; Brt I:4, 7;
>Met I:5; Met III:6

reason
>- raises an answer out of itself **Met I:7**
>- and belief Met I:1
>- and faith Met I:2
>- and hope Met I:3
>- and logic Met I:8
>- and temptation Met:9

self
>
> annihilation of - Sym II:5; Mor I:3
>
> knowledge of/knowing the - Mor I:3; Met III:10
>
> the thought of - **Mor II:1**
>
> losing the thought of - Ins III:9
>
> the vehicle of the - **Brt I:8**
>
> the limited - Scb II:8
>
> the natural - Evd I:1
>
> the true - Brt I:8
>
> the unlimited - Mor I:3
>
> the - the miniature of the universe Sym II:9
>
> -assertion, Mor III:10
>
> -confidence Ins I:3; Met I:2
>
> -consciousness Mor I:10; Mor II:1
>
> -control Brt I:5; Brt II:7; Met I:10
>
> -defence Ins III:8
>
> -denial Sym I:3; Sym II:10; Mor I:2; Mor III:6
>
> -discipline Scb II:8; Met II:4
>
> -effacement Sym I:3; Mor I:2; Mor II:5; Met I:4
>
> -interest Mor I:7
>
> -respect Mor I:8; Mor III:3
>
> -sufficiency Sym I:4; Evd I:9

selflessness
>
> **Mor II:10**

sense
>
> the feeling - Met III:9
>
> the inner - Brt I:9
>
> the one - beneath the five -s Ins II:5
>
> breath the light of all -s Brt I:9
>
> the -s the instruments of the will Met II:4

shadow/shade
>
> the psychology of the - **Scb II:10**
>
> - and reality Ins II:2; Evd II:5, 8
>
> bad impressions are a - upon the soul Evd II:3
>
> inharmony is a - Evd II:5
>
> no form exists without a - Ins III:6; Sym II:2
>
> two -s Brt III:2

shame
>
> - means want **Met III:9**

Shiva/Mahadeva/Maheish
        Ins I:3; Ins II:10; Sym I:9; Sym II:5; Brt II:7; Evd I:5;
        Met III:4+QA; QA-Met III:8
sight
       aspects of - Ins I:1
       qualities of - Ins I:10
       - one aspect of trinity Ins I:2
       man's - and God's - Met III:1
sin
       - an attitude, an action, a situation and a result **Met III:3**
sobriety
       - necessary for spiritual evolution **Evd I:9**
soul
       the being of the - is happiness Evd II:3
       the five bodies, vehicles of the - Sym III:8
       the instruments of the - Ins I:1, 2; *also* Sym II:1; *also* Evd I:1
       the journey of the - to immortality Sym III:8
       the light/illumination of the - Scb II:10; Ins I:2, 3; Sym I:2;
          Mor I:7; Mor II:7; Met I:5
       the material body/mortal abode necessary for the
          experience of the - Scb II:8; Met II:10
       - realization Met II:10
       - and ego Mor I:7
       - and mind produce joy and wisdom Sym III:8
       - and spirit Met II:10
       the - of man and the Spirit of God Sym II:1
       the - born to be immortal Scb III:4
       the - born again Sym I:3; Sym II:5
       the - represented by the body Ins III:2
       the - sees/witnesses from within Scb III:10; Mor I:9
       making the - independent of body and mind Ins I:1
spirit
       the independent - becoming dependent Met II:8
       the nature of the - Sym II:4
       the power of the - Sym I:4
       a skeleton plan of man's - Scb I:4
       - and matter Scb II:8; Sym I:6, 8, 10; Sym II:4; Met II:10;
          also Sym II:3 and Scb III:10
       the - of Guidance Sym III:7, 10
       the - of man and the Spirit of God Mor II:2
       the - of objects Ins I:10

sun
>the - nature's symbol of God **Sym I:2**
>the - and the moon Scb III:9; Sym I:4, 6, 8
>the - is life giving Scb II:10
>the - represents divine light Scb III:9

superstitions
>**Scb I:1–10; Scb II:1–10; Scb III: 1–10; Ins II:6;**
>>**Mor II:4**

symbol
>-s **Sym I:1–10; Sym II:1–10; Sym III:1–10**
>Chinese -s Sym I:10; Sym II:1, 2
>the - of spiritual progress Sym I:6

sympathy
>- the awakening of the love element **Met III:2**
>- the manner of God Mor III:1
>- gives insight Ins I:5

teacher
>the true and the false - Scb II:10
>the greatest -s have been the greatest pupils Sym I:6

temptation
>- a momentary illusion **Met I:9**

things
>- and beings Sym I:7; Sym II:3; Brt III:9; Met II:2
>the unfolding/uncovering of - Ins I:3; Sym I:1
>all - speak to the seer Scb II:8
>- are not what they appear to be Ins I:3
>the mystery hidden behind little - Scb III:8
>*see also* object

thought:
>every - connected with a deep feeling Ins II:2
>evil -s and evil feelings Evd III:1
>- and breath Brt I:6; **Brt II:1, 4, 5;** Brt III:3
>- and feeling Ins II:2; Brt II:5; Evd III:1
>- and movement Ins III:3
>- the outcome of mind Evd III:3
>- a wave of the mind **Met II:7**
>-reading Ins II:2, 7; Brt II:5, 10; Brt III:3; Met II:7

time
>the influence of - **Scb III:9**

will

    free - Mor I:1; Met I:2

    the senses instruments of the - Met II:4

    - human and divine **Met III:4**+QA

    - necessary for concentration Evd II:2

    - should control activity Met I:4

    - the king, reason the minister QA-Met II:4

will-power

    the best use made of - Met II:4

    faults come from lack of - Mor I:4

    - is soul-power **Met II:4**+QA

    - the secret of peace Ins III:10

    - in man is the secret of God Met II:4

    - not always sufficient Brt I:3

    - the only power to control activity Met I:4

    - strengthened by endurance Met II:3

    - works through the glance Sym II:7

    there is no - in fighting with others Evd II:10

wine

    - comes from the annihilation of grapes **Sym II:5**

    the eye symbolized by a cup of - Sym II:7

    ecstasy called - by Sufis Scb I:6

    divine love is the sacred - Scb I:7

wisdom

    worldly and spiritual - Ins III:4

    the object of - Sym II:1

    - a great teacher **Mor II:10**

    - a puzzle Sym II:6

    - is followed by insight Ins I:10

    - leads to understanding Scb I:1

    in - both heart and head are at work QA-Met II:6

wish

    the tree of -es **Sym II:9**

    -es granted Scb I:7; Scb III:1+QA

woman

    -'s intuition Scb II:5

    seclusion of - Scb I:8, 9, 10

    - and man/feminine and masculine/female and male Scb I:9, 10; Sym I:4, 8

    see also mother

Index to Gatha Series and Subjects